NIKKI

Ruth J. Freedman

authorHOUSE®

AuthorHouse™
1663 Liberty Drive
Bloomington, IN 47403
www.authorhouse.com
Phone: 1-800-839-8640

Published by AuthorHouse 1/26/2012

ISBN: 978-1-4678-5872-4 (e)
ISBN: 978-1-4678-5871-7 (sc)

Part One

Reflections of the Past

Chapter One

Nikki walked out of her apartment building. She experienced a feeling of well being when she noted what a glorious day it was. She could hear the sweet voices of the children singing at the church nursery school that was connected to her apartment building. She loved to hear the small children singing their French songs. To her, it was amazing that the children were singing so well in French until she would realize that they were French. She wished that she could speak as well as they did.

She had arrived in Casablanca in May of nineteen forty-seven. Now it was June and she was already into the routine of life here. She walked to the corner and hailed a horse and buggy and told the driver, *"Marche s'ill vous plait!"* As she rode down the main boulevard of Casablanca, the Boulevarde de la Guerre, and passed the most popular café in the city, *Le Roi de la Bierre,* on her way to the market, she thought to herself, *"It's really unbelievable. Who would have ever thought that I would wind up living here in French Morocco?"*

Until she had seen the movie "Casablanca" with Ingrid Bergman and Humphrey Bogart, she had never known that such a place existed, but never in her wildest of dreams did she think that at the age of twenty-two she would be living here. She smiled to herself as she rode down the boulevard and thought, *"If the kids back home could only see me now!"* and as she clutched her market basket, she secretly wished they could. There were few taxis in Casablanca and for the most part, people rode in the horse and buggy. The driver was called the coche'.

She had married before any of her friends and she supposed that they were still living in their same little world, not knowing or caring what went on outside of their little circle. Her sister, Nora, had been keeping her posted about the news at home; who had married and moved away and all of the gossip that she had heard about Nikki's old friends.

Nikki Parker had married Roger Carpel when she was eighteen. It had been a wartime marriage and he was a brand new Second Lieutenant, a *"shave tail,"* they called it. He was almost eight years her senior. She was not really sure if she was in love with him at first, but he was so worldly and she was fascinated with his sophistication. He was very continental and had traveled all over Europe, as well as having been in Hawaii before he had gone to Officers' Candidate School. He had lived in Casablanca from the time he was a young boy as his father was an importer and exporter.

On their first date, he had taken her to the door and kissed her hand as he said goodnight, which she found so different from all the other boys she had dated. Most boys her age would have tried to kiss her or cop a feel at this point in the evening, but Roger was different. She had only seen things like this in the movies and suddenly he became Cary Grant to her. He told her goodnight in his fluent French and although she did not understand French, she knew what he was saying. They continued to see each other every night that Roger was not on duty and on week-ends they would go out on picnics. She had never learned how to cook as her Aunt Emma had been so meticulous about her kitchen, and she didn't want anyone to mess it up. After much pleading, Nikki finally managed to talk her into helping her fry a chicken, make potato salad, and bake a devil's food cake for Roger.

On a steamy Sunday afternoon, Roger sat at the dining room table with stern Aunt Emma and a frowning Uncle Frank with chatty Nora and silent Bob. The room felt hot, crowded and airless and Nikki held her breath wondering if the food was even edible. She had spent the entire morning in the sweltering kitchen pouring over the recipes trying to make it all perfect. She couldn't eat a bite of it. She had no appetite. Her armpits were sweating and her hair was beginning to frizz. The condensation on the outside of the iced tea glasses was slowly trickling down the glass as Roger finished his second helping of potato salad and his third piece of fried chicken.

He wiped his mouth and set his napkin in his lap and declared, *"That is the best food I have eaten in recent memory"*. Nikki let out a sigh of relief and felt as if she might pass out as she stood up to clear the plates. She was wondering what he would have said if he knew that the only thing she knew how to do was broil lamb chops and boil corn.

Some week-ends they would go to one of the dude

ranches about 35 miles away. Although Nikki was already supporting herself, she was still living at home and so she had to adhere to the rules of her aunt and uncle and could not stay out as late as she wished. She had thought of moving into an apartment with one of her many friends who had come to San Antonio to work during the war but her family was against it, as it was considered the wrong thing to do if you were unmarried and living in your home town. So when she wanted to go to the dude ranches she would tell them she needed to stay with Nora because Bob was on duty and Nora hated being home alone. Fortunately Bob had the type of job in the service where he remained at the same place throughout the war and was often on weekend duty.

Nora and Nikki were all each other had in the world since their parents had died when they were just young girls. Aunt Emma and Uncle Frank took them in because they were the only family members who could take the two sisters without splitting them up during the years of the Great Depression. This childless couple, though they did their best to raise the girls, were strangers to them. They were strict and kept a house that was difficult to feel at home in. So it was no surprise that the girls married young as a way out of that place and into a world that would be of their own making.

Chapter Two

On the night that Roger had proposed to her, three months after they had started dating, she was flattered and in awe. Here was a man who had been around, and had known all kinds of beautiful, exotic women and he wanted her. She could not help but ask him why he selected her over all of those other women in his life.

His answer was, "*I knew that when the time came to get married that I would want a beautiful girl who I will be proud to take home to meet my parents. One who was naïve and whom I could respect. I could never marry any of those women I have spoken about. They were for the young, wild days, not for marriage.*" She could not refuse such a romantic proposal.

Aunt Emma and Uncle Frank were not too happy about it when Nikki came home that night and woke them to tell them that she was going to marry Roger. They knew that she would be moving far away and that they would rarely see her. They felt that they were losing her, but they finally agreed to the marriage. Unbeknownst to Nikki, her Uncle Frank had already checked with the Chaplin at the base to make sure that Roger was not a married man and that he had no record with the police.

As with most wartime marriages, there was no formal engagement and they were married in a small ceremony at Nikki's aunt and uncle's house. They invited only their family and a few close friends. After the ceremony, she gave them a little reception with a buffet supper and a small wedding cake. Nora was her Matron of Honor and Roger's best friend, Nick, was his best man. Although it was small, it was beautiful. Aunt Emma cried, which made it complete.

It was not but a month later that Roger received his orders to go to Georgia and as they drove off, Aunt Emma and Nora both cried. They knew that outside of a few leaves of absence, when they would come home for a visit, Nikki would never live in San Antonio again. Nikki was too excited to cry. Roger had promised to show her the world and she felt that this was the beginning of a new adventure. Now she was free and she knew that no one could tell her what to do anymore. She wondered to herself as they drove along if that was why she had accepted Roger's proposal of marriage, just to get away. But she reproached herself, convinced that she had married him because she really did love him very much.

Roger was never assigned to one base for very long. About the time they would start making friends he would be transferred to another base. Nikki never seemed to have any trouble making new friends as they moved around, as she had always been a very out-going girl. Most of her friends were older, as she had married so young, but they seemed to like her and soon she was into the routine of packing and moving and making more new friends. She decided not to let herself get too attached to any of them because she knew that in a short time either the friends or she and Roger would move on. They were stationed in almost every state in the south. She had hoped to see the west coast, but they always remained in the south. The only good thing about it was that it was easy to go home for visits when Roger would get leave, but he finally told Nikki that the next time he got a leave he wanted to take her to New York City. She was looking forward to their New York trip when Roger got his orders to go overseas. When his parents were told about it, they insisted that she come and stay with them. She was nervous about going to meet them for the first time alone, but consented to go.

Chapter Three

After Roger left, Nikki went home to say goodbye to her family. She stayed for two weeks before they put her on the train to New York. Nikki was heartbroken that she and Roger would be separated and the last night they slept in each other's arms all night, but neither one of them had slept very well.

The train to New York was anything but smooth. The train was late and the Pullman train had not waited for them in Dallas and she had to sit up all night. The problem was, the train was so full of soldiers that there was not even a seat available and she stood up all the way to Dallas. When she was told that there would be no Pullman car, she was in tears. She had seen several soldiers flip coins to see who would sit with her and when offered a seat she would refuse it.

Finally, at about two in the morning, a nice soldier came up to her and said, *"I know you must be very tired. Please take my seat. My buddy over there is out cold and he won't bother you."*

Nikki thanked him for being so kind and finally sat down. She noted that the soldier had gone over and doubled up with another of his friends, therefore she didn't feel too guilty about taking his seat away from him.

As the night went on, all kinds of thoughts were going on in her mind. She knew that Roger's parents had always wanted a daughter and they were very anxious to meet her. His brother, Bill, was six years older than Roger and was in Iwo-Jima. He had never married. She was picturing the scene when Roger's parents would greet her. She could see them opening the door, looking her up and down critically, and coldly saying, "*Come in.*" She became so overwhelmingly upset when she thought of this that she tried to change her thoughts and pictured them grabbing her and kissing her and saying, "*Welcome home daughter*!" Although not quite so dramatic, the latter did happen. They had been anxious to meet their new daughter-in-law and were happy to have her live with them until Roger's return.

Nikki was looking forward to seeing New York with its bright lights. She had always dreamed of seeing Times Square as she had seen it so many times in the movies and she wanted to see all of the other famous land marks as well. She felt terrible when she realized that Roger would not be the one to show it to her, as she had always dreamed of the day that he would. However, she was informed by mom that New York was browned out for the duration of the war and that she would not be able to see the bright lights until the war ended. As it looked at the time, it was a long way off, as it was the fall of nineteen forty-three.

About a week later Roger called. He was in San Francisco

about ready to be shipped out in the Pacific, God only knows where, when they discovered that there was already another unit of the same number over there. He informed her that his overseas orders had been cancelled.

Nikki was delighted as she asked, "*So what happens now?*

Roger's reply was "*Well, I get a two week leave and come to New York to pick up my wife and visit with my folks, and then you and I will go to Dallas, Texas to wait for my next assignment.*"

Nikki was so elated that she could not believe her ears. So it would be Roger to show her New York after all, and so he did. They were out day and night. Roger was in uniform and so they got into the shows and clubs for half- price. The highlight of the whole trip for Nikki was the night that they went to the Aster Roof where *Harry James* was playing. She and Roger had always loved to dance and they were perfectly matched. The most incredible part of the whole evening for Nikki was that *Betty Grable* was there. She was so beautiful with her peaches and cream complexion. She was much prettier in person than she appeared on the screen. This was the first celebrity that Nikki had ever seen and she was quite enthused over it. Roger took her to all of the places of interest and they saw several shows that were playing at the time. They had two marvelous weeks of fun. One night as they were walking along, they saw a long line of people standing at one of the theaters. Roger asked someone what was going on and was informed that *Ingrid Bergman* was playing in *Joan of Arc* and would be arriving at the stage door momentarily. A few minutes later, a car pulled up and out stepped the most beautiful woman that Nikki had ever seen. Her hair was cut short because she was playing Joan of Arc and she wore a beret. She had no make-up on and had so much natural beauty that it was breath taking. Nikki remembered reading that they never had to do very much make-up on her, as her coloring was so magnificent.

They saw several musicals, *Bloomer Girl* with musical score by *Harold Arlen and E.Y. "Yip" Harburg,* performed by *Celeste Holm, Oklahoma* alumni. They also saw *On the Town,* score by Leonard Bernstein, and Lyrics by Betty Comden and Adolph Green, a team of remarkable newcomers at the time.

They also saw *The Song of Norway* which used the melodies of Norwegian composer Edvard Grieg.

Nikki enjoyed all of it so much. She had never been to the theater before and decided that she really did enjoy it.

When the two weeks were over, they boarded the train for Dallas.

Chapter Four
Roger

When Roger first spotted Nikki at the USO dance, he couldn't take his eyes off of her. As he watched her being tossed from one GI to another, dancing gracefully, as if she enjoyed every second of it, he knew that this was one girl he wanted to meet. He didn't want to cut in on her as he knew that in a few seconds someone else would follow suit. There was no doubt about the fact that she was the most exquisite looking girl he had ever seen. He decided that he would watch and use his eyes as he had learned to do from Marcel, his best friend in Casablanca. He had the technique down pat. Roger had watched and learned, but he knew that he never would be as good at this as his friend was. He made up his mind to use these tactics on the beautiful girl in the red formal. He stood with one foot on the chair, leaning on his knee, and every time the girl came by him, he looked her up and down until he finally began to get her attention. He noted that she was watching him as she danced. They were playing a rumba and since Roger was exceptionally good at this dance he finally decided to cut in on her anyway. He executed every step that he knew and was surprised to see that she followed him with such ease, it was as if hey had been dancing together all of their lives. When the dance ended, he quickly ushered her off of the dance floor and brought her over to his table. He was taking no chances that someone would cut in on them. He was one of the few officers there. Most of them were enlisted men and he saw the dirty looks that were coming his way and ignored it. He knew how they felt, as he had just graduated from Officers' Candidate school, but had been an enlisted man way before the war America had become involved in it. After the European war had started and things had gotten bad, he and his family knew it was just a matter of time that America would get involved and they all came back to the states. They had stayed in Casablanca trying to save their property, but once the Vichy French were in power, they decided that they should go back to the States. Roger knew it was just a matter of time that war would become part of the American history so instead of looking for a job he enlisted in the Army.

After his basic training, he had been shipped to Hawaii and had been assigned to the original Twenty-Fourth Division. He was living at Scoffield Barracks in Pearl Harbor, and since there was no war at that time, he and his buddies were living it up, getting drunk every night and sleeping with every skirt that they could find. Every night was party time, but especially Saturday night. On Sunday, December the seventh, nineteen forty-one, when Pearl Harbor was bombed by the Japanese, they were all sleeping off their hangovers.

They were totally unprepared for the surprise attack. They ran out on the veranda to see what was happening and couldn't believe their eyes. The planes were flying over, bombing the island and flying low and strafing the tents below the barracks where the new recruits were temporarily housed. The screams were terrifying as the tents caught fire and he could smell the human flesh burning, something that he would never forget for the rest of his life. As he turned to his buddies who had also run out on the veranda, he realized that they too were being shot at.

From that day on, the men worked and drilled and had maneuvers to prepare for another invasion. President Roosevelt declared war on Japan and Germany and America was now at war. Play time was over and the men were serious, as they knew that in a matter of a short time, the Twenty-Fourth Division would be shipped out to the islands that were already occupied by Japan and that they were in for some rough times. They were served Spam and Powdered eggs, which Roger found he could not manage to get down his throat and he began to live on coconuts, bananas and pineapple.

He had applied for Officers' Candidate School when he first was sent to Hawaii and assumed that he would never be able to go now, but to his complete surprise, one day his commanding officer called him into his office and informed him that because of his knowledge of the French language and the customs of the French people, he had been accepted into Officers' Candidate School in Miami, Florida and was told to pack and be ready to leave immediately. Roger was elated, because he had applied for the Army Air corps and that was the school he had been accepted into. He was hoping that they would send him to the European Theatre of War and that he would be able to get back to Casablanca, because as far as he was concerned, that was home to him. His mother had written that Marcel had not been inducted into the service as he had married Juanita, the woman that he had been living with and had had two children with. He married her to keep from going into the service. His brother Jon was already seeing action and was already a big war hero.

Try as he may, Roger could not picture Marcel a married man, but married or not, he was sure that he was still living the same life as before, as he had run around on Juanita even when he had been living with her. He knew that he was not the type to be faithful to any woman, because he loved making new conquests too much and the women all seemed to fall for him.

Chapter Five

At the end of August, 1945, Roger finally received his overseas orders for the second time, but this time it was definite that he would be leaving. He knew that he would be sent to the Pacific since the European War had ended shortly after President Roosevelt had died. He was hoping the war would end with Japan, as he did not want any part of the Pacific action. He knew that his dreams of getting back to Casablanca would not come to pass. There were still American bases there, but with the war still going on with Japan, they needed men in that area. It was odd, he thought, he had been selected for Officers Training because of his knowledge of the French language and people and they continued to send him to the Pacific. He had been there when the war began and in his heart he always felt that he would be there when it ended. He was sent to Manila, but by the time he reached his destination, the atomic bomb was dropped on Hiroshima and Japan opened peace negotiations. On September 2, 1945, Japan signed the terms of surrender.

At least he knew that he would not have to fight. His only concern was getting home to Nikki and starting his life again. His main goal in life was to go back to Casablanca.

He tried to keep busy while waiting to get back to the states. However, it was not to be until December 1st as they were sending the men home in the order of how long they had been there and he knew that he would be in the last group. There were not enough ships to get them home any faster. He wrote to Nikki almost every day and received daily letters from her. He was happy to know that she had made a good friend and was not as lonely as she had been at first. He made friends with some of the fellows that he had gone over with and they spent most of their time at the Officers' Club. He didn't have much money to spend as he had not thought he would need it. Most of his paycheck was automatically being sent home to Nikki. He hoped that she was saving it. He knew that they would need it once he got home and out of the service. He was glad that it was going to her as he knew himself well and was sure that if he had kept most of it he would be blowing it on nonsense and losing it in poker games. However, it was quite boring to be overseas and idle, without much money in his pocket to spend.

It was difficult to find things to write about, as there was nothing happening in his life and he knew that his letters were dull, as all he could write about was the guys he had met and that he was anxiously waiting to go home. He was angry about the whole situation. At least if he were in Europe he could go and visit with his friends in Casablanca and his cousins in Paris. As it was, all he did was listen to the other guys complain and he couldn't blame them, as he felt the same way. One by one his friends started running around on their wives and he found himself with more time on his hands, but he was determined to remain faithful to Nikki. He began to think that the day would never come for him to finally go home.

Chapter Six

Before Roger left for overseas he had taken Nikki home to visit her family in San Antonio before she was to leave for New York. Her Aunt Emma and Uncle Frank were living a completely different life since she and Nora had married. Her Uncle traveled for their living and now Aunt Emma was able to travel with him. She no longer lived the lonely life with her husband gone all the time. They knew that Roger's parents wanted her to live with them and she planned to go there.

When Roger left for San Francisco, Nora and Bob took Nikki and Roger to the airport. When Roger saw how heartbroken Nikki was he had to be brave and not show his feelings. He promised her that he would not try and become a hero and that he would come back to her in one piece. In his mind he knew that if he stayed with her for too long that he would break down and finally said, "I guess we had better say our goodbyes now, as I will have to board the plane." Nikki was crying as he kissed her and he could taste the salt of her tears. He begged her for a smile. "*I don't want to remember your face all scrunched up.*"

Nikki laughed and finally said, "*It reminds me of the song "I'm smiling with Tears in my Eyes.*"

As he boarded the plane, she managed to keep a smile on her face as she waved to him, but when the plane revved its motor to take off, she broke down and sobbed. When he looked through the window and saw her, he thought to himself, "*When will this damned war end!*" Nora and Bob tried to comfort her, but there was nothing they could say that would console her.

Nikki was to stay there for two weeks. The first week would be with Aunt Emma and the second one with Nora. When they arrived at Aunt Emma's house she was sitting on the front steps waiting for them. She knew that Nikki would need a shoulder to cry on and she cried along with her.

She told her that she wished that she would stay with her while Roger was gone and she replied,

"*Aunt Emma, when you took Nora and me to live with you, you made a big sacrifice. Now that I am married I realize how lonely you must have been with Uncle Frank gone all the time. Now you are traveling with him and if I were to stay you would feel obligated to stay at home with me. I love you too much to do that to you. I want you to know that I appreciate all that you have done for me, but no more sacrifices!*"

Aunt Emma cried and told her that she had never felt that it was a sacrifice. "*I love you girls as if you were my own. I was not blessed with children and I felt that God had given you to me when your mother and father died at such young ages. I have never considered it a burden and I wanted both of you.*"

Nikki replied, "*You have given up your own life for us, but now it is time for you to have your life and I want you to have it.*"

Aunt Emma decided to sleep in Nikki's room that night so that she wouldn't feel so alone. In the middle of the night she did cry out and Aunt Emma woke her and told her she was dreaming. She had fallen asleep easily, as she was so emotionally spent.

Chapter Seven

Two weeks later they took her to the train. Roger told her that she could fly to New York, but Nikki had never been on a plane and said she was afraid. She told him *"I'll take the train. "That way I know I will be alive and waiting when you come home!"* He had laughed and told her she was silly, but she stuck to her guns.

By the time she arrived in New York she had become very thin as she had never been able to swallow food when she was upset or excited. This time mom and dad were waiting for her at the station and they hardly recognized her.

When she greeted them mom said, *"Nikki, I hardly recognized you, you are way too thin!"*

Dad interrupted, *"Don't worry Millie; we'll fatten her up before Roger gets home."* Nikki didn't want to be fat, but didn't say anything.

She felt very much at home with Roger's parents and loved hearing all about the things that he had done as a small child. It seemed that he was the one that was always getting into mischief. Nikki was getting to know him better even though they were thousands of miles apart. By the time she reached New York the war had ended and of course she and mom and dad were happy to know that at least he was not in danger now. However, it would take months to bring the men home and they knew that Roger would have to wait his turn, as he was in one of the last groups to go over. Therefore, he would have to wait longer than the ones who had been there for a while which was only fair.

Mom and dad were having financial problems, as they had left Casablanca when it became too dangerous to stay and in turn had left their livelihood. They owned a plant where they made suede and sheep casings to ship to the U.S. Now that they had been forced to leave it all behind, dad had taken a job in New York and mom had gone to work as a secretary. Ever since the European war had ended, dad had been commuting back and forth to Washington trying to obtain a new passport so that he could go back to Casablanca to try and pick up the pieces that he had left behind. This had been going on for a long time, but because of so much red tape it was taking much longer than he had hoped. He was a kind hearted man and had helped some of the refugees who had sifted into Casablanca when the Vichy French were in power. He had actually hidden some of them in his basement and had helped them to eventually get their papers to go to the United States. These people had come to him with jewels, wrapped in rags to bring to the states for them so that when they got there they would be able to sell them and use the money to start a new life. The Vichy French were guarding their home constantly, as word had leaked out that he was helping these people. Mom, being a kind hearted person as well, felt sorry for the men who were guarding their house and when the weather was warm she had made pitchers of lemonade and taken it out to them. The people that dad had so generously helped now came to their apartment in NY and boasted about all of the money they were making. Not one of them offered to help him out. Nikki would be furious when they would leave and would express her feelings.

Dad would say, "*When you do something good for someone, never expect them to repay you. You only pray that they will in turn help someone else who is in trouble.*"

Nikki thought, "*What a great man he is,*" and she respected him very much.

Dad finally got his passport and left for Casablanca. Nikki and mom were alone and mom worked all day. New York people were not friendly like the people back in Texas were and Nikki was very lonely. After straightening the house she would usually go out for a walk, sometimes just for the fresh air, as she loved the autumn. It was such a change from Texas where it went from summer into winter and winter into summer. She had forgotten how beautiful the four seasons were. Sometimes she would do the grocery shopping, but there was very little to buy for just the two of them. The women in the building would take chairs out in the front where they would sit and gossip while their children played in the fresh air. Nikki would smile and nod as she walked by them, but there was never any response. She didn't know how to approach these people; they were like foreigners to her. She was homesick and lonely for her family and friends and missed Roger more than ever. Some days, she was sorry that she had come to New York, but there had been no real alternative.

One day when she stepped into the elevator to go out, a woman with a small baby in a carriage and child of about 3 years old got into the elevator with her. This had happened several times before and the woman smiled and said,

"*We always seem to be going and coming at the same time, why don't we walk together?*"

Nikki was beside herself with happiness and said, "*My name is Nikki Carpel and I thought I would never make a friend here in New York! My husband is overseas and I am staying with his parents until he comes home. I am from Texas.*"

The woman answered, "*I know what you have been going through, as I went through the same thing. . As long as I worked it was fine, as I became friendly with the other models that were also from other cities and states, but once I stopped working I found it very lonely. By the way, I am from Georgia. My name is Jean Eiders and I moved here ten years ago to become a model. Then I married and my husband insisted that I quit working and I was very lonely.*"

Nikki could see that she would have been a model, as she was tall and carried herself beautifully. Here they were, living on the same floor and from that day on they walked together and talked about their lives and became very close friends. Jean was about 10 years older than Nikki and she became her confidant. She met Randal, her husband, and they seemed to be very happy together. They invited her out to dinner with them several times, but Nikki felt like a fifth wheel and really didn't want to leave mom alone. She told them that when Roger got home they would make it a foursome.

Chapter Eight

One morning at about 2 A.M. the phone rang. Nikki ran to answer it and when she heard Roger's voice she was ecstatic. He had forgotten about the 3 hour time difference and seemed surprised to hear the sleepy voice on the other end of the line.

When Nikki heard his voice she was immediately awake and asked, *"Where are you?"*

Roger answered, *"I'm in San Francisco. I will be flying into New York today. God Nikki, it's so great to hear your voice. You don't know how much I have missed hearing it!"*

Nikki felt a lump in her throat and could hardly speak. Finally she said, *"Oh Roger, I just can't wait!"*

At that point mom came stumbling in to see what the noise was all about and Nikki realized that she would have to turn the phone over to her. When mom finished talking to him he asked her to put Nikki back on.

Nikki asked, *"About what time will you be home?"*

Roger's reply was *"As soon as they get me there. All I know is that it will be some time this afternoon or tonight."*

They finally said goodbye and when they hung up Nikki knew that there would be no more sleep for her. She was much too excited to sleep. She wished she could so as to make the time go faster, but her mind was full of what she had to do between now and when Roger would arrive. She finally got up and put the coffee on. In a few minutes mom joined her, as she couldn't sleep either, and the smell of the coffee had lured her into the kitchen.

Nikki was wondering what she should wear for Roger's homecoming. She was sorry she had not bought a new dress. As soon as she thought that Jean would be awake she ran down the hall to her apartment to tell her the wonderful news and of course Jean was very happy for her. By this time she depended on Jean's opinion for just about everything. Jean was a marvelous cook and had taught her everything she knew. She asked her what she should wear.

Jean laughed, *"He'll be so happy to see you that he probably won't notice what you are wearing. You could be naked and he wouldn't know the difference!"*

Nikki laughed and said, *"I think he would prefer it that way, but I think his mother would be a little embarrassed!"*

In a matter of hours they would be together; she would be in Roger's arms and she was so happy that nothing could upset her that day. She finally decided on a blue dress that Roger had always liked on her, because he said, it matched her lovely soft blue eyes.

As soon as she got her clothes on, Nikki ran up to Broadway to buy some colors and a poster board. She hurried home and made an elaborate ***"Welcome Home"*** sign to put on the door. Everyone had ***"Welcome Home"*** signs on their door when their loved ones returned from overseas. On her return from the store there was a telegram from dad. Mom told her that he was coming home at noon. Nikki said, "*What perfect timing*!" Of course mom had not gone to work that day, as she had wanted to be there to greet her son. Now she would have her husband at home again as well.

When Roger hung up the phone after talking to Nikki he had a feeling of such guilt that he was actually depressed. He tried to make excuses to himself for his activities in the past month. He loved Nikki more than life itself, but he decided that he was only human and he didn't do anything that the other guys hadn't done. When he first arrived in Manila he was faithful to her, but as time went by so slowly, being a normal young male, he was beginning to feel a desperate need for his sex life. One night at the club he had met a cute girl. She was not as beautiful as Nikki, and he knew that he didn't love her, but after a few drinks he had taken her to a hotel and they had ended up spending the night together. The next day he had been sick with guilt and tried to blame it on the fact that he had been very drunk, but try as he may, he could not stay away from her once they had started their affair. He began seeing her steadily and she had finally taken an apartment so that they could live together. He had explained that he had very little money, as most of it was being sent to his wife, but she insisted that she would pay for the apartment. The days had been dragging up until then, as from the first day that he had arrived in Manila he had been doing nothing but waiting to go home. He found the days to be long and the nights unbearable, as he had no way of expending his energy. After he met Donna, he was with her constantly. He knew that he didn't love her, but he needed her desperately. Most of his friends were doing the same thing and others were with different girls every night.

When the news came that he was going home, he decided to go to the hospital and have some tests made. He didn't want to take the chance of bringing any disease home to Nikki. He loved her with all of his heart, but he had had his needs and had weakened.

When he heard Nikki's eager voice on the phone his stomach flipped over. He felt like the biggest heel in the world. Her voice sounded so sweet and innocent that he felt like crying. He hoped to God that Nikki would never learn of his escapades and decided that he would never contact his friends in New York who had been with him. He felt that someone might slip and say the wrong thing, especially when they were drinking. He had promised all of the guys who lived in New York that they would get together with their wives and have a reunion. They had exchanged phone numbers with each other and were planning to get together soon. If they called, he would just make an excuse. As it turned out, none of them called and he figured that they were thinking the same thing he was. They were all afraid of a slip of the lip.

Chapter Nine

Dad arrived home around noon and when he was informed that Roger was coming in that evening he was beside himself with happiness and also was glad that he had timed it so well. Of course mom was delighted to have him home again as she had missed him. He announced that their plant in Casablanca was still in tact, but that he planned to sell it and start a new business there. He said that the people were desperate for so many things and felt that they would live there and import those things from the states. He was sure that he would make a lot of money.

As it turned out, Roger never even got to see the sign on the door. Nikki ran and opened the door every time she heard the elevator stop and finally, there he was, running to her and her to him. He dropped his bag when he saw her so that he could run faster.

"I don't think I have ever been so happy in my life!" Nikki shrieked. She felt as if her heart would burst with joy as it was pumping so fast.

Roger looked at her with his dark, serious eyes and said, *"I pray that we will never have to be separated again. Thank God the war is over. I've imagined this scene so many times and it is finally happening exactly the way I have pictured it."* Though he had been unfaithful, he knew that he was telling the truth. He knew that no one could ever take Nikki's place. She looked beautiful in an apron and glamorous when all dressed up. Even when she woke up in the morning she was a knock out. There was not one woman who he had ever known before who could equal her in looks and she was the only woman he would ever want in his life.

Roger's parents stayed away until the big reunion was over and then ran to greet him. Dad led the way into the living room and said, *"This calls for a celebration. I have been saving two bottles of champagne for when my sons came home."* There was a feeling of festivity when he popped the cork on the champagne, though he was always looking for an excuse to drink, since mom did not approve of it very much. He filled their glasses and offered a toast, thanking God for Roger's safe return and to his beautiful daughter. When the bottle was empty, Nikki was feeling a little dizzy. She was not sure if it was the champagne or the excitement of having Roger home again. She decided that it was probably both. Then Dad announced, *"We will save the other bottle to celebrate when Bill comes home."* Two weeks later Bill arrived from Iwo- Jima and Nikki finally got to meet her brother-in-law whom she had heard so much about.

He looked at Nikki and held up his glass and said, *"My compliments little brother. How did you ever win over such a beauty?"* Roger answered, *"With my charm, dear brother!"*

Nikki felt like a queen, as between dad and Bill they constantly complimented her and they could not imagine what she had seen in Roger.

Dad said to her one night, "*It couldn't have been the uniform, as you had so many of them there. What did you see in him?*" Roger was not exactly handsome. He was small in statue and build, but he had beautiful dark eyes that seemed to see right through her. Sometimes she wondered if he had hypnotized her. The thing that got to her the most was his *savoir faire*. He was sophisticated and she had never known anyone like him before. He was capable of ordering their dinner in French when they went to the small French restaurants and he had a mannerism about him that enthralled her. He was the one who made all of the decisions and he became a father figure to her. The main thing was, he knew how to make love. Though she had no way of comparing him to other men, she wondered if all women found their husbands so exciting in bed. Her own family had questioned her in the same way and she couldn't find the words to explain her feelings so that they would understand. Bill was completely different than Roger and didn't seem to have the fire in him that Roger had. He was more dependable, according to mom and dad, and it seemed that Roger was always the one who had given them the most trouble when the two were growing up. But she liked Bill and found him very easy to talk to and they became good friends. She really felt like she had a brother now.

Bill had been corresponding with a girl while he was overseas. He had never met her, but a mutual friend had started them writing to each other. Bill had been looking forward to meeting her and decided to call her to make arrangements. She lived in Long Island, but worked in Manhattan, so he called her and they met the next evening when she got off of work. They had a few drinks together and then dinner. Her name was Eileen and she seemed like a nice girl from the way he spoke about her. After seeing her just about every night for several weeks, Bill announced that he would like to bring her home for dinner. Of course mom and dad were anxious to meet her as it was beginning to look serious. Nikki and Roger were also becoming eager to meet her and were looking forward to it.

The night that Bill brought Eileen home, Nikki started the dinner and set the table with the good china and silver before mom got home from work. Everyone was waiting to meet her and in a way, Nikki felt sorry for her. She knew how she had felt as she was remembering her first trip to New York alone. At least Eileen had Bill with her, but Nikki assumed that she must still be very nervous. When they finally arrived, Nikki liked her immediately. Although she was not a beauty, she had a pleasing personality and a cute petite figure and knew how to dress. In a matter of a short time, Bill announced that they were getting married. From that day on, Nikki found her to be beautiful. She had that happy glow on her face that only a girl in love could have and she showed her happiness.

The night of the wedding Dad was proudly introducing Nikki to all of his friends as the beautiful daughter-in-law and someone asked if she was the one who would marry Bill. Nikki was so embarrassed that she felt like running away. She loved Eileen and didn't want to take any of the glory away from her on her wedding night. She finally walked away from her father-in-law so that he would not continue to do this. He had an eye for beauty and he was very proud of Nikki, but she felt that he was not being fair to Eileen. This was her big night and dad was making Nikki the center of attention. Roger had always said that his father was a ladies' man and now she could understand what he meant.

Chapter Ten

While Roger was waiting to be mustered out of the service, he was still in uniform and he and Nikki took in as many movies and shows as they could, as they were admitted at half price. They knew that once he was out of the service that they would not be able to afford very much, as it would take time for Roger to start making a decent living. Nikki had managed to save some money while he was away, and outside of pitching in on the food bill and taking in a few movies, she had put the rest in the bank. However, they could not afford to dip into their savings until Roger had a job. They went to several radio shows which were free and it seemed that she was always chosen as a contestant. They just seemed to pick her out of the crowd, no matter where they were sitting. She asked Roger why and his reply was, "Because you are a lovely looking young lady." He decided that they spotted their contestants as they came in the door and noted where they were seated. They did all the things that tourists did. New York was lit up again since the war had ended and Nikki was fascinated with Times Square. She couldn't get over the bill boards, especially the one with the Camel Cigarettes where the smoke rings kept coming out and the one with the coffee where the coffee was pouring and the steam was pouring out. She was sure that she could smell it. She loved to watch the current news bulletin going around and around and they even went into Ripley's Believe it or Not and all of the other places where they took the tourist's money and gave them nothing for it. Roger was enjoying his job of showing her New York. He loved watching her face with every new experience. It was sheer joy to see her and he realized that he loved her more than ever. They even walked the steps up into the torch of the Statue of Liberty. The elevator was out of order that day, but they were so full of energy that they decided to walk up the steps.

Roger was finally mustered out of the service and it was time to start looking for an apartment. He felt that it would be for a short time, as he was sure that he would be going to Casablanca after his father went back and got things started. Nikki was looking forward to getting an apartment as she had felt very self-conscious whenever Roger made love to her. She was afraid that mom and dad would hear them and felt quite inhibited. Besides, now that dad had gotten things started in Casablanca, he and mom were planning to go there soon to live. They could have taken their apartment, but the rent was more than they could afford and they didn't need such a large one. They had finally sub-leased it to mom's niece who had two children and needed a larger apartment. They had hoped that Nikki and Roger could get her niece's apartment, but there was a waiting list and they were unable to talk the owner into giving it to them. They were having a difficult time trying to find a decent place to live, as all of the better apartments had waiting lists and you had to give them at least two thousand dollars for "key" money to go on the top of the list. In their case, this was impossible, as they would have to give up their entire savings. Finally, through some friends of the family, they found an old brownstone apartment on the first floor in deplorable condition between West End Avenue and Riverside Drive in the west nineties. Housing in New York had reached a point where people would sit around in hospitals waiting for someone to die so they could apply for the apartment. Though their apartment on West Ninety-Seventh Street was not exactly what they were dreaming of, in fact, it was a far cry from what they wanted, they decided they had better grab it while they could. They assumed that it would only be temporary anyway.

The apartment was dark and the lights had to be on all day, but they cleaned it up and got the land lord's permission to paper the walls.

As they worked all day and half the night, Nikki commented, "*He should be paying us to do this!*"

Roger answered, "*We were lucky to find anything at all the way things are.*" Nikki knew that he was right. When they finally finished, after much cursing on Roger's part, it was at least presentable, but not exactly a place that one would want to call home. It was clean and neat, looking much like a home made job, but colorful if nothing else. It was much nicer than dirty walls.

Chapter Eleven

Roger went to work for a vacuum cleaner company, selling from door to door. He had no trouble selling them, as people were in need of new appliances since there had been no new ones since before the war. Most of the factories had become war supply plants. He was to receive a commission on each vacuum cleaner he sold, but what the company failed to tell him in the beginning was that he would not receive his commission until the machine was delivered. He was then informed that they would not be able to deliver for six months. At this point their savings was going down and Nikki was depressed staying home in the dark apartment and had become very homesick. She longed for the houses on the large lots with the back yards and trees and flowers. However, she was smart enough to realize that the wise thing for her to do was go out and find a job. Roger didn't like the idea very much as he was old-fashioned about women working, but he finally consented to her going to work. He also knew that they could use at least one steady salary since his was so uncertain.

Nikki went to an agency to apply for a job as a secretary as this was what she knew she could do. She hated secretarial work, but she didn't know what else she could do. She thought of working as a sales clerk in a department store as that way she would be able to meet people all day long and wouldn't be stuck behind a desk. The woman at the agency told her that she would not make as much money as she could working as a secretary so she decided that she would go ahead and call on some of the people who were looking for secretaries. They gave her a list of names and a letter of recommendation. While she had been sitting around waiting for an interview she had befriended another girl who was looking for a modeling job.

Nikki said, *"That sounds like it would be fun to do, but I don't have any experience. Besides, I don't think I am tall enough."*

The girl insisted that Nikki go with her on some of her interviews. *"Who knows"* she said, *"you are a very pretty girl and something could come from it!"*

Finally Nikki decided to go with her, knowing that she was wasting a day, but there was something about it that fascinated her. She was sure that it was the fact that she would be wearing good looking clothes all day long, which she otherwise could not afford. Maybe she was thinking of Jean and remembering all the things that she had told her.

The first show room that they entered, the man looked at Nikki, ignoring the other girl, and asked her if she had ever modeled before.

Nikki said, *"No, I just came along with my friend. Besides, I don't think that I am tall enough to be a model."* She was very self conscious and embarrassed and felt her face turning red.

The man looked her over and said, *"Turn around."* Nikki

obeyed. Then he said, "*Take off your coat, I think that would help!*" Nikki again obeyed and took off her coat and turned around again. Finally he asked, "*Are you a size seven?*"

Nikki answered, "*Yes sir.*"

"*Perfect!*" the man said excitedly. *We have a very fine junior line as well as the ladies line. How would you like to start training?*"

Nikki was astonished that it had been so easy. She finally managed to ask, "*Why me? Surely there are a lot of girls who have already had the training and are looking for jobs.*"

The man smiled at her and said, "*That is true my dear, but you have the elegance. It is rare that one with your looks walks into this showroom.*" He almost seemed too eager and Nikki became frightened.

She finally smiled and said, "*I will have to get my husband's permission.*"

The man smiled and said, "*You ask your husband dear, and call me tomorrow.*" He then gave her his card. He had never even noticed the other girl and Nikki was feeling sorry for her.

When they left the girl said to her, "*If I were you I would be careful. He was a little too eager!*" She finally added, "*Believe me when I say it is not sour grapes, as I knew that they would like your looks and that is why I asked you to go with me.*"

Nikki finally said, "*I feel badly though, after all, you were the one who was looking for the modeling job and he didn't give you a chance.*"

The girl smiled and said, "*There are plenty of other showrooms, but I'll have to admit that I think that after lunch you and I should part company. I don't think that I'd like that kind of competition all the time! However, I think you ought to check this one out, as he was just ga ga over you!"*

Nikki was excited about the fact that she had made such a good impression on the man and decided to phone Jean when they stopped for lunch and see if Jean knew anything about the company. She was already picturing herself getting large sums of money to model beautiful clothes. She thought that she was dreaming. She excused herself after they had ordered their lunch and went and called Jean.

When she told her what had happened Jean said, "*The girl is right, you had better be careful. It is not often that they want a girl with no experience or training. Give me his name and I will have the company checked out for you.*"

Nikki hung up and went back to the table. She informed her new friend that she had a very close friend who had been a model and that she was going to check it out for her.

"*That's good,*" the girl said. "*It could be legitimate, but you can't be too careful in this city.*"

Nikki was wondering what Roger would have to say about it. She knew that it would pay more money than secretarial work and it was by far more glamorous.

When they finished lunch the other girl wished her luck and said, "*Maybe if we split up I'll have some luck. I really need to get busy and look for a job.*"

Nikki realized that the girl was not too happy with the competition that she had presented her with and decided to go home and call Jean and see if she had found out anything. When she walked in the door the phone was ringing. It was Jean and she sounded excited.

She said, "*Nikki, you must have made quite an impression on that guy. He is legit and I understand that it is a very prestigious company to work for with very fine clothes. You hit the jackpot, honey!"* Nikki became excited and thanked her and when they hung up she could not wait for Roger to come home to tell him the news.

She went into the kitchen and started preparing dinner. She was eagerly waiting for him to return home when she heard the key in the door. She ran down the hall to kiss him before he could get into the living room and he could see that she was excited. She immediately began to inform him of the events of the day.

Before she could finish he was already in a rage. Nikki was startled, as she had no idea how possessive and jealous natured he was. He said, *"There is no way that my wife is going to be a model! I will not permit it! Those men will put their hands all over you!"*

Nikki argued that Jean had checked out the company and found it to be a very legitimate one, but Roger was against the whole idea.

Finally she said, *"I guess I will look for secretarial work. Let's hope that my boss doesn't have roving hands!"*

She was being sarcastic and Roger knew it and could see her disappointment. He tried to cheer her up by saying, *"Nikki, please God, you won't be working for very long. I expect to hear from my father soon and I know he will be sending for us to come over to Casablanca. It would really be foolish for you to go through a training period and then have to leave. It would not be fair to your boss either."*

Nikki knew he was right and the next day she took a job with an insurance company.

Chapter Twelve

At this point their life was not very exciting. They got together with Eileen and Bill once a week to have dinner and play bridge. Occasionally they would go ice skating. Two of Nikki's friends from home had married New York boys and were now living in New York. They all lived in different areas and therefore didn't get to see each other very often. Outside of that, they worked and managed to live and Nikki had stopped brooding over the apartment, as she was not at home during the day. The only time that she was not happy about it was when some of her father's family would come to New York and it would embarrass her for them to see the apartment.

Bill was busy opening his hardware store in Long Island. He had managed to save quite a bit of money because of the fact that he had been overseas for so long and had not been married at the time. Eileen had continued to work after they were married and she was bringing home a fairly good pay check, as she had been working for the same people for many years. She was ten years older than Nikki. They seemed to be very happy and were living in Long Island with Eileen's parents. They had already decided that when the hardware store opened that Eileen would quit her job and work with Bill at the store. Nikki figured that would be the end of their weekly get-togethers and that depressed her, as she looked forward to it every week.

About a month after she had started working, when she returned home one evening, she found Roger in a state of excitement as she had never seen him before. He rushed to greet her with the telegram he had received from his father.

SENDING MONEY STOP PREPARE TO COME TO CASABLANCA WITH NIKKI STOP LOVE DAD.

Nikki was overjoyed. Now she was finally going to see the world as Roger had promised her. He was more like the old Roger and she could see how pleased he was. Since she had started working he had not been the same. She knew it bothered him that he was not able to support his own wife and he had lost his spark. Now it was back as he started making plans.

He told her that he had already checked with the steamship lines and that it would be three weeks before they could leave, as there was nothing available until then. He had booked passage for them traveling on one of the beautiful luxury liners that Roger had described to her, but they were still in the process of converting them back to passenger liners. During the war they had all been converted into troop ships. After two years in New York, Nikki was eager to leave. She didn't like it at all and wondered how people could spend their lives there. Of course she knew that those who had money had a good life, but for those who didn't, it was no life at all.

Roger informed her that if she wanted she could go home and visit with her family for a week or ten days before they left. He had decided that he would pack and ship all of their belongings while she was gone. She agreed that she would like to see her family since it had been two years since she had seen them. She called her Aunt Emma that she was on her way and they were very excited. Nikki had mixed emotions about leaving Roger alone to do the work, but she knew that it would be a long time before she would see her loved ones again. When the train pulled in and she saw everyone there to meet her, she knew that she had done the right thing. As Roger had said, "God only knows when you will see them again."

Her aunt had prepared a lovely meal for the family. She saw and talked to all of her family and friends who were still living there and the week went very fast. Most of her friends had married and moved away, like Nikki, they met boys who were stationed there, married them and moved away. She did miss Roger and was ready to return to New York when the time came. When she got on the train both she and her family were crying, since they had no idea of how many years it would be before they would see each other again. She especially hated leaving Nora with whom she had been so close, and her heart ached when she thought of not seeing her for such a long time. She wondered how old Betty would be before she would see her again. She knew that when she returned one day that everything would be changed.

Book Two

Casablanca

Chapter Thirteen

When Nikki arrived in New York, Roger was at the train to meet her. He seemed happy to see her, but he looked very thin and pale. He immediately told her that he had been very sick with the stomach flu and that he had had a rough time going through it alone. His parents were already in Casablanca and therefore his mother could not help him. Nikki felt badly that she had not been there to take care of him, but she had no way of knowing that he would become ill while she was gone. In a way, she was slightly irritated because she felt that he was putting a guilt trip on her. She thought he was being a bit of a baby and could not handle an emergency alone. Even when he had had colds he always acted as if he were dying.

Finally she said, *"If you had called me I would have come home right away!"*

Roger replied, *"I didn't want to cut your visit short."*

"Now he is being a martyr," Nikki thought. She didn't really know why she was so irritated, but assumed that she

was still feeling the heartache of telling her family goodbye. Finally she asked, "*How long do you really think we will be gone before we can come home to visit the states?*"

Roger looked surprised and asked, "*Are you having misgivings about leaving now? Don't you think it is a little late for that?*"

Nikki tried to explain her feelings. Finally she said, "*You said that you didn't know how many years it would be before I would see my family again. I was just wondering if we will be able to come home and visit from time to time.*"

Roger was a bit impatient and she could see it. "*How come you haven't asked me that before now?*"

Nikki thought a moment and said

"*You will be with your family. I am the one who will be making all of the sacrifices. It just doesn't seem fair.*"

Finally Roger understood and said, "*It will depend on how well we do financially. If we are making enough money, we will be able to come home for a visit now and then.*"

Nikki seemed satisfied with his answer. She finally said, "*As I left home and saw my family all standing there crying, I too cried for the first time. Suddenly I got a terrible feeling inside of me and wondered if I would ever see them again. I couldn't stand the thought of it.*"

Roger put his arms around her and tried to console her. "*You will visit your family, honey, even if I can't go with you. I promise.*" He added, "*We are leaving on Sunday at three o'clock.*"

Suddenly Nikki realized that the big day was only two days away and she could feel the excitement churning inside of her. She turned to Roger and said, "*I love you so much! I promise not to give you a hard time of it. I am really looking forward to this."*

On Sunday afternoon Bill and Eileen and all of their friends came to see them off. Even though it was a freighter there was the feeling of festivity as they had their farewell party on board. They brought chocolates, bottles of champagne, baskets of fruit and wine and all kinds of good foods to eat. They took pictures on deck, all of the girls hamming it up and posing cheese-cake and a good time was had by all. Nikki was worried about her favorite cartoon, Lil Abner, who kept saying *"I'm ready for Freddie"*, and as yet, no one knew who Freddie was. They were teasing her when she said that she would never find out now and they promised that as soon as it became evident who Freddie was they would let her know. They were full of nonsense because they were so sad having to say goodbye for God knows how long. They were enjoying their last hour before leaving American soil. When they finally took off at five o'clock, Nikki was very excited. As they passed the Statue of Liberty Roger said, *"Take a good look honey, as it will be at least two years before you see her again."*

As they got further out and looked back at New York, it looked like a fairy land to Nikki. When they passed Long Island, a car was parked at the beach and blinked their lights in Morse code, *"Goodbye and good luck."* The captain asked them if there was anyone they knew in Long Island and they told him that there was. They were sure that it was Eileen and Bill. He answered them with the ship's whistle in Morse code, *"Goodbye and thank you."*

Nikki was happy that she and Roger would have two long

weeks alone since they had never had time for a honeymoon. There was only one other passenger besides themselves, a young man who was going to see his mother for the first time in many years. He had lived with his father after his parents divorced and his mother had gone to Casablanca. As it turned out, they didn't have as much time alone as they had hoped for, as the poor fellow was lonely and wanted to talk. Sometimes they would lock themselves in their cabin just to be alone, but after a short while there would be a knock at the door. At times they would pretend to be asleep, but they did feel sorry for him and most of the time they would invite him in.

They ate with the ship's officers. The captain was a very nice man and very interesting to listen to. There was a larder where they could go and help themselves if they felt hungry at night, but it got to the point that Nikki could hardly stand to walk in there. It smelled of cheese, as the Norwegians eat a lot of cheese and this was always their dessert. Nikki would go to their cabin and bring out the chocolates to pass around after dinner and they were very happy to have them, as there was nothing sweet, outside of fruit, on board ship. Toward the end of the trip, they had even run out of fruit. The meals consisted mainly of fish, which was not one of their favorite foods. Roger had always enjoyed fish, but even he was getting tired of it. They both had visions of a big, thick steak. There were always cold cuts for lunch, but not what they were used to and outside of tasting it, they barely ate any. They had two long weeks with nothing to do except read and make love. They couldn't even look forward to meals, as they left so much to be desired. The only meal they actually enjoyed was breakfast, as there was always plenty of bacon and eggs and fried potatoes.

Throughout the voyage, Nikki kept having visions of the romantic *Kasbah* when she thought of Casablanca, as that was the impression the movie had made on her. She thought of it as being the most romantic place in the world. Roger had talked about it so much since they had been married and even before. Most of the time he had spoken of Marcel, his best friend, and there were many stories about their escapades. Marcel was the type of man that women chased after. They had literally thrown themselves at him, according to what Roger had said. Nikki was curious to meet this man that she had heard so much about. When she would try to picture him, he always ended up looking like Humphrey Bogart. She knew that he was now married and had three children. Nikki felt that they would be very good friends and they would be running around with Marcel and his Spanish wife, Juanita. She had been a famous Spanish dancer and Roger had told Nikki that she was a beautiful woman. She wondered if she had let herself go after having three children, but couldn't picture a man like Marcel living with a woman who did not keep herself looking her best. She knew in her heart that she would never let herself go as Roger was much too proud of her looks and loved to show her off. At times she found herself worrying about it, as she knew that as she grew older her looks would fade and wondered if Roger would still love her. Then she would realize that he was almost eight years older than she and he would certainly be looking his age as well. She had always taken pride in herself, as it had been drummed into her and Nora by her Aunt Emma that it is easy to get a man, but the most difficult thing is to hold on to him. She would say, "*Never let yourself get fat and sloppy.*" Nikki always remembered this. She had also said, "*If you don't get up in the morning and fix your husband breakfast, he will go to a restaurant where he will see the pretty young girls looking fresh and all made up and he will think of you at home with your hair uncombed and dowdy!*"

Nikki had always remembered that and had always fixed a good breakfast for Roger after fixing her hair and make-up. She always looked lovely for him when he returned home in the evening, even when she was tired and not feeling at her best.

Chapter Fourteen

On their arrival, Nikki was feeling dizzy and confused when she realized that she had come to live in what seemed to be an uncivilized country. Dad was there to meet them, as were a million Arabs. They were all screaming at each other in what she assumed was Arabic and dad spoke it fluently, in fact, many dialects. She was afraid that one of them would hit him as he was screaming as loud as they were. When Nikki expressed her fears, Roger laughed out loud and explained to her that this was just the way they talk. They were not arguing with each other, but although he did not speak the language, he understood a good part of it and said that his dad was telling them to bring their bags to the customs. Nikki breathed a sigh of relief when she finally realized what was going on. As she looked around, she saw all of these people dressed like ghosts. At least that was the way she had always seen them drawn as a child. They were wrapped in things that looked like white sheets and even their heads were covered. All that she could see were large, brown eyes.

She held onto Roger and asked what they were and again he laughed and explained to her that the Arab women dressed like this. They could not show their faces in public. He also explained that the ones who could afford it wore Jellabas, which were long coats with hoods that zipped down the front. With that, he explained that they wore fancy veils over their nose and mouth. Suddenly all of the romance of Casablanca was gone. Nikki's image of the romantic cafes and the intrigue was lost. They were taken to customs and Nikki just stood there feeling helpless while their luggage was being searched. She had handed over her passport and a chill went through her when she thought that they may not give it back to her and she wondered if she would ever be able to go back to America again.

Roger and his father were jabbering away with the customs officers in French, which sounded like one long word to Nikki. She wondered if she would ever be able to learn this language, when suddenly she remembered that Roger had told her that many of these people did speak English, especially since the Americans had been there during the war. But even before that, they learned English in school and they imported teachers from England so that they had a good pronunciation. However she knew that she was much too curious a person and that she would not be satisfied if she didn't learn to speak French, as she would miss out on too much. As she stood there looking around, suddenly a wild looking man with uncombed hair and large eyes appeared in front of her and before she knew what was happening, he grabbed her and started kissing her. She was terrified and must have shown it when he said in broken English, "*I am sorry that I am late! I have been waiting to meet you for so long and wanted to be here when you arrived!"*

Nikki had pushed him away and was sure that her eyes must have looked as wild as his she was so frightened. She was so shaken up and wondered why Roger had not tried to rescue her from this crazy man.

Suddenly Roger looked up and saw him. He rushed over to him and they embraced and kissed each other on the cheeks, chattering away in French in excited voices. Then he said, *"Nikki, this is Marcel, my best friend! Don't be afraid of him, he is only greeting you and came down to welcome you to Casablanca!"*

As she breathed a sigh of relief she wondered to herself why the women fell at his feet. After coming to her senses she said, *"I'm sorry if I was rude, Roger has spoken about you constantly, but I didn't realize who you were. I'll have to admit that I have been terrified since our ship docked. They are all yelling in languages that I don't understand and I have felt so strange since our arrival. I suppose I should have known you, as Roger has spoken of you more than anyone else since I first met him, but I have never seen a picture of you and had no idea what you looked like!"*

Marcel smiled and said in his broken English, *"I am sorry if I have frightened you. I should have realized that you would not know me since we have never yet met, but Roger has sent me pictures of you and I was looking forward to meeting you in person for years. I suppose that I am a very impulsive person!"*

Nikki smiled at him and realized that he did have the most beautiful, expressive eyes she had ever seen. Now she could understand why he was a ladies' man and wondered if she would be able to resist him if he ever made a pass at her. As they spoke, she suddenly realized that it was as if there was no one else around. She completely forgot that Roger and some other people were standing there watching them

He told her to speak slowly, that even though he spoke English, he was not as fluent in English as Roger was in French. It was then decided that Marcel would take Nikki home while Roger and his father finished with the customs. They asked her to leave her purse and Marcel then led her to his car. Almost everyone drove Renaults, which was what he had.

As they drove through the city, Nikki was aware that it was a different looking place, much different than she had expected. All of the buildings were white, which was where the name Casablanca came from. Also, they were very modern, in fact, more so than in the states. The traffic was heavy because it was lunch time and there didn't seem to be any laws about driving. Everyone seemed to have the right of way, including the many bicycles on the streets. The cars were all going fast and honking their horns. It seemed to Nikki that they came close to at least ten accidents before they arrived at the apartment.

She was holding onto the door with all of her strength when Marcel looked at her and laughed and said, *"Don't be afraid. This is the way people drive here."* As she discovered later, very few women did drive.

As they drove the rest of the way she was watching Marcel. Roger had talked so much about his reputation for being a great lover and she could not help but wonder what it would be like to have him make love to her. Now he was married and had three children, but he was still a ladies' man.

Her curiosity became more and more aroused as she looked at him. With his eyes alone he could embrace you. The glare from the white buildings was beginning to make her eyes water and she put on her sunglasses which had been perched on top of her head. Marcel startled her when he said, *"Please, Nicole, don't do that!"*

Surprised, Nikki asked him why. His answer was, *"Because, Nicole, I cannot see your lovely blue eyes!"* She liked the sound of her name in French. When Marcel said it, it sounded so romantic. Suddenly she realized that all the time that she had been watching him, he had been looking at her through the mirror. As if reading her mind he said, *"Yes, I saw you watching me!"*

She was embarrassed, but she laughed and asked, *"Do you have eyes on the sides of your head too?*

Marcel laughed and said, *"No, but I do have a mirror and I angled it so that I could watch your reaction as you saw our city."* He lied. He was watching her because he found her to be such an attractive woman and he was still human.

Nikki laughed and said, *"I'll have to admit that it is at least a million times better than my first impression at the docks."*

Marcel agreed that he could understand that and added, *"But after all, any port in the world is not what a person dreams of."*

"That is true" Nikki said, *"But if you speak the language it is not quite as frightening, at least you understand what they are saying."*

Marcel admitted that he could see where it must have seemed strange to her, especially where they were speaking both in Arabic and French.

Just about that time he drove up in front of a small apartment house. Roger had been telling her that Marcel still ran around on Juanita and later on was to find out that most of the men had mistresses and when she was introduced to "*Madame*" she never really knew if it was the wife or the mistress.

As she looked up, mom was standing at the door watching for them. It was difficult to get phones in Casablanca and since they did not plan to stay in that apartment for very long they had not even tried. Therefore she had no idea if the ship had arrived on time or at what time they would be arriving.

After embracing Nikki, she welcomed Marcel in French and suddenly Nikki felt envious that she was the only one who didn't speak French. When she expressed her thoughts, mom assured her that it would not take long as she was young. *"I was much older than you when I first came here and as young as you are, you will be speaking French much better than I do."* She asked Marcel if he would like to stay for lunch, but he explained that his mother was expecting him home.

Nikki remembered that Roger had told her that Marcel and Juanita still lived with his widowed mother, as did his brother Jon and his wife. It also amazed her that he was concerned about his mother, but not his wife and she wondered why the women here put up with being treated this way. They were simply ignored once they were married in many cases, from what Roger had told her. About that time Roger and dad were coming toward the door. They were finally home and she was glad.

Marcel explained that he was just leaving and informed everyone that his mother was expecting them for dinner.

He said, "*She is very anxious to see Roshay and to meet Nicole.*" With that, he said goodbye and left.

Nikki kept hearing *Roshay* and *Nicole* echoing in her ears and loved the sound of their names in French.

Chapter Fifteen

At eight thirty they all climbed into the Renault that dad had bought and drove to Madame Beret's house. Nikki was surprised to see that she was still wearing widows' black since her husband had been dead at least six years.

She grabbed Roger and hugged and kissed him. She was an extremely emotional person, but Nikki could already see that most of the French people showed more emotion than the average American. She kept repeating *"Mon fils, mon fils!"*

Mom explained to her that he was like a son to her because he and Marcel had been inseparable since they were very young boys and Roger had practically lived at Marcel's house. She then grabbed Nikki and held her face in her hands and ranted and raved saying, *"Elle est une jeune fille! Elle este. tres belle! Sa yeux etes tres bleu!"* Roger turned to Nikki and said, Marcel's mother thinks that you are very young and beautiful and that your eyes are very blue. Tell her *"Merci."*

"Merci beaucoup, Madame Beret. "Peller moi ma mah!"

Roger told her that she wanted her to call her *Ma Mah* and so she did.

About that time she saw a young woman whom she was sure was Juanita. She knew it had to be her, as she was the most exquisite Spanish woman she had ever seen. She held her head high as would a classical Spanish dancer and she carried herself proudly. Nikki spoke a few words to her in Spanish, as she had studied it in school and although she was not very good at conversational Spanish, she was at least able to speak to her. Juanita seemed pleased to see that they would be able to talk to each other as she did not speak English. She was introduced to Jon and Theresa, his new wife, who was a very pretty Italian girl. Jon was Marcel's brother. His children were adorable. The girls had their mother's classic Spanish features and their father's large, expressive eyes. The baby, who was a boy, was also good looking and Nikki could picture him growing up to be a lady killer like his father.

Marcel's mother announced that she wanted to give Nicole a gift that she had been saving for her. When Roger explained this to Nikki, she again found herself saying "*Merci, ma mah*!" Everyone laughed at her attempt to speak French and she found herself laughing good naturedly at herself. When she opened the box she could not believe her eyes. She was sure that they must have popped right out of her head. It was a very large ruby and by far the most magnificent gift she had ever received. Mom, dad and Roger were all speaking at once and Nikki was sure that they were telling her how generous she was. Her answer was, "*Rien est aussi bon pour l'femme de Roger*!" Roger told Nikki that she had said *"Nothing is too good for Roger's wife."* Nikki went and put her arms around her and kissed her.

All evening everyone seemed to be talking at once and she kept hearing her name over and over. All she could do was smile until her cheeks started to ache. She was wishing they would go on to another subject. Every once in a while Marcel would look at her and smile knowingly.

Finally he said, *"I bet your cheeks hurt!"* With that, Nikki laughed out loud and admitted that he was right. *"You will have to hurry and learn French so that you will know what they are saying! Believe me when I tell you that it is all good. My mother has fallen in love with you as we all have!"*

Nikki felt her face turn red. She had never had so much praise before and though it made her feel good, it also embarrassed her.

Finally they were ushered into the dining room. The table was very long and elegantly set. They had beautiful china and silver and a magnificent hand made table cloth.

When they started serving the meal, Nikki could not believe that people could eat so much and she wondered why they were not all as big as houses, but the only person who was heavy was Madame Beret.

First they served fish, then soup and then the main course which was a huge leg of lamb with mint sauce, browned potatoes and peas on which they poured rich, thick cream. When she thought that dinner was over, they served the salad. Her face must have shown her surprise, as they immediately explained to her that the salad course is always served last, as it is light and helps to wash down the heavy food.

By this time she was feeling dizzy, as she was not used to drinking wine, which was all they served. There was no water on the table and she learned later that the water in Casablanca was so bad that no one drank it. They had changed the wine with each course and Nikki found herself drinking it all. For dessert they served a variety of soft, aged cheeses and fruit. When they passed the plate to her and she got a whiff of the cheese, she refused it, saying that she could not eat another bite, which was in fact true. She didn't dare look at Roger as she knew that they would both burst out laughing, as he knew that she didn't care for any cheese after their steady diet of it on the ship. She also noted that he did not take any. After that they served coffee and brandy. When she drank the liquor, she turned red in the face and started coughing. Everyone laughed and explained to her that liquor was to sip, not to drink.

When the servants removed the food and plates from the table, Juanita followed them into the kitchen to supervise and Nikki went with her. After the servants ate, they threw the bone from the leg of lamb out of the window and to Nikki's surprise it had barely touched the ground when it was snatched up by a poor Arab. Later when she mentioned this to mom, she explained that they would split the bone and make soup. She added that they had no garbage problem in Casablanca. The poor Arabs raided the trash cans. All of the bottles and cans went into one sack to be sold for recycling and all of the food scraps into another to be eaten. Being that the French people were very thrifty and did not believe in waste, there was very little garbage to begin with, as they used the left over vegetables the next day for lunch, served cold with vinegar and oil.

Chapter Sixteen

After the war, as in America, apartments were difficult to come by in Casablanca, as building had halted during the war. Also, the population had grown considerably because many European refugees had poured in during and after the war. Roger's parents had only one bedroom and it had been decided that Nikki and Roger would stay in a hotel until they could get into a larger apartment for the four of them.

After dinner Marcel went with them to help take their luggage to the hotel. When Nikki entered the hotel room she discovered that it was very large, which pleased her very much since they were going to have to live there for a while. Dad had a lead on a large apartment and had given a deposit on it, but the people were not moving out for another month.

When she walked over to look at the bathroom Marcel was behind her. To her surprise there were two toilets, one with a seat and lid and the other without. She assumed that other one was a urinal and thought it strange that they should put a urinal in hotel bathroom. Suddenly Marcel started laughing and Nikki jumped, as she didn't know that he was behind her. He said, *"All Americans think that the one without the seat is for making pee pee, they have never seen a bidet before!"* When she asked him what it was for he told her that she would have to ask Roger to explain it to her.

They decided to go to the club across the street, as it was around midnight and the clubs were just getting into full swing. People dined late in Casablanca, never before nine o'clock, and they made such a production over dinner that it was usually over around eleven. The clubs would start getting busy around 11:30. As they walked out of the hotel to go across the street to the most popular hang out, Nikki couldn't believe her eyes when she saw a man standing there with his penis in his hand, aimed at the wall of the building relieving himself. It was explained to her that this was normal here. She was to find out later that many more unusual things were common in Casablanca.

When they went to the beaches the men would pull off their wet trunks in front of God and everyone and change into dry ones. She found that men and women shared the same laboratories in the rest rooms and to get to the ladies' toilets you had to walk through a room with urinals lined against the walls where the men were urinating. The first night she came flying out of the rest room. She was sure that the sign had said *"Dames"* but when she saw all of the men, she assumed that she had made a mistake. She went back to the table immediately and when Marcel saw the look on her face he exploded with laughter saying, *"I'll bet you thought that you were in the wrong room!"*

She was furious with Roger for not warning her and he told her he had not thought about it and apologized. She could not believe how uncivilized these people were. Nikki had always been very modest and it had taken a year before she had been able to undress in front of Roger, and even then, it was because he made her do it. Now, she found herself in a total state of shock. She asked Roger to take her to the hotel room, as she did not want to go back in the restroom again. Laughing, Roger got up and escorted her across the street. She asked him about the bidet and what it was for and he explained to her that women used it to clean themselves after having intercourse. She replied, "*The French seem to think of everything when it comes to sex!*" Roger was amused by the way she reacted to these things.

When they arrived back at the club, Marcel was dancing with some young girl. By this time many of Roger's old friends had discovered that he was there and they came over to the table to greet him and welcome him back. They all wanted to meet his lovely wife whom they had already heard about. Most of them spoke English and Roger introduced her as Nicole. It was the first time she had heard him use her French name and it sounded strange. From that night on, every time they walked into the club the band would play "*Deep in the Heart of Texas.*" The men surrounded her. They were fascinated with her blue eyes, which was rare in Casablanca and they all wanted to know if she had a sister that looked like her.

After Roger started going to the office to work with his father, Nikki would go to her mother-in-law's. They would go to the market and make lunch. Lunch was their main meal of the day. After lunch the men would take a siesta for a couple of hours. At three o'clock they would meet at the tea room for tea and pastries. It was a very easy life.

Chapter Seventeen

By this time Nikki had made some very good friends at the club. Monique Dubose was her closest friend, as she spoke perfect English. Though she didn't look it, she was ten years older than Nikki and she had a lovely ten year old daughter. They confided in everything and she was so glad to have someone to talk to.

One day they were talking about the gossip going around, there always was, and Monique said, "*You have to understand why, Nicole. Since many of us do not always have the liberty of selecting our spouses, we do not always love the person that we are forced to marry. In many cases the parents arrange the marriages for their children. Some are promised to each other from birth and others make financial arrangements between themselves, which was the case in my marriage. My mother died when I was very young and my father had very little money. Michael fell in love with me and wanted to marry me. His father had a lot of money and he asked to visit my father and offered him a large sum of money if he would promise my hand in marriage to his son, Michael. I had nothing to say about it and I have never been in love with my husband."* She went on to say, *in this country the majority of the people who are not Arabs or Jews are Catholics and it is very difficult to obtain a divorce. We have been married for twelve years and have a ten year old daughter, but I do not love him as a woman should love her husband."*

She went on to say that during the war Michael was sent to England and she was alone when she had met an American major and fell deeply in love with him. "*We lived together for two years. He wanted to marry me and take me back to America with him. This is why I speak English so well. When Michael returned home, my American major had already been shipped back to the United States, as they were beginning to close the American bases here. We continued to write to each other and still do. He sends the letters to my sister's apartment so that Michael will not see them. At the time I told Michael that I wanted a divorce, that I had never loved him and I also told him about my affair with the American and that that was why I wanted my freedom to marry him. His response was not what I had hoped for. He forgave me for having the affair and said that it is not easy to be alone for two years and then said that he could understand why I was unfaithful to him and he would never hold it against me. He pleaded and cried; he even got down on his knees and told me that he worshiped the ground I walk on. I wanted my American more than anything in the world, but I felt sorry for Michael and I stayed with him."* She went on to say, "*If I were to meet someone now who appealed to me, I would still have affairs, but there is no one here that I care about. My heart belongs in America with my wonderful major!"*

Nikki thought about Roger and her love for him and she

felt sorry for Monique. She knew that Roger had been raised in this country and had had affairs with married women before the war and suddenly she wished they could go home. She felt insecure and was afraid that Roger would tire of her and start having an affair with someone.

As if reading her mind, Monique asked, "*What would you do if you found out that Roger was having an affair?*"

Nikki wondered if she knew something that she herself did not know and she felt a lump in her stomach. "*I just don't know, but I suppose I would go home and get a divorce.*"

Monique looked at her unbelievingly and said, "*Then you are a fool, Nicole! If you love him you won't leave him. Most of these affairs only last for a short time and do not mean anything. You must remember that Roger was raised in this atmosphere and is accustomed to seeing men do these things.*"

Suddenly Nikki decided that she didn't want anymore of this conversation and suggested that the others were waiting for them on the tennis court and that they had better join them.

Chapter Eighteen

When Marcel had received the pictures of Roger and Nicole after they had married he thought that she was a real beauty, but he was not prepared for the effect that she would have on him when he first saw her. She had taken him by complete surprise and he could think of nothing but her. He had her on his mind when he went to sleep at night and when he woke up in the morning and during the day he could not concentrate on his work. He could think of nothing but having her in his arms and could not get over the fact that he thought he might be in love for the first time in his life and that it was with his best friend's wife. He could not think of doing anything about it since she was Roger's wife. Roger was like a brother to him. He knew in his heart that if he could be married to her, he would never stray again. He would never look at another woman. It was strange to him as he had always loved variety. Now he found himself envious of his closest friend and could not do anything about it.

Since he had married Juanita he had had many affairs

and at the present time was having an affair with her best friend. He also knew that if she were to find out that he was with Yolanda she would be terribly hurt and this was the first time he had actually kept an affair under cover and had made it a point not to be seen out in public with her.

Yolanda had hated him at first, as she knew how he was treating Juanita. One night she followed him into the restroom. She told him that he was a dirty bastard, who was treating Juanita like a servant and she had actually spit on him. Juanita had taught her how to dance and she loved her very much. He always liked women with a lot of fire and decided that he would have her. The next night he went back to the club and watched her, using his eyes as he had done with so many other women. It always worked for him. He could see that she noticed it and was not quite sure if she was angry or interested. That night, when he went to the restroom she followed him again, but this time she threw herself down at his feet and with tears running down her face said, "*Take me, I am yours!*" At first he considered it just another conquest, but they started meeting every day in borrowed apartments and he realized that he was drawn to this woman as he had been drawn to Juanita in the early days of their affair. There was definitely something about these Spanish dancers that appealed to him. They danced with such passion that many times they would even faint at the end of the dance.

He had thought of nothing but Yolanda until he had finally met Nicole. She was different. He was not sure if she had the fire in her that the Spanish women had, but he dwelled on how it would be to go to bed with her. She seemed so soft and loveable and he had a strong desire to fondle her. He could think of nothing else, except that she was married to his best friend who was like a brother to him.

He had missed Roger when he had been forced to leave Casablanca and had looked forward to his return for all of these years. He valued his friendship and could not forget about all of the years that they had been so close and all of the conquests they had made together. He decided that he would keep his hands off of her until the first time he found that Roger was straying, and if he knew his friend, he was sure that he would eventually weaken and try and see Carla, as he had been madly in love with her when he had left Casablanca. He had already asked about her and had wanted to know if she had remarried after her husband was killed in the war.

Marcel managed to be with Nicole and Roger just about every night since they had arrived in Casablanca. He was testing her and trying to see if she was the least bit interested in him. He was sure that Roger had told her that he was a ladies' man and he could tell that she was just a little curious about him. When the slow dances came on he would always ask her to dance with him. This was a very natural thing since Roger was aware of the fact that he did not like to dance to the Latin rhythms or the jitterbugs. On several occasions he had found himself with an erection while dancing with her. The lights were always turned down low for the slow pieces and he was interested in the fact that Nicole did not try to pull away from him. As a matter of fact, she had seemed to dance even closer and he knew that she was enjoying it. Being a very passionate man, he felt that one day they would have an affair, as he knew that she was definitely attracted to him.

One night when they were at the club Carla came in and he saw Roger and her looking at each other and if he knew Roger, they were passing signals to each other, although Roger never mentioned it to him. In the old days they had always confided in each other when it came to women and although he confided in Roger about his affair with Yolanda, Roger hadn't mentioned Carla lately. He wondered if Roger sensed his own interest in Nicole, though he had been very careful not to show it.

Marcel decided to do a little spying. Roger's parents had left for Italy and he and Nicole were alone. He was sure that this would be the time that he would try and see Carla, when he was not under the prying eyes of his father and he would not be there to see if he showed up at the office or not. He knew that Roger was afraid of his father because of money reasons and that he would never do anything that he would disapprove of, as it was obvious that his father was very fond of Nicole and also very proud of her.

At times he would laugh at himself and think, "*This is the first time in my life I have not pursued a woman that appealed to me.*" That was using the term lightly, as not only did Nicole appeal to him, but he wanted her more than anything he could think of. Sometimes he felt that it would be worth losing Roger's friendship, but he felt a loyalty to him as he would to his own brother. He would tell himself, "*What is best is worth waiting for. The time will come.*"

Chapter Nineteen

Nikki found herself daydreaming more and more about Marcel. She thought of his burning eyes and his sex appeal. She looked forward to the slow dances with him when she could feel the hardness in his groin. She was sure that he knew that he was causing her to climax right on the dance floor. She could think of nothing but this, but in her heart she knew that she could not hurt Juanita or Roger. She felt that she should get her mind off of him, but found it to be impossible.

Poor Juanita, she never joined clubs and Marcel never took her out. She stayed at home with her babies and her only friends were Yolanda, who would sometimes go to see her and herself, who Juanita had started confiding in. By this time they had moved out of Madame Beret's house and had bought a villa. Marcel was now doing very well financially. He owned a factory where they manufactured knit wear and everything was selling these days. One night when they had gone over to visit with Juanita and Marcel, Juanita had confided in her that she knew that Marcel was seeing another woman. She said, *"I have never let myself get fat as so many of the women do after they marry and have children, but he has always had to have other women. I have never let it bother me, as I knew that these never meant anything more to him than a few rolls in the bed. The day we moved in to our villa, I found out that he is having an affair with Yolanda. We had moved most of our things over to the new house, but I still had some packing to do and Marcel suggested that I go home and finish packing and that he would stay here to guard the house and all of our belongings, as you cannot move things into a villa without the thieves knowing about it and if the villa is left alone they will break in and take everything. The next morning I came over early to bring him his breakfast and he didn't want me to come in. I finally pushed my way in and when I looked in the bedroom I saw Yolanda. She cried and got on her knees and pleaded with me to forgive her. I really don't blame her because I know how Marcel is when he decides to go after a woman. However, I am very hurt by this and I do not see how we can ever be friends again."*

Nikki felt like crying, she felt so sorry for her and she realized that she would have to start refusing to dance with Marcel, as sooner or later she was afraid that something would happen between them. She was determined to stop thinking about him. She knew that she could not hurt this poor woman whom she had grown to love. Nikki had found out about Marcel's affair with Yolanda when she had gone to Tangier with Roger and he was there with her. She could not help but feel jealous for Juanita, or, she wondered, maybe for herself. She hated to even think about it. After that, when he knew that she was aware of their affair, he had brought her to their apartment from time to time when mom and dad had left. Nikki was always polite to her and could not blame her for being attracted to this sensuous man, but she always felt a pang of jealousy when she saw him with her and then would wonder why she had a right to feel this way. She had mixed emotions about the whole thing and didn't like to dwell on it. After all, she did love Roger, and she had no business even thinking about this. She wondered if Roger had the same feelings about other women.

Before Roger's parents had left for Italy they had moved into their new apartment. Since their bed had not yet arrived, Marcel insisted that they stay at their villa that night. They had already given up their hotel room, so they gratefully accepted his invitation. Nikki was remembering how happy Juanita had been at the time, as Marcel stayed at home that night. Nikki had gone into the kitchen with her as she prepared dinner and watched her cook a fantastic Spanish dish and decided that she would have to learn to cook some of these dishes. Juanita was flattered and told her that she would love to teach her. Then she said, *"I wish that you were staying longer, it is so good to have Marcel want to stay at home!"* Nikki had felt so sorry for her at the time and knew that she could never live this kind of life. She would never put up with it.

In the morning the maid had rolled a portable bidet into their room and filled it with warm water. Roger saw the expression on Nikki's face and roared with laughter. *"In this country they assume that if you are young you will need a bidet in the morning."*

Nikki shook her head and said, *"Sex seems to be the most important thing in the world here!"*

Roger replied, *"It is at home too, but we are much more subtle about it."* Nikki suddenly realized that this was true. Americans liked sex as well as anyone else, but they just didn't talk about it as much. It was a very private thing.

Chapter Twenty

After they were settled in their apartment, Roger's parents made the announcement that they were leaving for Italy for a month. Nikki was glad that they would have the apartment to themselves for a while and was hoping to fix dinner and insist that Marcel bring Juanita over for dinner. However, things did not work out as she had hoped.

She had noticed a big change in Roger. She was not sure when it started, but suddenly he was not as eager for sex and sometimes was completely disinterested in sex. He had always loved it when Nikki made the first move, but when she did, he had turned her down saying that he was tired. She was not sure what was going on, but she had a strange feeling that he was having an affair. Most of the time he would leave as soon as lunch was over, saying that he had a lot of work to do at the office with his father away. She would not have suspected anything except that his affection for her did not seem to be as strong as before and he would usually turn his back and go to sleep. After about a week, he started making excuses to be out at night alone. He would tell her that he wanted to go out and drink with his old buddies and added that she was lucky that he took her out at all. She realized that he was becoming more and more like the other men in this country. He had told her about Carla during their dating days and she knew that she had become a widow.

One night when they had been at the club, shortly after mom and dad had left, someone had pointed her out to Nikki. She was sure that she would have recognized her anyway, as Roger had described her many times and even before someone mentioned that it was Carla she was wondering if it was her. She had seen Roger and her looking at each other and he seemed to be imitating Marcel as he looked at her, unaware that Nikki knew who she was and unaware that Nikki saw him. She had talked herself out of the idea that Roger was still attracted to her but she was feeling sick inside. Now she was sure that he was with Carla all of these nights that he was supposed to be with his friends.

One night Roger came home and informed her that he had to leave early in the morning for Tangier on business. Nikki begged to go with him, but he said that he was going in a private plane and there would not be room for her. Nikki had made friends with an Italian girl who lived just above them. Her mother and father owned the building that they lived in. About a week later Madame Licia said, *"Nikki, I saw Roger in Tangier. You should always go with him when he takes a trip. It is very nice there."* Nikki realized that Madame Licia was trying to tell her something and she was certain that she had seen him there with another woman and assumed it was Carla. She knew in her heart that it was Carla, but she could not approach him on it as she didn't have proof.

Finally she called Marcel and asked him if she could see him. He told her that he would be right over. When he arrived she asked him outright if Roger was seeing Carla again. His answer was *"I don't know, but if it is true my friend must be crazy! It is true that I have been unfaithful to Juanita but it is different. She was not the respectable girl that you are. She had been with many men before me, but your situation is different. Roger was the first man to have you, therefore he should respect you!"*

Nikki was certain that Marcel knew what Roger was doing and she realized that she should have known better than to ask him, as he would never tell on his best friend.

Soon after the Tangier trip, Roger told her that he didn't love her anymore and was afraid that he might be tempted to take a mistress. Nikki said, *"I think you already have one!"* She cried and told him that she wanted to go home. He ignored her and walked out of the apartment. He stayed out night after night and she couldn't eat or sleep. She grew thinner by the day and became reclusive. When her friends called her to come to the club she would make excuses. She could not bear to face people, as she knew that they would see the misery on her face.

She paced the floor every night, peeking out over the balcony that faced the street, waiting for Roger to come home. She could hear the sounds of the horses, "clickity-click, clickity-click," on the cobblestone streets and it became a very lonely sound to her. When he would drive up, usually between four and four-thirty in the morning, she would jump into bed and pretend to be asleep.

Chapter Twenty-One

About ten days after her lonely nights began; Nikki was pacing the floor as usual when there was a knock at the door. She looked at the clock and saw that it was after midnight and cautiously asked, *"Who's there?"*

"Marcel, let me in!"

She opened the door and as he walked in he said, *"Juanita and I had a fight and she has locked me out of the house. Do you think that you and Roger can put me up for the night?"*

Nikki said, *"Roger is not at home, but you are welcome to sleep in his parents room."*

He asked her where Roger was and she broke down and poured her heart out to him. She told him what had been going on, including the part where he told her he didn't love her anymore. Suddenly she realized that she was crying and Marcel had his arms round her trying to comfort her. He assured her that he would have a talk with Roger.

Nikki gave him a pair of pajamas and went in to draw him a bath. After he took his bath he told her not to worry and went into the bedroom. She realized that Roger would not be home for many hours and went in to take her bath. When she started running the water, she found herself pouring a scent into the bath, something she had not done in a long time. She stood in front of the mirror looking at her naked body and thought to herself, *"I may be thinner, but I still have a good body."* She realized that she missed being fondled. Roger hadn't touched her in days and there was a space missing in her life that she needed badly. As she dried herself, she ran her hands over her body and sensed a feeling of excitement and pleasure when she thought of Marcel in the next room and wondered if he was asleep. She knew that he had always wanted her from the times they had danced together. Her nipples were erect and hard when she thought about what she was going to do next. She slipped on her most revealing gown, one that she had not worn since she and Roger had started living with his parents, but now she knew that tonight was the night she had been saving it for.

She went to the door of his room and when she looked in it was dark, but he was smoking a cigarette and when he took a drag on it she could see that he was not wearing Roger's pajamas. She could also see that he had an erection.

He said, *"I have been waiting for you, Mon Cherie. I have waited for you ever since I first laid eyes on you."*

As she walked towards the bed, she felt as if she were hypnotized. When she stepped out of her gown and slid into bed with Marcel she was already wet between her legs. As he took her into his arms and kissed her, she realized that she had been waiting also, ever since that first day that they had met. In her ecstasy she forgot about Roger and Juanita, she was in heaven and she was in the arms of the man whom she wanted more than anyone or anything in the world. This was the one night that she would never forget, nor would he. They blended together as one and he made her feel like the most desired woman in the world as he brought out all of the passion in her that she had ever known that she had. She knew that one night would not be enough and she prayed that he would never tire of her.

There had been many times that she had never even climaxed with Roger, but tonight she did, over and over again. "*Oh God,* she thought, *no wonder poor Juanita could never leave him.* She felt no remorse now, as she was doing what she had longed to do since she had first arrived in Casablanca. She hoped that Roger would continue to see Carla as she knew that she was getting the best end of the bargain. This night would never be forgotten, nor would the many nights that followed. She didn't care if Roger were to find out after the way he had treated her. As far as she was concerned, she wished she would never have to see him again. She knew that any love she had felt for him in the past was gone.

Marcel began talking for the first time. "*From the day I first saw you; I have wanted you more than anyone in the world. I have wondered what it would be like to have you and I am not disappointed. Roger must be insane! I have known what he has been doing. Juanita and I did not have a fight tonight. I knew that you were here alone and I have started to come over before now, but my friendship with Marcel is so strong that I felt that I could not do it. Tonight I weakened and I am not sorry. I know now that I love you more than life itself and I will forfeit anything to have you.*"

After that first night, Nikki decided to let the servants off at night so that there would be no talk, as they were faithful to Roger's parents since they had worked for them before the war.

Every night Marcel would come to the apartment after Roger left. He and Nikki had a signal. If she was not waiting for him on the balcony, it would mean that Roger was still at home. But every night she was on the balcony and he would look up and smile at her. She hoped that Roger would never tire of his affair with Carla, as she wanted to continue seeing Marcel. She lived for the hour that he would arrive and thought of nothing else. She saw less and less of her friends. They would call to see if she was alright and she would answer that she was fine; but with her mother-in-law away she had a lot to do. She was certain that by now they all knew about Roger's affair.

One night she mentioned to Marcel that she was concerned about how they would manage when Roger's parents returned. He told her not to worry, that he would manage to find a place for them to meet in the afternoons. She could always say she was with her friends playing tennis or bridge. She knew that she would eventually have to let Monique in on it so that she could cover for her. She was sure that she would do it.

Marcel would usually leave around three o'clock, just in case Roger decided to return early one night. When he would arrive home she would turn her back and pretend to be asleep. He would climb into bed very quietly and go to sleep. Some nights he would be drunk and would reek of liquor and would breathe heavily or snore and Nikki would move to the other bedroom as it would keep her awake. She wondered why he slept in their room at all and then she realized that he was afraid of what the servants would think and perhaps say something to his mother when she returned. This continued for almost three weeks and it was nearing the time when Roger's parents would be coming home. She hated the thought of it.

One morning, shortly after Marcel had left, Nikki started feeling sick. She was nauseated and doubled over with pain. She was trying to make it to the bathroom when she passed out on the floor in front of the bedroom door. When Roger came home he almost stumbled on her. He panicked when he realized that she had been lying on the cold marble floor for God only knows how long and thought, *"She could have died and no one would have known it."*

He was suddenly filled with remorse when he thought about the fact that he had brought her to a country so far from her home and had treated her so badly. He had not noticed how thin she had become until he picked her up with no effort at all, realizing that it was dead weight. As he laid her on the bed he was thinking, *"What have I done to my poor little Nikki. I must be insane!"* His overwhelming love for her surfaced and he knew that he could never treat her badly again. He also knew that his affair with Carla was over.

Chapter Twenty-Two

The first time that Roger saw Carla he could not believe so many years had passed. She was still beautiful with her long dark hair and fiery brown eyes. She still had a radiance that many women would have lost after having three children and losing her husband in the war. Suddenly he remembered her passion when he had his torrid love affair with her before he left Casablanca. He wondered if it could still be the same. He felt the familiar excitement that he had always seemed to have when he was with her and his groins began to ache and he wondered if he dare try and see her.

Nikki would never put up with it if he were to start seeing her and she should find out. She would never be able to accept it. In Casablanca most of the women knew about their husbands affairs, but it was a way of life and many of the women were having their own affairs, but he was sure that if Nikki would find out about it she would react in a completely different way and he knew that she would never even think of having an affair with anyone.

He tried to get Carla out of his mind, but found himself thinking of her when he was in bed with Nikki. It was true that he and Nikki had enjoyed their sex life, it had always been good, but when he compared it to Carla it was not as fiery. However, he also realized that they had now been married for four years and after that length of time couples can start to take each other for granted.

When he and Nikki had been at the club with Marcel and some of his friends, Carla had walked in on the arm of an Air France pilot. She did not see him at first, but he was watching her every move. He knew that if he stared at her long enough that she would notice him. Suddenly, when she got up to dance with her date, just as they walked onto the dance floor, she saw him. He could see the surprise on her face and then noted that she was looking at Nikki. He was not sure if it was curiosity or if she was just sizing her up. She glanced back at him and suddenly she smiled at him. Carla had a generous, sexy mouth and when she smiled, her white teeth glistened. It was unbelievable that she had been two years older than he, which would put her at about thirty-one. In the dim lights of the club, she still looked fantastic and he wondered if her firm body had become flabby after having three babies. He watched her, being careful not to be too obvious. He knew that Marcel was fond of Nikki and he had given him a lecture on behaving himself when they had first arrived, saying that Nikki was a respectable girl and that he should keep his eyes off of her. For that reason he didn't want Marcel to know that he was excited over seeing Carla again. It was ironic, he thought, since he and Marcel had always been so close and shared these things in the good old days. When they had seen a woman who appealed to them they had always confided in each other and would talk about how it would be to get into her bed. Now he didn't want Marcel to know that he was thinking of taking up with Carla where he had left off. Even though he ran around on Juanita, he didn't want him to know that he was thinking of cheating on Nikki. He was saddened by the fact that their relationship was not as close as it had been in the past.

He also noticed how Marcel had looked at Nikki on many occasions and he knew that he would like to have an affair with her. He knew his friend well. He also knew that Marcel would never make a move unless he himself started playing around and at that moment he decided that his affair with Carla would have to be very discrete. His mind was already made up that he would have to see her and be alone with her once more, if only to prove that he didn't love her anymore. He had not been this stirred up over anyone since he had left Casablanca; not even when he had cheated on Nikki when he was overseas. He had never punished himself very much for that, as they had been separated for three months and he had needed a woman at the time. After that, he had never even considered cheating on her as he loved her and enjoyed teaching her how to please him.

This was the first time since he had married that he knew there was someone he wanted more than her. He would make some inquiries tomorrow, he decided, but he would have to put on an act of curiosity. He could not even check the phone book, as even if she did have a phone, he did not know her married name. He would have to find out from someone who did not know Nikki and who would not reveal the information.

Roger knew that he would have to find out if there was anything left from the old days. She made him feel young again, as though those seven years had not passed. Not that he was old, but he was living in the past; as he was before the war, and the excitement that stirred inside of him when he saw Carla was the same as it had been in those days.

Chapter Twenty-Three

Carla

When Carla had first seen Roger it was a very emotional moment for her. She had heard that he was back and that he had a very pretty, young wife. She was not sure that he would try and contact her. She had heard that Americans were more faithful to their wives than Latin's were. She also realized that the rumors were true. His wife was a beauty and she was very young. She felt pangs of envy when she saw her. She had been proud of the fact that she had kept herself looking so young after all that she had been through and at the age of thirty-one, she felt that she looked more like twenty-five. Most of the men told her that and would have believed it if were not for the children.

When she saw Roger, her first instinct was to run up to him and throw her arms around him, but she knew that this was not possible. She was sure that he had told his wife about her. Their affair had been unsurpassable. They had been very good together, especially in bed. She had always been amazed at Roger, as she had thought that Americans were not as hot blooded as Latinos, but in his case it had not been true. He had always been very considerate as well, much more than the other men she had known. He had always made sure that she had reached her climax before he did. She had longed to have Roger back in her bed many times after he left Casablanca.

She had heard that he had seen action in the Pacific, as she kept in touch with Marcel and he would tell her what was going on and keep her in touch with the where-abouts of Roger. Even after she married she still wanted to know about him. She had hoped that he would manage to get sent over to Casablanca or at least close enough where he could come and visit. After her husband left for the war, she especially hoped that he would be sent there. Even though she had married, she knew that she was still in love with him. When Marcel told her that he had married she felt a deep hurt inside of her. She had never hoped that he would marry her, as he had told her that his family would never approve. He had said it in a discrete way, never hurting her feelings, but they would want him to marry an American girl. She knew that what they were really saying was they would want him to marry a respectable girl who had not slept around as she had.

She assumed that his wife had been a young, naïve girl when he had married her and wondered if he was bored with her by now. She had seen her and knew that she had those lovely blue eyes. The eyes had always been a weak spot with Roger. He had liked her eyes as they were full of fire. He liked eyes that were expressive, but she had not been able to see his wife long enough or close enough to see if they were expressive, only that they were large and blue. The biggest blow of all had been when she saw how young she was and it made her feel very old. She knew that she could not compete with one so young and fresh and she was sure that Roger would never try and contact her. She felt envious as he had been her man first.

She wondered how he would react if he were to see her in the morning when she first woke up and if he would show the interest that he seemed to be showing her at the club. She knew that she would have to see him alone, but would like to see him at night when she could have the lights turned low and soften her image. His wife was soft looking, but of course she too had been in the soft lights when Carla had seen her. She decided that she would have to manage to see her in the daylight.

The next morning she decided to go to the market as she was sure that Roger's wife went there every morning to buy their food for the day. All of the housewives went to the market in the morning. Though she was not an early riser, she managed to get there early and she meandered around, keeping her eyes on the entrance as she watched for her to arrive. Around ten-thirty she saw her. In the bright sunlight she was breath taking. She had a certain virtue about her that showed she was quite superior to the others around her and she disliked her even more. She was certain that it was jealousy, as the youthfulness that glowed from her was something she had not known for many years. She hoped that she didn't have that spark of fire in her that had appealed to Roger in the old days, but she doubted that he would have married her if there had been no fire. At that moment she decided she would make an attempt to contact him.

When she arrived home from the market she decided on her next move. She called her sister and asked her to keep the children for the rest of the day and night. Then she got busy and gave herself a facial. When she felt that she looked her very best she sat down and wrote her name, address and phone number on a piece of paper. Now that she had started making her move, she found that she was excited as she left her apartment. She realized that he might not respond to her message, but couldn't control the emotions inside of her. He had been back for three months and had not tried to contact her and she wondered if she was making a fool of herself, but she had to find out.

Going to the corner she found a *coche'* and instructed him to take her to Jon's office. At one time she would have confided in Marcel, but for.some reason she felt that Roger would not want Marcel to know about it if they were to get together. Marcel was fond of Roger's wife, as he had told her so, and she felt that he would not approve of what she was about to start and would not deliver the message to Roger.

So far, everything was working out. Her sister was willing to take the children as she had done so many times before. She understood that Carla needed to have some man in her life from time to time. She had never met anyone she wanted to marry after her husband had been killed. Though he was fairly good to her, she had not really liked being married. She was a flirt and she liked variety. Roger had been the only man that she had ever been faithful to for a whole year and she knew that no one would ever be able to hold her love as he had. As she thought about it, she realized that the old feeling was still there. Though they had not been together for seven years and she had been married in the meantime, she knew in her heart that she would have left her husband in a minute if Roger had come back. It had never occurred to her that Roger would be married when he returned and this had upset her very much, especially when everyone had raved about his wife. She decided that she would show that bitch that youth was not everything and that she could get Roger away from her. As the *cocher'* moved along, she hated Roger's wife more and more and was determined that youth was not everything. She was going to break up the marriage.

Suddenly it occurred to her that Roger may not even want her. Since he had not tried to contact her in three months, why would he suddenly want her now? She remembered the look on his face when she had seen him at the club and decided that there was only one way to find out.

When she arrived in front of Jon's office she decided she had chosen the perfect messenger, as she knew that she could trust him not to talk to anyone about it. When Jon looked up and saw her, he smiled and immediately knew why she was there, as he had been at the club the night before and had seen what had happened. Marcel said nothing to him, but he too was wondering if Marcel had plans for Nicole, as he had watched him dancing close with her and he had noted the way he was looking at her. He knew his brother well and knew that he respected friendship up to a certain point, but when it came to a woman that he wanted, he was not sure what he would do. He himself had found Nicole to be appealing and would have loved to have moved in on her, but he knew that his brother would never put up with it, especially since he wanted her himself. He could see the fire works start shooting now that Carla was making the first move to see Roger and was sure that it would not be long before Marcel would be in Nicole's bed.

Chapter Twenty-Four

Jon stood up as Carla entered his office and said, "*I think I know why you are here.*"

Carla gave him one of her wide grins and said, "*He has not tried to contact me since his arrival in Casablanca, but I saw the way he looked at me last night and I knew he would be out today trying to find me. Since he does not know my married name, I thought that you could help us along a little by delivering this note to him.*"

Jon looked at the piece of paper in her hand and decided to give her a hard time of it. "*Do you think that you can compete with his beautiful, young wife?" She is almost eight years younger than he is and you are older than him. He seems to be very much in love with her.*"

Carla answered haughtily, "*Sometimes experience is much better than youth!*"

Jon teased, "*Aren't you ashamed of yourself! What do you think Nicole would have to say about this?*"

"*Oh, so that's her name!*" Carla replied indignantly, "*Well, all is fair in love and war and I saw him first and it was before the war!"*

Jon laughingly said, *"I will see that he gets your message. If he doesn't call you it will not be my fault, as I will put it in his hand when I see him at the café this afternoon."*

Carla seemed satisfied and looked like the cat that ate the canary. She gave him another one of her wide grins and left the office. When she was gone, Jon shook his head and wondered what all of this would lead to. He was sure that Nicole would never put up with it, as he knew about how American women were and he knew that if Roger went for it he would be a complete fool, as if Nicole were to find out she would probably fly home as fast as possible and get a divorce. He wondered if he should give him the message, then decided that he would. After all, Roger was a big boy now and he probably knew what he could or could not get by with by now.

At six o'clock, when he went the Café and saw Roger, he walked up to him and shook hands. As he did so, he slipped the note into his palm. Roger looked surprised. He took him aside and asked, *"Why did you give me this?*

Jon answered, *"Because she brought it to my office this morning."* He then added, *"You are looking for trouble if you use this information. I doubt that Nicole would put up with it and I am sure that sooner or later she will find out. Carla is not known for being discrete and would most likely boast about the fact that she took you away from your young wife!"*

Roger looked at him and reminded him, *"It's my business, Jon. I know what I can and cannot get away with. Besides, what makes you think I want to see her? It has been three months since I've been back and if I had wanted to see her I would have before now!"* Jon knew that there was too much anger in his answers and was sure he planned to take advantage of the information.

Roger was overwhelmed with anxiety to see her. He knew that he would have to be discrete and would have to make Carla swear to him that she would keep quiet and he was sure that she would if it meant that they could go on seeing each other. He called Nikki and told her that he could not come home for dinner, that business problems had cropped up and he would have to have dinner with a customer. He was thankful that his father was gone, as he knew his father would know that he was up to something. He then called Carla and asked if he could come over.

Jon watched as Roger made his fast exit. He was thinking about Nicole. He would not mind having an affair with her, but he knew he would have to wait and see if Marcel would try and take advantage of the situation. It occurred to him at that moment that men were such predators, waiting for their chance to move in on their prey.

Chapter Twenty-Five

When Roger hung up the phone he was so excited that it didn't occur to him to feel guilty for what he was about to do. All he could think of was getting to Carla's without anyone seeing him. His heart was pounding so hard he thought it would leap right out of his chest as he left the café.

He stopped at a perfume shop to buy her favorite perfume. He just lucked out, as they were already closed, but the owner knew him and unlocked the door. He asked if he could buy a bottle of Shalimar which happened to be Carla's favorite fragrance. The owner asked him if it was for his father and Roger was not quite sure what to say. "*Your father comes in here to buy this all the time for your mother.*" Roger was stunned to hear that the old buck was still playing around. He knew that it had not been for his mother, as she never wore perfume because she was allergic to it. He decided to buy two bottles and give one to Nikki in case anything came up about his being in there.

In response to the man's question, he merely said, "*My*

wife likes it as well." He could hardly keep from smiling as now he had something on his father. If the old man should find out about his meetings with Carla he would not be able to say a word.

He drove to within a block of her apartment. He was not about to take any chance of his car being recognized in front of the building. Most of the cars were alike, but one never knew. He realized that he had been smart not to take one of the American cars that his father had imported, as he had been tempted to do. As he got out of the car he looked around to see if there were any familiar faces in the vicinity, but it was aperitif time and all the men were at the cafes and the women were at home preparing dinner or dressing to go out. He had picked the perfect time to have his first rendezvous' with Carla. It was definitely the safest time of the day to go there without being seen.

As he walked up to her apartment his heart was beating even faster than before and he was afraid that he would have a heart attack right on the stairway. He finally reached her door and rang the bell. He heard a voice asking who was there and the sound of her voice brought back even more memories, it had not changed. "It's Roger!" he said and found that he was trembling as he stood there. He was not sure if he was trembling at the thought of being there with her, or if he was afraid that Nikki would find out. The door opened and there she stood, smiling at him with tears in her eyes. It was such an emotional moment that even he felt his eyes becoming moist at the sight of her standing there.

"Oh Roger!" she said, *"I was afraid that you would not come. You have never tried to contact me in the three months*

that you are back and I felt that you didn't want to see me anymore. When you called I couldn't believe my ears. I couldn't understand why you did not try and find me after the way things were between us when you left." She then added, "*I am being rude, please come in.*" She took him by the arm and almost pulled him inside. He realized that she was just as anxious to have this meeting as he was. He handed her the bottle of perfume and she looked at it and started to cry with happiness. "*You didn't forget!*" She whispered. They were both so emotional at the moment that they just stood there and looked at each other. They had not yet touched or kissed. Finally she threw her arms around him and they embraced.

He knew that he had made the right decision. "*Why should I deprive myself of this pleasure?*" He thought. "*Most of the men have their other women and there is no reason why I shouldn't if I am discrete about it.*" He knew that he was making excuses to himself, but he also knew that he wanted this affair more than anything in the world at this moment.

Carla was the first to speak. "*You have a very lovely wife, Roger. Are you not afraid that she will find out?*"

Roger's answer was "*Yes. Why do you think that I have not come here before now? If I had not seen you at the club I doubt that I would be standing here right now, but when I did, I knew that I would not be able to stay away. However, I want you to know as of now that we will have to be very discrete. I do not want Marcel to know about it and I only hope that Jon doesn't tell him about your note. He is very fond of Nikki and I think he would be very angry with me.*"

Carla answered, "*Are you afraid that he will want to have*

an affair with your Nicole?" Roger had thought of that, but didn't want to admit it to himself.

Finally he said, *"I don't think that Marcel would try anything with my wife, you know that we are like brothers."*

Carla replied, *"As long as we can be together, I will be happy. I promise that no one will hear about it from me."*

To ease the tension Carla fixed them a drink, but before they could get their glasses to their lips they were locked in an embrace and she was pulling him into the bedroom. He was so full of passion and ecstasy that he forgot about Nikki and everyone else in the world. This was what he had dreamed of for so long and now he realized that this was also the reason he had been so anxious to return to Casablanca. The only person he wanted was Carla and he realized that he would have to continue seeing her. At the moment he almost hated Nikki, as it was she who had kept him from his beloved Carla. It was as if time had stood still and waited for them. Carla had not changed as far as her passions went. In fact she seemed more eager than ever before and he assumed that it was because of their long separation. He did notice that she was not as firm as she had been and her breasts had fallen, but she had not forgotten how to please him in bed. She was like a disease with him, there was no use trying to fight it. He didn't know that he was still good for three times in one night, but he knew that Nikki would wonder when he would not be able to perform and decided that he would not go near her.

Many nights, when he got in bed he knew that Nikki was pretending to be asleep. He was glad that she did not try to seduce him. He had started to go into the other bedroom and use the excuse that he didn't want to wake her, but he realized that the servants would know that they were not sleeping together and that they might say something to his mother when she returned. He also wondered what he would do when they did come back. He mentioned this to Carla and she suggested, "*We will just have each other during the day.*"

Roger knew that he would have to go to the office or his father would start asking questions. He didn't want to be burdened with these worries now, as he was too happy, and decided that he would figure it out later.

Night after night he and Carla were together and they were living as though it were the good old days. Roger was getting tired of always hiding in the in the apartment with her, he wanted to take her out to dinner and dancing. He knew that it would be impossible to do in Casablanca, as until now, no one was actually sure of what was happening. He was sure that they suspected something, as he had not been out with Nikki in a while and they had been going to the club every night up until he had started seeing Carla.

One night he said thoughtfully, "*Carla, I have an idea. Maybe we could go to Tangier, and with luck and being careful, we won't run into anyone we know.*"

She was elated at the idea and asked, "*When shall I start packing?*"

Roger laughed when he saw how eager she was and then realized that he too was very eager. "*I will tell Nikki that I am going there for business. Then we can be together day and night and I will not have to leave you in the middle of the night to go home. I want to go out and have dinner with you and dance with you like we did before I left.*" Carla was happy when he left her that night. She realized that he wanted her companionship for more than just the bed and it made her feel that he truly did love her.

On the way home Roger decided to tell Nikki that he was going on a private plane and then decided that they would. No sense in taking chances of running into people on the plane or the at he regular airport. He decided to make the arrangements in the morning and then tell Nikki at lunch that he would be leaving the following day.

Chapter Twenty-Six

The first thing he did when he got to the office in the morning was to call a friend who had a private airplane service. He was informed that they could leave the next morning at seven o'clock. When he went home for lunch he informed Nikki that he was leaving for Tangier. She asked why she could not go with him and he told her that there would not be room on the plane.

That night he told Carla to be ready at six o'clock in the morning and that he would pick her up. He knew that at that time there would be no one around to see them together.

She was delighted. He had never seen her look so happy. The next morning they were on their way.

They had a marvelous time in Tangier. Every night they went to the clubs to see the flamenco dancers and had dinner out. The only time that Roger became concerned was when they went into a small Spanish restaurant and Fabia's mother and father were there. He had hoped that they did not recognize him in the dimly lit room, but he was not sure.

If so, he was sure that Nikki would know about it. Somehow it didn't seem to matter much anymore. He was sure that by now Nikki assumed there was another woman in his life, as he had not gone near her for at least 3 weeks, since he had first started seeing Carla.

Chapter Twenty-Seven

Roger laid Nikki on the bed and called the doctor who lived only a few blocks away. By the time he arrived, Roger had managed to revive her. The doctor examined her and told him that she would have to go to the clinic immediately as her appendix were bad and had to come out. He said, *"I only hope that they have not ruptured. She does not look well at all."*

Nikki cried and said, *"I am not going to the hospital. I want to go home to have my operation, where there will be someone who cares if I live or die!"* The tears were pouring out of her eyes and down her face.

Roger leaned over her and said, *"Nikki, I care, believe me. If you wait you won't stand a chance. You don't have time to go home!"* Then he added, *"I have been a fool, honey, please forgive me."* He prayed for God to forgive him as he carried her to the car and promised to make things up to her if she would be spared. The whole way to the clinic he prayed that God would spare her and he was very frightened that she would not make it, as he knew that she would not be fighting for her life as she would be if she felt wanted. He told her over and over that he loved her and that she had to fight for her life. In Casablanca only the poor people went to the hospital. Those who had money went to the private clinics.

When they wheeled her into surgery, Roger sent a telegram to his parents. They arrived the next day on the first available flight. After the surgery the doctor asked Roger when she had started to feel sick. Roger found himself stuttering on his words as his guilt became more intense. He wondered if Nikki had been feeling sick and had not told him. They had barely spoken to each other for the past several weeks and if she had been ill, she would not have said anything, as he was sure that she would have been afraid that he would think that she was looking for sympathy. He was glad that this had not happened when he was in Tangier, as she could have died with no one there to help her. He finally managed to tell the doctor that she had complained of stomach pains on the ship coming over to Casablanca and that everyone assumed that it was only seasickness. However, he did suddenly remember the Captain reading from his medical book and when he had asked him why the Captain had said, *"Just reading up on what to do if I have to perform an appendectomy!"* Luckily the pains had subsided and Nikki had not complained anymore. He said, *"I realize now that it was foolish of me not to take her to a doctor and have her checked when we arrived here, but she never complained anymore and I was sure that the Captain must have been mistaken."*

The doctor informed him that if they had waited just an hour more her appendix would have ruptured. He also informed him that she had had several other things wrong which he had corrected. "*She had a four-in-one operation, Roger, and she will be a very sick girl for a while. When she does come home, if you don't want to have children, you will have to be careful, as now it will be easy for her to become pregnant, whereas before the operation she could not have conceived.*"

Nikki opened her eyes and looked around the room and finally saw a nurse sitting on the couch. She was disoriented, but she asked where her husband was and then realized that the nurse did not speak English. She did understand because she opened the blinds and showed her that it was dark out. She had no idea of how long it had been since she had had her surgery and was not even sure what day it was. She also had no idea that mom and dad had returned and assumed that Roger was with his beloved Carla. She wondered if Marcel knew what had happened. She was sure that he had gone to the apartment and wondered what had happened to her.

With Marcel on her mind, she dozed off again and did not wake up until later on in the morning when another nurse was taking her blood pressure. As she looked up she saw Roger walking into the room carrying a beautiful bouquet of flowers. He kissed her and asked her how she felt. She was in so much pain that she could barely whisper, "*I feel terrible!*"

He sat down next to her and took her free hand and begged her to forgive him. He said, "*I didn't realize how much I really loved you until I thought that I was losing you. You don't know what a scare you gave me. You would not have made it if it had been a few hours later. Mom and dad flew home when I wired them that you were seriously ill and in surgery. They will probably be here at any time now, but I want to talk to you alone and ask you to forgive me for treating you the way I have. I realize now that I had to have been a fool!"*

Nikki could see that he was afraid that she would tell his parents what had happened while they were gone. When she thought of Marcel, she knew that she could not hold a grudge against Roger, as he had actually done her a favor. In all of her pain, she managed a little smile and said, *"Don't worry Roger, I won't tell your parents."*

Roger looked at her and asked, *"Do you think that is my only concern? I really do love you Nikki, don't you understand that?"*

Nikki replied, *"If that is love, I'd rather have hate. Do you love me as much as Carla?"*

Roger looked stunned. Then he asked, *"How long have you known?"*

Nikki was feeling sick and found it hard to speak by this time, but managed to say, *"When you went to Tangier, someone told me that I should always go with you when you have to travel and I knew that she had seen you with her."*

Roger couldn't believe that all this time Nikki knew and had not said anything to him. *"It had to have been Fabia's mother Roger guessed. I was afraid she had seen us. Nikki, I want you to know that Carla doesn't mean anything to me. It was something that I had to find out."* He realized that he was speaking the truth. *"I had to get her out of my system, as when I left Casablanca at the beginning of the war I thought that I was madly in love with her and I had to find out if she really meant anything to me or if it was just a physical attraction. I know now that it was strictly physical, as we have nothing else in common and I know that I don't love her. She could never take your place, honey, and I will never hurt you again, I promise. That is if you will give me another chance."*

Nikki told him that she was too sick to make any decisions and when he saw that she was going to be sick he grabbed the basin and put it up to her mouth. She was nauseated all day and would fall asleep and wake up and throw up again. Because of the fact that her stomach was empty she was having dry heaves and was desperately ill. From time to time she remembered seeing mom and dad and Roger all trying to help her and then she would fall asleep again. They had given her a shot for the nausea and pain and it was making her very drowsy.

Chapter Twenty-Eight

Nikki kept waking up and hearing bits of conversation between Roger and his parents. She heard mom saying, "*The poor dear, she is so terribly ill.*"

Sometimes when she awoke, dad would be standing over her and stroking her head and shaking his head. She heard him tell Roger that she had become so thin. He said, "*Surely she has not become this thin since the operation, Roger. What has been going on here?*"

Roger was speaking in a low voice, but she could make out that he was saying that they had not been getting along very well and that she always lost her appetite when she was unhappy. From time to time she could hear mom say something, but she was so drowsy that she could not make out what they were saying and she would doze off again and wake up in a different part of the conversation. Everyone seemed to be so far away, it was as if they were in a different room. She could see them when she managed to open her eyes, but they were blurred. She could not remember ever having been so sick in her life. She was praying that she would not die in this strange country so far away from her loved ones. By the latter part of the day she was finally awake and was able to take part in the conversation. She still felt a great deal of pain, but it was not quite as severe as it had been and the nausea was about gone. They brought her some kind of herb tea to drink and it tasted terrible. Mom insisted that she drink it and she fed it to her with a spoon and she obediently drank it. They told her that it would give her some strength and she knew that she would need all of her strength to get well again.

After the first day, mom would stay with her during the day and when Roger and dad were finished with work they would come to the hospital. She had received many flowers from people she didn't even know, mostly friends of mom and dad. The third day the flowers arrived from Juanita and Marcel. Nikki was relieved to know that Marcel was aware of what had happened. She wondered when she would be able to see him again and felt sad when she thought that their affair was probably over, because everything had changed now that Roger was back in her life. That night, shortly after Roger had left, the door opened and Marcel came in. He went over to Nikki and said, "*My poor darling,* Then he added, "*When I left you that night you seemed to be fine!" What happened? I didn't know anything until Roger called me the day after the surgery and told me what had happened. I have never been so surprised in my life. It must have happened shortly after I left you."*

Nikki said "*I don't know when, but I suppose it was shortly after you left that I started feeling nauseated and my stomach hurt me terribly. I started for the bathroom thinking that I was going to throw up and the next thing I knew, Roger was bending over me and trying to talk to me and then the doctor came and they took me to the clinic. It hit me all at once, and I don't ever remember being so ill! I have thought of you day and night and wondered if you knew until your flowers arrived today.*"

Marcel explained, "*Roger told me that you were too sick to see anyone. That is why I have not been here. Today when I saw him he told me that you were feeling better and able to see people. I used all of my will power to stay away. I wanted to be with you, but my hands were tied. I knew that he had wired his parents to come home and that they were with you.*

Tonight I parked up the street and when I saw Roger leave I came up, as I wanted to see you alone."

Nikki was sad when she said, "*I don't know what to do now. I still love you with all my heart, but Roger has been terribly worried about me and has begged for another chance to prove that he can be a good husband to me. I don't know what to do. I know that I love you, but I also know that our situation is impossible for right now. He told me that he is through with Carla and now mom and dad are back, I just don't see any hope for you and me. I suppose I am going to give Roger another chance, even though I can never love him again, as I cannot love two men at one time, and you are the one who I really do love now.*"

Marcel looked unhappy, but said he understood and then he said, "*No matter what happens, please remember that I love you and always will. I know that we can't do anything about it right now, but one day, who knows?*" In his mind he knew that sooner or later Roger would stray again and that they would be back together. He kissed her goodbye. There was so much emotion between them that he felt it would be best to leave, as he didn't want Nicole to have any complications to keep her from getting well. They were both in such a turmoil that neither of them could talk. As he left the room he said, "*Some day, you will see.*"

Chapter Twenty-Nine

When Nikki returned from the hospital three weeks later she was barely able to walk. They had not let her out of bed until two days before. She felt that she was much wiser, because she had been forced to speak French, since no one at the clinic spoke English, not even the doctor. At least she had learned something. She felt that she had learned even more about life because of her affair with Marcel, as it made her realize what was lacking in her sex life and since she had decided to try and make a go of it with Roger, she decided that when she was well enough she would experiment with him and maybe he would not be looking for other women to satisfy him. She imagined that because of the fact that she was inexperienced before she married him, she may not have given him what he wanted. She knew that she would have to be careful not to give herself away, as she was afraid that Roger would suspect that something had happened during the time that they had been estranged.

As the doctor had ordered, two weeks later Roger took

her back to the clinic for her check-up. When she walked in, he spoke to her in perfect English asking, "*Well Miss America, how are you feeling?*"

Nikki couldn't believe her ears. "*Doctor, you spoke English and all that time you made me struggle to speak French!*"

Smiling, he said, "*Well Nicole, you do speak French now, don't you?* He added, "*Your day nurse spoke English, but I told her not to let you know; I did you a favor!*"

Nikki laughed and admitted that he had. Now she could talk to people and even though she made some comical mistakes, she was able to make conversation. As time went on she got better and better and by the end of the year she was even thinking in French. Sometimes she forgot what a word was in English.

Life settled down to its usual routine, Nikki and mom never had to worry about doing housework, as they had two servants. What had surprised Nikki the most was that the servants slept on the floor in the kitchen. They were not used to beds and could not sleep in them. What drove them mad was when the Ramadan holiday came each year. It was a religious ritual when they fasted from dawn to sunset every day for a month. They had to abstain from food, drink and all carnal pleasures. They would feast all night and during the day they would be so exhausted they would lie down on the floor in the living room and sleep. During that month they would have to do their own housework, as they couldn't get any work out of them. All of the Arab women were called *Fatima* and the men *Mohammed*. Nikki wondered why they did not get all mixed up when they referred to each other, but she was sure they had other names as well.

Roger and his father would come home every day at noon for their main meal and siesta and they would go back to the office at two o'clock. At four they would either come home for tea, or Nikki and mom would meet them at the tea room for tea and French pastries. At six o'clock the men would go to the café where most of the business was transacted. Everyone talked in millions and most of them didn't have much of anything, but in Casablanca during the post war days, everyone was wheeling and dealing and they had to act as if they had money even if they didn't, or they didn't stand a chance to make any deals at all. Dad had sold the building where they had made the sheep casings and suede before the war and had started importing from the United States. There were so many things that were needed in Casablanca that they were selling everything as fast as they brought it in and they were selling everything from food to used cars. It was the land of opportunity, and those who were able to bring in these things were making money hand over fist.

Nikki would go to the market every morning while mom would start cooking lunch. The mornings were the busiest time of the day for the housewives. The only problem that Nikki ran into was the Arab merchants knew that she was an American and most of them did speak English, but they would always try to over-charge her in the beginning. She watched as the other women argued prices with them and she followed suit. They would finally realize that even though she was an American they could not cheat her.

Nikki and Roger had become very good friends with Fabia and Pasqual, the daughter and son-in-law of their landlord. They lived directly above them. Monique and

Michael lived on the other side of the building and Roberta and Antoine lived only a block away. They saw less and less of Juanita and Marcel and in a way Nikki was glad, as she was afraid that if she was around Marcel she might give herself away.

She thought of Marcel often and sometimes she could almost feel him next to her. She wondered if he thought of her as much. Sometimes when she slept with Roger she would close her eyes and pretend that it was Marcel. She didn't feel guilty about it, because, after all, Roger had been the cause of it all. Had he not treated her as he did she would never have dreamed of having an affair with anyone, no matter how much he appealed to her. It was the way she had been raised and she could not feel that it was the right thing to do. In her case, she felt that it was different, as Roger had asked for it. She knew that she was going to have to stop thinking this way if they were going to have a normal relationship again, but she couldn't help herself. She was in love with Marcel and there was nothing she could do about it. She often wondered if he was back with Yolanda and would feel a twinge of jealousy when she thought about it. She was not so stupid as to believe that he would have not seen another woman once he tired of her. He was not the type of man who could ever be faithful to one woman for very long, she was sure, and she felt that she was no different than the rest as far as he was concerned. He had spoken of his love for her, but she wondered how long it would have lasted had she not gotten back on good terms with Roger.

Nikki had always been a very loving and affectionate person and Roger noticed that this had changed. He wondered if it was because he had hurt her, or if there had been another man in her life during the time that he had been with Carla. She had stopped nagging him about going out every night and sometimes he even felt she was anxious to get rid of him. At the time, he had imagined that it was just that he had made her so angry and that she did not give a damn anymore. He did know that Nikki had a jealous nature and suddenly she had stopped going into tantrums about his leaving her alone. She had seemed to accept the fact that he was going out and not putting up any fuss the last few weeks. He could not shake the feeling that she had changed. At least her feelings for him had changed. He, on the other hand, became very possessive and jealous if she so much as looked at another man.

Chapter Thirty

Their social life went on as it had before all of the events of the past couple of months. With the war so newly ended, Casablanca was swinging with gaiety and craziness. They would stay out until six in the morning many times, especially on Saturday nights and would come home to change clothes and go fishing. After that they would return home again to shower and dress to go to the horse races. Nikki knew nothing about horses, but would select a horse by its name and most of the time she would win. It reached the point where all of the gamblers who were friends of Roger asked her who to bet on. Most of the time she would select the right horse, but she did not always bet on them, as she was not much of a gambler. When the horse would win she would be mad at herself for not betting. Everyone was making money on her hunches except her.

After the races they would wind up at the club or at one of their apartments playing bridge. The fact that Roger was making no attempt to be with Marcel and Juanita made

Nikki wonder if he suspected something. Marcel rarely came by and when he did he never stayed long.

Fashions were coming back in nineteen-forty seven. During the war the dresses were short, just below the knee or to the middle of the knee. They claimed it was to save on fabric. Now the skirts were full and dropping almost to the ankle with fitted bodices and cinched waistlines and plunging necklines. All of the girls envied Nikki, as the styles were made for her figure. She had a tiny waist and well rounded breasts and did not have to wear the wasp waist girdle to hold her in. Most of the women would not be able to eat when they went out as they had a hard time breathing with their girdles pulled in so tight. There were times when one of them would faint and they would have to take her to the ladies' room and take off her girdle.

They had their clothes made by couturiers. There was no such thing as buying clothes already made in the stores. They were not stylish and were not well made.

Autumn was the peak of the social season when the charity balls began and everyone wore elegant, elaborate gowns with their hair swept up in stylish hairdos.

Nikki went to have her hair combed every day as it was only a half dollar in American money to have it done. Her hair dresser was very handsome. He was gay as were so many hair dressers in Casablanca. Nikki thought maybe it just seemed that way, as they never tried to hide it there as they did at home. When she went to her first ball, she went to the salon to have her make-up done and her hair combed. She took her gown and changed there as well. Most of the women made beauty dots on their faces and he told Nikki that they did it to show off their best feature. Then he placed one just below her right eye at the top of her cheek bone. He said *"Your eyes should be seen above all, as they are your best feature."*

Her gown was elegant. She had gone to one of the top couturieres in Casablanca. The fabric was a heavy brocade satin, mauve colored with purple ostriches brocaded on it. There was a crystal sewn into the eye of the ostrich. The bodice was strapless and the skirt had yards of fabric. She wore long gloves that had been dyed to match the dress and they went up past her elbows. The entire effect was perfect.

When Nikki would walk down the street the men would speak to her and say, *"Vous et tres joli, vous et tres belle!"* She would think about the difference in the Frenchman and the American. She liked the way the Frenchmen complimented her. At home the men would whistle and make you feel cheap. Here they made her feel more desirable and it gave her a feeling of self confidence. At times they would approach her and speak to her. She would very naively say *"Jet no comprends pas le François!"* It meant *"I don't understand French."* The men would shrug their shoulders in their French manner to show their disappointment. She enjoyed teasing them and realized that she would miss it if she ever left this country.

Chapter Thirty-One

Nikki had not been feeling well and was concerned about it. She was sure that something was wrong with her, but had never had the symptoms before. Her breasts had become very tender and she was feeling nauseated most of the time. She had not mentioned it to Roger, but one morning when Fabia had dropped by for coffee with her she told her about it. Fabia started laughing and Nikki could not understand what was so funny about it. Finally, she said "*You're not sick, but I think that you are pregnant. You have all of the symptoms!*"

Nikki had not even thought about the fact that she could be pregnant and said, "*You are teasing me!*"

Fabia said "*No Nicole, I am serious. I know the symptoms of pregnancy and you've got them. I know how it is as I have been there.*"

Nikki called and made and appointment with the doctor for that afternoon. When he examined her he informed her that she was about three months pregnant. "*But that is not possible!*" She exclaimed, "*I have not missed that many periods!*"

"This happens occasionally. A woman keeps having her periods and finds that she is getting fat and wonders why." he explained.

As she left his office she was not happy about the situation. She was sure that Roger would start cheating on her again. The marriage was still hurting and she felt that she could never trust him again. She thought of being stuck at home with a baby while he ran around. She was uncertain how he would react when he found out that they were about to start a family. Once when the subject had been brought up, shortly after they were married, Roger had said, "You are young and we have plenty of time to be tied down with a family. We should enjoy each other." That had been when he was still in the service and was afraid that he would be sent overseas. They had never talked about it since then, and now Nikki feared that he would not be too happy about it.

She finally decided that he would have to know sooner or later. When he came home for dinner she took him into the bedroom and informed him that he would be a father in six months.

He was surprised and asked, *"Why have you waited so long to tell me?"*

Nikki explained that she had just found out that day and explained to him what the doctor had told her. She was surprised and happy to see that he was excited at the thought of becoming a father in such a short time. He reacted much differently than she had expected. They went together to inform his parents of the coming event, and as usual, dad had to pop a bottle of champagne to celebrate. They were all thoroughly elated that there would finally be a baby in the family. Nikki was the only one who was not sure if she was so happy over the fact, as she was also thinking about Marcel and the fact that nothing could ever bring them back together again. She realized more and more as time went on that she was in love with him, but she was trying her best to love Roger. She found that she was having a difficult time coping with all of this. However, she also knew that Marcel had a wife and children and nothing could ever come from their relationship anyway. Finally, she decided that she would look forward to a baby and hope that Roger would behave himself and be a good husband and father. She made up her mind then and there that she was going to make a go of her marriage since there was a baby coming and she had to think of the baby as well as herself. From now on, there would be someone who would be more important in her life than just herself.

Part Three

Paris

Chapter Thirty-Two

A few days later Roger came home and told Nikki to start packing that they were going to Paris. Nikki was elated and asked, *"Why, all of the sudden are we going to Paris?"*

"Because I want to show you Paris before the baby comes. I know that we can always count on mom to baby sit, but I am afraid that you won't want to leave the baby for a while. You will probably nurse it, as I don't trust the milk over here and we would have to depend on shipments from the states."

Nikki was excited and she had heard that Paris was a fantastic place to visit, especially in the spring and it was spring, and all of the songs that had been written about it. As she packed, she was humming *"Paris in the Spring"* and Roger joined in. They were acting like children because they were so excited. She had always dreamed of going to Paris and now she was going. She realized that when she wrote home the news about the baby she would also be able to tell them about going to Paris. Roger told her to set a date with them and they would call them from Paris. She couldn't believe that she would finally be able to talk to her family, as they could not call the states from Casablanca. It seemed as if everything was happening at once and she discovered that she was not dreaming about Marcel now. She hoped with all of her heart that she and Roger would be able to make a go of it now that there was a baby on the way.

When she wrote home she told them what date and time they would be calling. She knew that they would all congregate at Aunt Emma's to await the call, so she decided to make it on Sunday at noon. That way they could all be there. It was almost a year since she had left home, and she knew they would be just as eager to talk to her as she was to them. She also decided that she wanted to tell them about the baby instead of writing them about it. Roger decided that they should send a telegram to be sure they would get the information, as a letter might take too long overseas.

"*Well,*" she said, "*It looks as if I am going to see more of the world!*" Roger could see that she was beside herself with joy and he was glad that he had thought of it. When he had asked his father if they could go, he had been very nice about it, and he gave him enough money for them to have a wonderful time. Roger was anxious to show her the beautiful city. He remembered how he had felt the first time he had gone there. Therefore, he knew the feeling that she was experiencing. Nikki broke into his thoughts saying, "*I am glad that I am not fat yet and can still fit into my nice clothes. I wouldn't like to go to Paris for the first time looking fat and ugly!*"

Roger laughed and said, "*You couldn't look ugly if you tried!*" Nikki liked the compliment. The strain of the past couple of months was gone and they were getting along well now. She hoped that they would continue to get along this well.

Nikki had always been nervous about flying, but she was so happy she didn't give it a thought. Their plane left at midnight, and Marcel, acting like the old family friend once more, offered to drive them to the airport. Since dad was having trouble with his eyes, he didn't like driving at night and he gladly accepted Marcel's offer. As they got ready to board the plane he kissed Roger on each cheek and said, "*Merde*!" Then he turned and kissed Nikki on the mouth. She was sure that he was not going to miss the opportunity to kiss her and she hoped that the electricity that went through them was not obvious to Roger as he stood and watched them. To take away from the awkwardness, she said in a light manner, "*Well, at least this time I knew who you were and didn't panic!*"

Nikki was speaking fairly adequate French by this time, though she still made mistakes and everyone would laugh at her and tease her. She asked Roger why Marcel had said "*Merde*", as she knew that the meaning of the word was "*shit*".

Roger explained to her that it was a superstition with the people here, just as in the states they would say "*Break a leg*" for good luck. He said "*I think the Americans are the ones who use the term "Bon Voyage"* the most.

As they found their seats and buckled their seat belts, Nikki could think of nothing but Paris. She wondered if any of her friends at home had ever been there and she doubted it. Tourism at that time was not yet happening very much. Since ocean liners had been the main means of transportation to

Europe before the war, most people were not into flying yet and the remodeling of the liners was taking time. It was still difficult to get booking on a luxury liner.

They flew on Air France and the food was served in courses just as in the restaurants. Everyone got a bottle of wine on their tray with their dinner. There were no women stewardesses as in the states. They were all men stewards. She was surprised when she saw them carry the trays into the pilot and co-pilot, as there was wine on their trays as well. She asked Roger why they would let the pilots drink alcoholic beverages when in flight, it made her a little nervous. He told her *"In France, they drink wine from the time they are very small children and it does not even faze them."*

It was a five hour trip and they pushed their seats back to relax when suddenly Nikki felt very ill and knew that she would lose her dinner. Roger rang for the steward and explained that she was pregnant and they gave her a bag to use. After she lost her dinner she was still so sick that the co-pilot had to come out and give her oxygen. She was embarrassed that she had created so many problems for them and apologized. The co-pilot smiled and said, *"Don't be embarrassed, this happens quite frequently and we are here to serve you."* She thanked him and realized what a handsome man he was. She especially liked his soft, kind voice and finally managed to smile at him.

By the time they arrived in Paris she was feeling fine again, though a little hungry. However, she was so excited that she didn't let a trivial thing like that bother her. They cleared customs quickly. There were not many people there at that time of the morning, as they arrived at five o'clock.

They took a cab to the hotel and as they drove there, Nikki was straining her neck, trying not to miss anything. She was fascinated with the different type of architecture that the houses had and noted that the roofs came down almost to the ground. When they arrived at the hotel it was six o'clock and the city of Paris was still asleep. She noted that there were shoes lined up in front of all the doors and asked Roger why. He told her that the guests leave them there to be picked up and polished. When they entered their room, Nikki saw immediately that there was a balcony facing the street. She walked out to see the famous city of Paris that she had always heard so much about. Suddenly she heard the sound, "*Clunkity clunk*", *clunkity clunk*" and in an excited voice said, "*Oh what fat horses they have here!*" She was thinking about the nights she had waited for Roger to come home and the lonely sound of "*clickety click*" that the horses in Casablanca had made.

Roger said, "*You notice it because the horses in Casablanca are very thin. You know, we do have fat horses at home in the states also.*" Of course at home they didn't use horses for this type of thing anymore and she had never really noticed what sound they made. In Paris and Casablanca the horses were put to use as they had been in America before motor cars were invented, but that was way before her time.

Chapter Thirty-Three

By the time the sun came up Nikki was dressed and ready to go. She had not slept a wink. She was so anxious to get out and see the city. Roger had slept off and on, but with Nikki moving around so much he had been awakened and didn't sleep as well as he could have. She was telling him to hurry and get dressed.

He enjoyed watching her in her excitement, as he remembered his first trip to Paris and he reacted the same way. He was, none the less, excited himself; as it had been a long time since he had been here. Before they knew it, they were literally skipping down the street, holding hands.

A policeman smiled and said, "*Lamoure jejune*!" The Frenchmen loved lovers and what he was saying was "*Young love*!" They laughed, as they were sure that he thought they were lovers who had just spent the night together at the hotel.

Roger had two cousins living in Paris and also a young friend who was a student there. They knew that they would have to contact all of them while there. However, they decided that they wanted the first day to themselves. They stopped at the Café de la Paix for a continental breakfast. It was the café where most of the Americans hung out. It was on the corner near the opera house and you could look up and see the Mount Sucre-Coeur Cathedral. Nikki found that everyone spoke in English and she was beginning to miss it, since it was almost a year since they had left the states. They had café au lait and croissants. Although they made croissants in Casablanca, Nikki had never eaten any as delicious as these. She was extremely hungry, since she had lost her dinner the night before and she ate three of them. She giggled and said, "*They must think I am an awful pig!*"

After breakfast they took a cab and Roger had him drive around and show them the points of interest that he knew Nikki would enjoy seeing. They found out that the cab drivers were not the most pleasant people in Paris. They went up to one cab and asked him to drive to the Arch de Triumph and the driver told them that he was not facing in that direction, to go to the other side of the street. Nikki laughed, thinking that he was teasing, but Roger informed her that he meant what he said. He remarked, "*After so many years, I had forgotten how independent the cab drivers are in this city.*" They finally got into a cab and drove to the Arch de Triumph and Roger showed her the tomb of the Unknown Soldier. Then they drove to a section where all of the grand jewelry stores were. He showed her how a thief could never get out of there. The stores were in a square and when a piece of jewelry was missing the jeweler would push a button and the iron gates closed automatically. It was very well secured. After that they drove to a section where the boutique shops were located and they spent a good part of the day shopping for gifts to send home and something for themselves. Nikki had never had anything from Paris. She selected a beautiful hand embroidered blouse. Roger couldn't decide what he wanted so he decided to wait and see if he would find something that he thought he could not live without. He wanted Nikki to have a good time and if he didn't get anything for himself on this trip it wouldn't matter very much. He was so thankful that she had taken him back after his affair with Carla.

That night they had dinner at Maxim's. Although it was expensive for their budget, he told Nikki, *"You can't come to Paris and not have at least one dinner at Maxim's."* Everything was cooked and served to perfection. The food was beyond her expectations, as well as the service. She could not get over the fact that every morsel of each course could all be so marvelous and, she told their waiter that she had never eaten anything in the world as heavenly as this. The waiter evidentially thought she had traveled the world and he was delighted with the lavish compliments she was handing out. He worked harder than usual to see to it that everything was to her taste.

Roger was amused, as he was sure that he thought that she was well traveled. As Nikki found out later on, the French took pride in their service and they went to school to learn how to do all of the fancy things they did. It was the same with the chef. They were always alarmed when a dish was sent back to the kitchen half full, and would send the waiter back to ask if there was anything wrong with the food. This happened frequently with Nikki, because she found it difficult to eat large amounts of food that were served at each meal. She was not used to so many courses, and by the time she would eat her appetizer and soup, she could never manage to eat the entrée. Roger ordered oranges for them and Nikki was surprised that he would order this instead of an elegant dessert, but she imagined he had already arrived at the amount he wanted to spend on a meal. When the oranges were served, she realized that he wanted her to see how artistically they served them. They never touched the orange with their hands. Nikki was fascinated watching the way the waiter peeled them with the fork and knife to perfection, even taking off all of the white part that usually clings to the orange. Then he sliced them in a circle on a plate and served them with a knife and fork. After that, she ordered an orange several times when they went out to eat just so she could watch this procedure.

Chapter Thirty-Four

The second day Roger called his student friend, Andre. He told him where to meet him for lunch. As they rode in a taxi to the restaurant, they noticed all of the student apartments with clothes hanging out of the windows to dry. From the outside, the restaurant was not fancy, nor was it on the inside.

There were red and white checkered tablecloths on the tables and Nikki was surprised to hear a lot of English being spoken, until she realized that there were quite a few American students there. To her surprise, she saw a familiar face and realized that it was a boy who had been on the debate team with her in high school. She had never particularly cared for him, but she was so happy to see a face from home that she rushed over to him and called his name. When he looked up and saw her he jumped up from the table and came over and gave her a big hug. Nikki introduced him to Roger and they sat and talked to him while waiting for Andre to arrive. As it turned out, when Andre did arrive, they knew each other, as they had some classes together. Nikki asked Paul if any of their other school mates were there studying and he said that if they were he hadn't seen them. He had always been a loner in high school and Nikki realized that he had come to Paris alone. She wondered how anyone could enjoy traveling alone, but she imagined it was a matter of likes and dislikes. She suddenly realized that he must have a lot of self-confidence and she could not help but admire him. He asked her what she was doing there. She explained that she was visiting, but was living in Casablanca. He seemed impressed.

He said, *"It's funny, but when we were going to school, we really didn't know each other. I didn't think that you would be the adventurous type of person. I pictured you getting married and living in San Antonio for the rest of your life."*

Nikki laughed and admitted that she would never have expected to see him in Paris. *"The only difference is,"* she said, *"I married a man whose family was in business in Casablanca and it was not a decision I made for myself. I would never have had the nerve to go to a strange country alone. I really do admire you, as you went alone and did what you really wanted to do. I would have expected you to go to law school at one of the prestigious universities in the states. You were so brilliant in debate. You certainly had the makings to be an attorney."*

Paul thought for a moment and said, *"I did think about it all through high school and the first year I went to the University of Texas with every intention of going into law school, but towards the end of the first year I realized that I wanted more than that out of life and I came here to see if I could find it. I still haven't gotten my degree, because I've changed majors so many times, but in the meantime, I love it here and I may decide to live here after I finally graduate."*

Nikki complimented him on doing his own thing. Most of the kids at home had their lives planned for them by their parents but he was not your run of the mill kid. They said goodbye and she went with Roger and Andre to their table. She whispered to Roger, *"I never could stand that guy in high school. He was such an egg head, yet I was so pleased to see someone from home. I guess when you are away for so long, anyone looks good. I used to call him Porky the Pig! He has that pug nose and round face and we all used to make fun of him. He really is a nice fellow."*

Roger commented *"It's a small world, you never know when you will run into someone you know, especially now that tourism is coming back."*

Andre asked if they wanted fish or meat. Nikki asked if they had veal and they did. She ordered veal and Roger ordered fish. She imagined that they didn't have a menu with items prepared in different ways, which was why they could serve such a meal so cheap. They counted at least five courses that were served to them with a large carafe of the house wine. Everything was delicious and she couldn't believe how well the students lived on so little money. It came to about a dollar and a half a person. They had cheap rent as well as cheap food. At home, or even in Casablanca, the meal would have cost a lot more.

Andre told them that they were in luck, as there would be an art student ball that night and he wanted to take them. He said, *"The art student balls are fun and I know you will enjoy it."*

When they arrived, most of the students were in costume. She had never seen so many drunkards in her life. They were to the point of not knowing what they were doing and it was early in the evening. As she looked around she saw another familiar face, but this time it wasn't anyone from home. She realized that it was Edward G. Robinson. His wife was on his arm. She was a tall woman with long dark hair and wore a large picture hat. From that night on, it seemed that everywhere they went they would see them. It occurred to Nikki that even though he was a great movie actor, he still enjoyed doing all of the things that the average tourist did. It made him seem more human to her and she liked that quality in him. By the time the dance was over, they were all drunk as they could possibly be. Outside of a cup of tea and croissant, they had not eaten since lunch. Andre took them to a restaurant that was upstairs. It was a large room with checkered tablecloths on the tables. By this time Nikki expected checkered tablecloths except in the elegant restaurants. Here they served nothing but onion soup and automatically a bowl was placed in front of them when they sat down. Of all of the delicacies that Nikki had eaten so far, this was more delicious than anything she had eaten. The cheese was thick on top and when you started eating it was stringy and it was almost as difficult to eat as spaghetti. He told them that this was the place to go late at night after the shows and she decided that they would have to come back here every night that they remained in Paris. Andre seemed pleased that she enjoyed it so much. When they left the restaurant, they said their goodnights and went their separate ways.

"Call me again if you get a chance," Andre said. *"There are a lot of other places I would like to show you that the average tourist does not get to know!"* They thanked him and got into a cab to go back to the hotel.

When they got to the hotel they were still feeling no pain and they looked at each other and seemed to get the same idea at the same time. They ran from door to door, switching the shoes around and then ran like small children to their room where they doubled over with laughter. How many people would be furious in the morning when they awoke to find someone else's shoes at their door?

`Nikki said *"Just think, this is something we can't do in the states!"* They were still laughing when they fell into bed exhausted.

The next day they laughed when they read in the paper about the student ball. It seemed that some of the students had stripped and driven up and down the Champs Elysees, jumping out of their cars, completely nude, and running to the cafes and sitting on people's laps. They were sitting on the bumpers of the cars and on the hoods stark naked. Nikki and Roger were sorry that they had left so early.

Chapter Thirty-Five

The next morning they slept late. They had been running so much that they were thoroughly worn out. This was the day they were to call Nikki's family in Texas and they checked the time difference and realized that they would have to put the call in at eight o'clock that night, as that would be twelve noon at home.

Roger told Nikki to get dressed; he wanted to go to see his cousins, Annette and Pierre. They owned a very prestigious seafood restaurant in the Montmartre that specialized in bouillabaisse.

Roger's cousins were delighted to see him and they took to Nikki immediately. They insisted that they come back that night for dinner. However, they wanted them to come at ten-thirty, as by then they could all sit down together and have dinner, since the regular dinner crowd would be thinning out by that time. It worked out perfectly, as they would have time to put in their call to Nikki's family. They walked around the Montmartre and Roger showed Nikki the landmark of the area, the famous Moulin Rouge, which had been built in the eighteen hundreds. He told her "*They are famous for their can-can dancers, and if we have time we will go there one night while we are here.*" Nikki was eager to see it and had wanted to see the can-can dancers.

They decided to have a good cup of tea and eat something more than usual, as it would be very late before they would have dinner. Roger said, "If they want us there at ten-thirty, that means we probably won't be eating until after eleven." They found a lovely tea room and enjoyed the delicious French pastries. Nikki was wondering if she would be fitting into her clothes by the time they went home. However, they walked so much and she realized that her clothes were not any tighter than they had been when they first arrived in Paris and decided that they were walking off the extra calories they were eating.

Finally, they decided to go back to the hotel and put in the call, as Roger was sure it would take time. At ten o'clock they cancelled the call as they realized they would not have time to wait. Nikki was disappointed, but Roger told her they would call the next day.

They arrived at the restaurant promptly at ten thirty and Annette and Pierre had their family there to meet them. They had a daughter and son-in-law about the same age as Nikki, and a beautiful little granddaughter. They asked if Nikki and Roger had any children and Nikki told them that she was expecting. They all acted very excited for them and wished them luck. At this point Nikki was beginning to get excited about it herself and she could tell that Roger was happy when she made the announcement that she was expecting. They were getting along so well now that the doubts she had had when she first found out had vanished.

By the time the other diners left it was after eleven and Nikki was starving. They finally sat down to be served dinner. Nikki tasted the bouillabaisse and found it to be different than anything she had ever eaten. Even though she was not a fish lover, this had to be one of the best things she had eaten, ever. There were huge, cracked lobster claws in it they were given small forks with handles that pushed into the claw and extracted the meat. It was spicy and a very heavy dish to eat at that time of night. They made plans to get together the next day as the restaurant would be closed on Monday.

They were both sound asleep when the phone rang at three in the morning. Nikki was in the middle of a terrible nightmare and Roger was out like a light, but they both jumped to answer the phone. They could not imagine who would be calling at this hour. It was the long distance operator saying, "*Your call has gone through!*" The call had not been cancelled as they had requested. Nikki heard Aunt Emma's voice saying "*Nikki, what happened? We have been here since noon waiting for your call, it is now seven and we have waited all afternoon.*"

"*We put the call through and finally had to cancel it as it would not go through and it was late. It is three in the morning here and we were sound asleep.*" Aunt Emma could not hear her and put Nora on the phone "*Are you having a good time?*"

"*How is everyone?*" There was no reply. Suddenly Aunt Emma was on the phone again and was asking the same question that Nora had just asked.

Nikki realized that they were not hearing her, though

she was hearing them. She turned to Roger and said, "*They don't hear me*!" She kept on talking to them and they kept repeating their questions saying they could not hear her.

Finally Roger took the phone and when he realized that it was a bad call he hung up.

Nikki asked, "*What are you doing?*"

He called the operator and told her that they had had a bad connection and to try the number again. The operator tried to get the number, but the call didn't go through. Finally Roger said, "*Operator, please cancel this call! We cannot stay awake all night to wait for it*!"

Nikki was disappointed, but knew it was a waste of money if they could not hear her. Besides, she was so sleepy she didn't know what to say to them anyway. In a few moments they were both back to sleep again.

The next morning Roger said, "*Get dressed. We are going to a studio and make a record to send to them.*"

Nikki was amazed that he had thought of it and decided that it was better than a phone call, as they could listen to it over and over. However, she would have loved to have asked them some questions also.

Pierre picked them up at the hotel at twelve o'clock as they wanted to make a day of it. He seemed to adore Annette, and Nikki knew instinctively that this was one Frenchman who did not cheat on his wife and she loved him for it. Annette had not been quite ready and Pierre had not wanted to keep them waiting and said, "*My little doll likes to take her time when she dresses, as she loves to please me.*" It was obvious that he took much pride in her and though it was very refreshing to see a couple so completely in love with each other. They worked together all day long, up until the restaurant closed and they never seemed to tire of each other. He then informed them that he loved to dress her and he always went with her to select her clothes. He was very informed on fashions and they always stopped at the better couturieres. Then he said, *"Nicole must have a Paris creation! We are going to Versailles and then we will go to one of our favorite boutiques to buy something for Nicole."*

Roger was a little nervous and embarrassed when he informed Pierre that he didn't know if he could afford to buy anything for Nikki in one of the exclusive shops, as he was sure that they were very expensive.

Pierre insisted that he was going to pay for it. He said, *"I want to buy Nicole something special as Annette and I love her very much."* When Nikki protested he said, *"Today I am the boss!"*

As he said this, Nikki realized that they had arrived at his home and Annette, who had evidently been watching for them, came out dressed exquisitely. Pierre said, *"You see, I dress my doll well!"* He was proud of her and it was obvious. In her mind, Nikki was hoping that Roger was paying attention to this, as she wished that he would be as loving as Pierre was. He had been good to her since they had their problems, but she was happy for him to see that there were Frenchmen who were faithful to their wives.

As they drove to Versailles, the scenery was breathtaking. Nikki could not see enough and only wished she had six pairs of eyes as she didn't want to miss anything. She remembered studying about Versailles in school and about the palace where Marie Antoinette had lived in her history lessons, and now she was actually seeing it. Never had she ever dreamed that one day she would actually see it. The palace and the grounds were beautifully groomed and they were taken to the spot where Marie Antoinette had supposedly met with her lover. Nikki wondered what it would be like to live in a palace such as this and she decided that she would not want to. She felt as if she were having a dream. Everything that she had seen in the history books was now before her eyes.

On their return to Paris, Pierre drove up to Maison de Couture and stopped the car. He quickly opened the door for Annette and Nikki and helped them out of the car. Annette had not seemed surprised and Nikki assumed that she and Pierre had decided on this together. How thoughtful of them, Nikki reflected. She explained that she was three months pregnant, actually in her fourth month, and wondered if she should buy clothes now.

Annette answered, *"My dear Nicole, you will not be pregnant all of your life, you know! I am sure that you will be able to wear it soon, as you will certainly not want to remain fat."*

Nikki replied that she did not intend to ever let herself get fat and Pierre and Annette both seemed to approve of her answer.

They modeled several dresses for them, when finally a girl appeared in a stunning moiré taffeta dress. It had a fitted bodice with a plunging neckline and the skirt flared out and was short in the front and longer in the back. As the girl walked, the skirt opened in the front revealing an apple green petticoat. It had a lot of sex appeal and Nikki thought she would have to have that dress. They could see the expression on her face and told the owner of the shop that she would like to try it on. When they zipped it up, it fit her to perfection.

The owner was surprised to see that it fit her so well. She said, "*Madame, it is rare that one comes into my shop and can wear one of my dresses without having alterations. If you were a little taller I would ask you to be one of my models!*"

Nikki was flattered and then explained that they did not live in Paris and thanked her for the compliment.

While the dress was being wrapped, Pierre said, "*What is a new dress without the perfect the shoes to go with it.*"

"*Enough is enough.*" I will buy the shoes and bag to go with it." Roger insisted.

Pierre replied, "*If you want to buy her shoes and a bag that is fine, but not for my dress.*" He told the owner that they would be back and led them to a shop where they had shoes and accessories, where they found apple green shoes that tied around the ankle and were the exact color of the petticoat.

Nikki thought about how bitchy she was going to look in that outfit and was becoming more and more excited as the purchases were made. She could not wait to put them on together when her hair and make-up was fresh. While they were fitting the shoes, Pierre found a hand beaded black evening bag that he thought would compliment the outfit and insisted on her having it, although it was very expensive. There was no use arguing with him, he was buying her the complete outfit and would not allow Roger to pay for anything.

Nikki could not imagine how much he had spent on her and she could not believe that Annette had not blinked an eye. Roger too had a surprised look on his face for the first time she could remember, as he had done it all before and was not over-whelmed by every little thing as she was. She could see him counting in his head the amount that Pierre had spent and he was impressed. When they were delivered back to the hotel with all of the bundles, Nikki and Roger thanked them over and over again and Roger said, *"Tonight is on me! We'll go out and you will be our guests!"*

Annette said, *"But Roger, you are the visitors here!"* Roger would not take "no" for an answer and they finally agreed that they would rest for a few hours and be back to pick them up at nine o'clock.

As Nikki and Roger entered the hotel she said, *"I can't believe it!" They must have spent at least five hundred dollars on me!"*

Roger said, *"Try nine hundred!"*

Nikki could not believe her ears. *"He must be very rich."*

Roger said that he was sure they were quite wealthy. Their restaurant was very famous and always full. It was one of the better restaurants listed on all of the tourist recommendations. Although they had not seen the menu, he was sure that was not a cheap place to eat.

When they got to the hotel, Roger immediately put in a call to the Lido. It was the finest show in Paris and the food was also excellent. He wanted Nikki to see it and he felt that he owed his cousins a fine evening. After making the reservations he said, *"Why don't we take a shower together and have some fun of our own?"*

Nikki was tired and was looking forward to her nap, but she didn't have the heart to refuse him. The whole day had been for her and she had no right to be tired.

After they made love, Roger called down to the

switchboard and told them to wake them at eight o'clock. Nikki felt that was cutting it close, but she knew that she didn't have to worry about what she would wear and could probably dress in forty-five minutes. That would give them fifteen minutes to get down to the lobby and be waiting for them. In a few seconds they were both sound asleep.

It seemed as if they had just gone to sleep when the phone rang and they were informed that it was eight o'clock. Nikki felt she could have slept through the night, she was so exhausted. She asked Roger to order some coffee to the room while she started putting on her make-up and combing her hair. She needed coffee to revive herself for the long evening ahead of them. He obediently did so. He felt he could use some strong coffee as well. By eight forty-five they were ready and Nikki looked in the long mirror, "I can't believe this is really me!"

Roger grinned, as he could see she was excited over her new clothes. He said, *"You look beautiful honey, but you don't need a Paris creation for that."*

Nikki liked the compliment. For the first time since they had had their problems, Roger was acting more at ease. He was the old Roger again and she was beginning to feel that she did still love him. She realized too that the new surroundings were necessary to get back their old feelings again. Then she suddenly realized that she had not one time thought of Marcel. She wondered if Roger had thought of Carla but she doubted it. She was sure that he had gotten her out of his system and was over it. She was not sure if she would ever get Marcel out of her system.

She had noticed Roger looking at her from time to time

when he thought she had not seen and she had a feeling that he might be wondering what she had done with herself all of those nights that he had not been at home. He had become more possessive after they had gotten back together and showed signs of jealousy when she so much as joked with other men. He would say, *"You don't joke with men like that in this country as they will think that you mean it."* She would answer, *"Maybe I do."* And then she would laugh so that Roger would not take her too seriously. She wondered if now that she had had an affair that she would be tempted to have another one. There was an excitement about it that she could never forget, and felt a tinge of excitement when she did think of it. Then she would think of the baby inside of her and that she would have to be a good mother and not even be thinking about such things. She told herself that if Roger behaved, then she would too.

She knew that Roger would not be happy being tied down with a baby and it worried her. She was afraid that he would start leaving her alone again. As much as she tried to think that all was well between them, she knew it would never be the same. She wanted the baby, but feared that the baby would force her to stay with Roger even if he messed up again. Despite the good time they were having, she continued having mixed feelings inside of her that she was not happy about.

Chapter Thirty-Six

At nine on the dot, Pierre and Annette pulled up in front of the hotel. When Roger and Nikki walked out to the car they both showed their approval. Annette was the first to speak. *"Nicole, you look absolutely ravishing!"*

Pierre smiled and said, *"I know how to dress little dolls very well, Nicole, and you show them off very well."*

Nikki felt herself blushing as usual, wishing she could get over that habit and said, *"Thank you again, very much."* She did feel good about herself that night and felt that she would turn many heads as she walked into the club. It gave her much pleasure to think about it. She wanted Roger to realize that he had something special. Maybe it would keep him from straying again if he saw the other men were interested in her. She decided that she would have to keep him on his toes.

When they walked into the Lido Nikki was in awe. She saw how elegant it was. As they were ushered to their table she could see the men watching her and it pleased her immensely. She realized that Roger must have given the maitre'd a large tip, as they were seated at a table right next to the dance floor and the place was full. She supposed that he wanted to make a good impression on his cousins and also wanted her to see the show without any trouble. All around them the waiters were serving and carving food and they did it with such show, only as she had seen in the movies. She felt as if she were in a movie. She had to pinch herself to be sure this was not a dream. As she looked around the room she saw Edward G. Robinson and his wife again. She poked Roger and asked, "*Are they following us?*" He laughed.

When they sat down she noticed that there was already champagne chilled on their table. Roger informed her that this was the custom in the expensive clubs in Paris. When you finished a bottle the waiter would put it under the table and if you didn't keep count, there were always more bottles than you drank under the table at the end of the evening. He had learned this the hard way before the war. He told the waiter to please leave the corks on the table. The waiter then knew that he was familiar with their racket and did not try to over-charge him.

Pierre laughed and said, "*Roger, I see that you have not forgotten the tricks of the trade here in Paris!*"

Roger replied, "*I am sure that it has not changed. I just hope that they got to the Nazis when they were here!*"

With that Pierre roared with laughter and said, "*We all did. Sometimes it didn't work, but when they were serious about their drinking they didn't seem to notice. We squeezed them for everything we could get!*"

Pierre asked Roger about his war experiences. Roger replied that he had been at Pearl Harbor when it was bombed and described what had happened. He added, *"I was always hoping to get over here. Wouldn't you know how a government could waste a man? They knew that I spoke French fluently and knew the customs of the people, and I was sure they would send me here to take advantage of it. But both times, it was the Pacific. Lucky for me, the war ended before I reached Manila, but then I had that long wait to get home."*

Pierre agreed that it was ridiculous that they didn't place a man where he could be of more use. They seemed impressed when Roger told them that he had been a Major when he got out of the service. Pierre said, *"When the Americans marched into Paris that day, I was hoping that you or Bill would be with them."*

Roger's answer was that he wished that he could have been. Then he quickly covered it up by saying, *"That is, until I married Nikki.* After that I hoped *they would not send me away."*

Pierre remarked, *"I don't blame you. I can't imagine how you would want to leave such a lovely young lady."*

It made Nikki feel good when they talked liked this, and she hoped that Roger would think about that the next time he decided to have an affair. It was on her mind constantly.

They left it up to the maître'd to select their dinner. Roger had always said that the specialty of the house is usually the best thing on the menu. He brought them other things that were not on the menu and the meal was delightful. By this time Nikki knew that anything she ate in a French restaurant would be good. There was no such thing as a bad meal. It was a far cry from the restaurants at home where they threw the food at you. Nikki nibbled on each course, but never finished anything. She knew that the chef would be upset, but she had decided that she was not going to gorge herself on food she didn't want to eat just to make the chef happy. Pierre and Annette ate every morsel of food that was put in front of them. By now, Nikki was used to the French custom of handling the fork and knife and she had mastered it well. In the beginning they had teased her saying, "*Americans waste so much time changing the fork from one hand to the other that the food gets cold!*" She had laughed and decided that she would start eating the way they did. She had even mastered getting the peas on the back of the fork.

Pierre looked at Nikki's plate and said, "*You eat like a bird! Don't you know that you are feeding two people now?*"

Nikki replied, "*I never want to get fat and if I eat it all I will!*"

They said that she would never have to worry about that, but she knew they were wrong.

When the show started, much to her surprise, the dance floor started rising and suddenly became a stage. The master of ceremonies was a comedian and she could not understand him as he spoke much too fast for her and though her French was getting better all the time, when anyone spoke too fast she could not catch all of it. The girls in the show were beautiful. Roger had warned her that they would have nude breasts, so she was not surprised. However, they had on very elaborate head pieces and skirts and she had never seen anything like it before. They evidently selected them for their looks, as they did not have to have much talent to walk around the stage as they did. She found it amusing to note the different sizes and shapes of their breasts, and wondered if some of them had

had operations, since they all stood out too perfect, especially those on the large side, as the French women were not known for having large breasts.

The talent in the show was very professional and it was all to perfection. The magician was unbelievable. They were sitting right there and he made things happen right before their eyes. They looked at each other as though to say it was impossible. Roger, Pierre and Annette were all watching Nikki. They enjoyed her face when the different acts came on as there was so much enthusiasm and delight on her face, especially when the back drapes opened and the stage turned and the ice-skating number came on. The only mistake they made that evening was that they went to the Lido first, as after that, the other shows in Paris were disappointing.

When the show was over and they left the Lido, Pierre said, "*Now I have a surprise for you. I am taking you to some places that you will probably never see in America*!" He made no mention of where they were going. He drove to a club and when they went in Nikki noted that all of the waiters were extremely handsome. She felt flattered when they looked her up and down as she walked to the table.

The floor show came on and a young girl did a very provocative strip act. She entered the stage as if she were just arriving home from a date. She began removing her clothing, very slowly, but determined, and as she removed each piece of clothing she would fold it very neatly and lay it over the back of the chair, which was the only prop on the stage. When she had finally removed the last of her clothing, Nikki was somewhat astounded to see that she was completely flat chested. She knew that most of the women who stripped usually had something to show. The girl then slipped on a very sheer night gown and lit a candle, threw a kiss and made her exit.

Finally they asked her what she thought of the place and she mused, *"It seems strange to me that they would use a girl who had nothing on top. She seemed so unfeminine!"* They informed her that this was a lesbian club and that all of the handsome waiters were women. They were all sitting there waiting for her reaction, as even Roger was in on the joke.

Nikki was a little shocked at first, then laughed and said, "I have heard of these things, and now I know it is true."

The next club they went to was called La Vie En Rose, where the men were all female impersonators. This night was a real education for Nikki. The show came on and she could not believe that these beautiful women were really men and she would have given her right arm for some of the lavish gowns and shoes that they were wearing. All around them there were men embracing and kissing each other and when the dance music began, they were dancing cheek to cheek. One of the men winked at Roger and they were all teasing him.

Nikki turned to him and whispered, *"I'll bet they pay them to do this. I can't believe it is really true!"*

The next day when they decided to go to a movie, one of the couples from the club the night before were sitting in front of them making out, and Nikki realized that this sort of thing did exist. She was learning the facts of life in a hurry.

Chapter Thirty-Seven

The next morning Roger called his other cousin to see if she was in Paris. He and Nikki both would have liked to have had the day to themselves but Roger felt that one cousin might tell the other and it had to be done. Claudette and Robert had a chain of theaters in Indo-China. Roger said "they're probably not in Paris anyway, but my father will be upset if I don't call them." His father had been born in Egypt and he had gone to America as a young man. Most of his family had settled in Paris. Annette and Claudette had been born there. As it happenened, they were in Paris. She told Roger, you got us at the right time. We arrived here last night. He was sorry he had not called them first, as then he could have told his father that they were not there.

Their apartment was exquisite. Something like you would see in Better Homes and Gardens. She insisted that they come to dinner. Roger declined saying, you just got home and I don't want to put you out. Maybe we should wait a day or two." She insisted that it didn't matter, as they had brought their Indo-Chinese cook and servants with them.

When they walked into the apartment they could immediately see what Annette had been talking about. Everything was in its place and there was a place for everything. They had very elegant, expensive furniture, and beautiful paintings and sculptures. They were extremely wealthy and Nikki could see the surprise on Roger's face. She could tell that she was not the only one who was impressed for a change.

The dinner was superb. Everything was totally different than anything they had ever eaten before and Nikki could tell that Roger was overwhelmed, as he had no idea that it would be so elaborate.

For the remainder of the trip they went and saw the things that tourists usually did; the Eiffel Tower, the Louvre and several Cathedrals. They climbed the hundreds of steps to the Mount-Sacre-Coeur Cathedral and found that it was a whole little city of its own up there. They went through the church, though it was being remodeled, and then sat at a sidewalk café and had a drink while the violinists played beautiful music. There were many artists there and many small shops with interesting paintings. They went through the shops and finally picked out a painting that they both liked. They were surprised to see how reasonable they were as most things in Paris were quite expensive.

Each day they would go to a tea room at four o'clock where the pastries were divine. Afterwards they would go to the hotel and rest. They never were able to get together again with Annette and Pierre, as they had used their only free night with them and the restaurant was open six nights a week. They went to the restaurant to see them and thank them again and say goodbye. Annette and Pierre begged them to come back soon and they agreed that when the baby was big enough to leave with Roger's mother they would be back.

When they finally boarded the plane to return home they were pleasantly exhausted. They had thoroughly enjoyed their week in Paris and Roger promised that they would come back again. Nikki knew that it would never be the same as the first time when everything was so new to her. She had fallen in love with Paris and wished that they could live there.

Now all she could think about was going home to relax and make plans for their first baby. She had seen so many unique, handmade embroidered baby clothes, but they had decided not to buy any since they didn't know whether it would be a boy or a girl and wanted to wait until the next trip.

Chapter Thirty-Eight

After taking Nicole and Roger to the plane, Marcel had gotten into his car and driven around. His heart was heavy that night. He could see that Nicole was determined to stay with Roger, which meant that he was out of the picture. The only thing that gave him encouragement was when he had kissed Nicole goodbye. He had felt her trembling at the time and was sure that the kiss had been as exciting to her as it had been to him. However, he knew that he would have to wait for Roger to stray again. He was dwelling on his feelings for Nicole and he knew that though he had an eye for women, she was different than any he had ever known and that he would never tire of her.

He couldn't understand why Roger had been drawn to an old has-been like Carla when he had a wife that was so desirable at home. Carla had told him that Roger didn't love her anymore. She said, "I think he just wanted to relive the old days. Let's face it, Marcel, too much has happened to all of us to go back to the days before the war. We have all had our bad times since then, but I too was curious to see if it would still be the same

Marcel now realized that Roger had meant it when he told him that his affair with Carla was over. He assumed that Nicole loved Roger and that she did not think about him anymore. Or else, she had decided that there really was not any hope for them to ever be able to marry and decided to stay with Roger. He had no idea that Nicole was pregnant until Roger's father had made a remark that made him feel that she was. As he watched her he didn't see any signs of pregnancy. Her figure was as good as ever. If it was true, he was sure that was why she had decided to remain with Roger after the terrible way he had treated her. He wondered how far along she was and felt that everything had gone against them from the time of her operation.

After they had gotten back together, he found that he had lost his desire for Yolanda and had settled down and was, for the first time in his marriage, being a good husband to Juanita. He could see the happiness on her face when he came home every night to stay and knew that he had been a cad from the day he had married her. This woman had given him three beautiful children and had been a good wife to him. He found that he could not develop an appetite for sex with her and he knew that it was probably breaking her heart, but he could not get his mind off of Nicole.

When he realized this, he thought to himself, *"I guess I really am in love with Nicole."* In fact, he realized that he was truly in love for the first time in his life. It was more than just a physical thing, as it had been with other women he had had affairs with. The thought shook him up. He knew that she was not free, nor was he. "*It's ironic,*" he thought. "*When I finally meet a woman I truly love, she has to be the wife of my best friend.*" He shook his head and felt that it was such a hopeless thing, but he could not do a thing about it. Nicole would have to make the first move.

Roger's father had told him when they were coming in and Marcel had nonchalantly offered to pick them up at the airport. He was disappointed when the old man had said, "*No thank you. We are going to pick them up. We are very anxious to hear about their trip.*"

Suddenly Marcel got a strange feeling that he suspected something. He had been very careful during those nights that he had been with Nicole. He made sure that no one saw him go into the apartment or come out. As far as he knew, no one but he and Nicole knew about it and he was sure that she would never give herself away. During that time she had even let the servants go on the nights that they were together.

When Roger had asked her why, she had told him that she was embarrassed for them to see that he was out every night and didn't want them to know anything. Except for the first night that he had gone to her, the servants had not been there when he arrived. He wondered if they had seen or heard something that first night and that Roger's father had been told. He would have liked to have asked Nicole if he had said anything to her. He noted coolness about Monsieur Carpel ever since his return from Italy. Then he realized that it was probably his imagination and guilt that made him think so. He decided to wait until the next day to go over and see them to hear all about their trip. He also wanted to see if Nicole would show any indication that there was still some feeling for him.

When he got home, he told Juanita, "*It's been a long time since we've had Roger and Nicole over for dinner. Let's have them over this week, as soon as they have had time to rest from their trip. I think we would enjoy hearing all about it and certainly Nicole must have found it exciting. It would be fun to see her reactions when she relates about all of their experiences.*"

Juanita smiled and seemed pleased. She said, "*Give them a couple of days to rest up and then we will ask them. I will fix one of my Spanish meals, as Nicole loves that kind of food.*" She was excited at the idea of entertaining again, and Marcel felt guilty when he realized that she did not suspect anything and that she really did love Nicole. He wondered why life had to be so complicated. Never in his whole life had he felt as he did now and it confused him.

Chapter Thirty-Nine

Nikki was happy to be home again. She had had a beautiful trip, one that she would never forget, but she was extremely tired and for the next few days decided she didn't want to do very much. After she unpacked she laid down, as she felt that she needed a rest. She stayed around the apartment most of the time.

Mom could see that she was thoroughly exhausted and was very sympathetic. She told her not to worry about going to the market that she would go. She said, "*You young people have a tendency to overdo things. You are pregnant, Nikki, and you will find that you need more rest. I hope that you and Roger will stay at home nights and get rested up before you start running again.*"

Nikki realized that since they had arrived in Casablanca they had never stayed at home at night. They had always seemed to have someplace to go; either to play bridge or to a club. Suddenly it seemed strange when she thought about long evenings at home, as outside of those nights when Roger had been running around and she had been there alone they had never stayed around the apartment. She felt that it would be boring, as there was really nothing to do and they had run out of good books to read a long time ago. She decided to write and ask Nora to send some new ones. She wondered what it would be like when the baby came. She knew they would be tied down at least until she was not nursing anymore. The idea didn't really appeal to her very much and she wondered whether she would like being a mother. Then she would reproach herself and think about how sweet a baby would be. It would certainly keep her from being bored.

She soon found that it was out of her hands. She was taking a nap, dreaming of having a baby. She dreamed she was having terrible labor pains, and suddenly she awoke and she was having severe cramps. She felt wetness underneath her and when she got up and looked, it was covered with blood. She was so frightened, and screamed for mom.

When mom came in and saw what was happening she told her that she was sure that she was having a miscarriage. She called for an ambulance and once again, Nikki was back at the clinic. She was heartbroken when they told her that she had lost her baby. The doctor said, "You are very young, and you will have many others.

One night after Roger had left the hospital for the night, Marcel came to see her. He told her that both he and Juanita were very sorry to hear of her misfortune. It was an awkward moment when he first came in, as they had not talked alone for a long time. Finally he said, *"Mon Cherie, it is very difficult for me. Though I love Roger, I realize that I love you more. If he proves himself unworthy of you again, we will be together."*

She asked, "*Do you really love me?*" Marcel looked into her eyes and he was more serious than she had ever seen him. He answered, "*Very much. I really do love you!*"

Nikki had to be sure that he truly did love her. She was thinking that she didn't care anymore who she hurt, as she had been hurt so much by Roger and now losing her baby. She wanted the world to know that she was indeed, in love with Marcel. He had told her that he really did love her and that was all she wanted to hear.

She said, "*It is difficult to be around you and not be able to touch you. I will always love you, but it seems so hopeless at the present time for us to be together. I wish that I could have your baby!*" She then added, "*I can never forget what he did to me. Even now, as I lay in the hospital, I wonder if he is with someone else. If ever he starts an affair again, I will leave him. So you see, my darling, it is you who did the favor for Roger when you had the affair with me. If not for that, I would be back in the states now.*"

"*If Roger starts treating you badly again, I will be the first to let you know. Then we'll make our own plans. We have to wait and have patience. Our day will come, I promise you. I have not had an affair since I have been with you and I am at home every night. You can ask Juanita. I have not even been with Juanita, because I cannot get enthused about sex anymore, because I think of you and it is you I want more than anything in the world.*" He bent down to kiss her goodnight. "*You must get your rest and I will be back tomorrow night.*" he said.

As they embraced, she knew that she could never live without his love and she hoped and prayed that Roger would make that one move that would that would permit them to get back together again. She wondered how long she would have to wait. Mom and dad had already said that since there would be no baby they would probably be going back to the states for a while.

Chapter Forty

When she returned from the hospital their plans were made. Mom planned to stay for six months, since her mother was getting old and she wanted to spend some time with her. Dad planned to stay only for a few weeks. In the back of Nikki's mind she was sure that Roger would take advantage of his father's absence once more, and she realized that she actually hoped that he would. She knew that Marcel would know if he were to start seeing another woman and this time he would tell her. Nikki wondered many times if Roger suspected something between Marcel and her, as he had never seemed to want to spend much time with them anymore. He never said anything to indicate that he suspected something, but when she had asked why they were not close as before his answer had been, "*We go out with other couples and Marcel never wants to go out with his wife. We have less in common now and I realized that it is not as it was in the old days. Marriage changes a lot of things.*"

Nikki knew that as long as Roger was good to her, and

he certainly had tried to make things up to her, she would have to forget about Marcel.

When they took Roger's parents to the plane, they spent the day together. It was a weekday, but Roger said, "*I declare this a legal holiday*!" They went to the tennis club and played a few sets of tennis, then showered and changed and went out to dinner and to another club that had become popular since their arrival. On the set of the slow music, the lights were turned down low and the faceted mirror ball on the ceiling turned, reflecting the soft lights. Nikki thought it was quite romantic and closed her eyes as they danced and thought of Marcel. She was trying to get him out of her mind, but he was there, and there was no use trying to fool herself. She would laugh when the lights came on, as some of the women were busily buttoning up their blouses. The slow sets were for lovers, there was no doubt about it and she was remembering the times when they had first arrived and she had danced with Marcel. It seemed so long ago, but she wished that they could dance together again. She would finally tell herself to quit dwelling on it. Roger was being a good husband now and she should stop thinking about Marcel. She just hoped that she would not have to see him, as then she would find it impossible. The floor show came on and first there was a Hungarian dancer, then a belly dancer and finally Yolanda did her "Danse de Feu" which she did exceptionally well. Roger mentioned to her that Juanita had been the one who did this dance so well and had been famous for it all over Europe. Nikki had not realized that Juanita had performed in Paris and other countries before she had settled down with Marcel and she realized that she had given up a lot for him. She had seen photographs of her when she was a dancer and they were very elegant. She had a classical look about her that she had not seen on any of the others. She wished that she could have seen her dance. She was still a pretty woman and would probably still be dancing had she not had children. Nikki felt sorry for her and was sure that she remembered those days as the best ones in her life, but she could not blame her for falling in love with Marcel. She would become confused when she thought of it, and realized that if it was not her, it would be someone else. He simply was not in love with Juanita. It was obvious that he was not in love with her and had it not been for the war, he never would have married her and she would have fallen by the wayside as Carla had with Roger. However he had married her to stay out of the army and she actually lucked out, as at least she had someone to support her and the children, a security that she would otherwise not have had. A dancing career does not last forever. The men want to see young girls, not washed out old women. Juanita was no longer in her twenties and would be considered a has-been no matter how good a dancer she was.

One night they had run into Jon and Theresa and were sitting with them at the club, the first club they had gone to when they first arrived. They still played "Deep in the Heart of Texas" when Nikki walked in. This club still seemed to be the main hang out for the old crowd of Roger's friends, as the owner was also a friend of theirs. She was just sitting there, when suddenly a man walked up and leaned over her and said, "Donner moi un feu!" He was leaning over her with a cigarette dangling from his mouth. Evidently this was one way a man tried to pick up a woman. Nikki could see that he was very drunk. Roger jumped up from his chair and grabbed the man and a fight began. She was so frightened that she tried to pull them apart. Suddenly she found that she was being picked up and carried away. Jon had literally pulled her away from them saying, "*Roger can take care of himself*!" Jon had been a big war hero and the women liked him almost as much as they did Marcel. It was said that he had taken a whole village alone during the war. The fight finally ended with Roger being thrown into the drums where he cut his eye on one of the symbols. Nikki ran to him and took him into the rest room to wash the blood off of his face. While they were in the rest room, the other man came in to clean his face. He had actually gotten the worst end of the fight. He had cuts all over his face and it was already beginning to swell and show signs of bruising. Just as he and Roger were starting to discuss what had happened in a friendly way, as they had both had enough, an attractive woman came flying in and walked up to Roger and shouted, "*Regarder a moi, regarder a moi! Why would my husband need your wife?*" She threw a dirty look at Nikki and was very angry and humiliated to think that her husband had made a pass at another woman. She began to wash her husband's face as Nikki was doing for Roger, showing them what a good wife she really was. A few nights later when they went back to the club, she was there with her lover. Her husband was a pilot with Air France and was often away, but that didn't stop her from having a man around. When she looked up and saw Nikki and Roger she smiled sheepishly and shrugged her shoulders.

Chapter Forty-One

When Roger had finally settled down to become a good husband to Nikki he decided that he would be faithful to her from now on. He knew that he didn't love Carla, but there was something about her that drew him to her. She had a passion that no other woman he knew of had ever had. He tried to throw off his guilt by telling himself that it was a natural thing for a man to want to stray. He had seen it happen all of his life and he felt that it was natural for a man to be able to get away with that sort of thing. He had been faithful to her ever since the night of her operation and he had no intention of ever hurting her again.

When she had been rushed to the hospital with her miscarriage he would spend the evenings at the different clubs with his friends, but he didn't try to flirt with the women there, even though some of them had appealed to him. He had not wanted to stay at home, as for some reason he had noticed that his father was asking a lot of questions about what had happened when they had been in Italy. Nikki had never told them what Roger had done, and he appreciated the fact that she had not said anything. His father kept repeating the thing about Nikki being so thin and run down and he had asked Roger several times if he had abused her. He denied that anything had happened, but finally his father had said, *"Roger, the servants have made some remarks to me about you leaving Nikki here alone every night and going out by yourself when we were gone. They also told me that Nikki had started letting them go at night. I have wondered if it was because she did not want them to know that you were leaving her alone. I want to know exactly what did happen!"*

Roger's answer had been, *"It's none of your business. You set the example, you know. What about all of the flings that you have had. You have no right to question me about my life!"* When his father saw how angry he became he dropped the issue but would say from time to time, *"You don't know how lucky you are to have a wife like Nikki. She's a good wife to you. I have wondered for years what she sees in you. She could have made a better marriage!"*

Roger knew that his father was not stupid, but he didn't want to go back to struggling for a living again. He'd gotten used to the good life, but he was not financially independent. He also was wondering about Nikki letting the servants go at night, as she had always been very nervous when he had been on duty and she had been left at home alone. It was true that she was older now than in those days, as she had been such a child when he married her. He began to wonder what had gone on when he had not been there and if she had possibly been seeing someone and didn't want the servants to know. It was possible that he wanted to think something like that in order to ease his conscience, feeling guilty for having treated her the way he did.

While she was in the hospital he made it a point to tell his parents where he could be reached after he left the hospital. He knew that he could not take the chance of arousing his father's suspicions again. He also wondered if someone had told him that he had been with Carla. He was sure that when he had told her that their affair was over that she had opened her mouth and told her friends about it. She had been furious when he told her that it was over and she would have wanted revenge. If it was all over town, he was sure that his father had heard it.

He was somewhat relieved when his parents announced that they were going back to the states for a while. He felt that at least he would not be under the prying eyes of his father, though he did tell Roger to behave himself when they left. Roger made up his mind that he would spend all of his time with Nikki when he was not working and they made the rounds of the clubs, took a trip to Tangier and played a lot of tennis and bridge. Nikki had been close to Monique and the four of them had been together a lot of the time. When his father returned he would see a happy Nikki, he made sure of that. Maybe he would stop bothering him about it.

From time to time his mind would wander back to Carla and he would wonder what she was doing and who she was with. He was sure that she would have someone, as she was not the type to be alone. There was something about her that was still drawing him even now when he was trying so hard to be faithful to Nikki.

Chapter Forty-Two

Roger could not understand. From the day he and Nikki had arrived in Casablanca he had seen the way Marcel had acted around her. He could tell that he had something on his mind, as he knew him well and had a feeling that he would like to know her better. He had also noted how Nikki had looked at Marcel. At first he figured that they had heard so much about each other and were getting to know each other. However, their looks had been different lately. It was almost as if they were sharing some kind of intimacy that they didn't want him to know about. He could not shake off the feeling that something had happened between them during the time he was with Carla. Marcel was the one who had avoided him around the time he had been having his fling with Carla and he wondered if he had tried to get to Nikki and had succeeded. He didn't think that she would play this game, but she had to be curious about him after all the things he had told her. Now he was sorry he had ever told her that he had a reputation of being a great lover. He finally shook off his feelings for the moment and decided that Nikki would never play that game. It was not her way of life.

Roger was busy that day, he had a lot of work to do and called Nikki and said, *"Honey, I won't be home for tea so go ahead and make plans with some of your friends. I have a lot of work to get out today."*

She had told him not to work too hard, that she would find something to do and hung up. He realized that at one time she would have been upset, but now she never made an issue out of things like this. Again, he wondered why. There were quite a few orders that he had to get out. He was bringing in some cars from the states. One was a yellow convertible which he decided to keep for himself if it was in good condition. It would be nice to have a larger car for a change, he decided, and the climate in Casablanca was perfect for a convertible. Now that he did not have to worry about anyone spotting his car near Carla's, he didn't have to drive a Renault. He decided that his father could drive it and he would have his own car. Many nights when he and Nikki had wanted to go out, mom and dad had wanted to use the car to go to the show and he and Nikki would have to take a *cocher'*. They should have their own car. He worked hard in the business and he felt that he was entitled to it and would tell this to his father if he complained about it.

As it turned out, his father remained in the states longer than he had planned. His mother had found out that she had to have a hysterectomy, so he stayed for the operation and made sure that she was on her feet before he left her. She was happy to be back in the states as she had a lot of family in New England and they had all come down to see her and she wanted to be with her mother for a while. Nikki and Roger invited him to go out with them when he did return to Casablanca, as they felt sorry for him being alone, but he would always refuse. He would say that he didn't care to go to the clubs anymore and that he had plenty of reading material. Some nights he would be invited to dinner with some of his old friends who he had known for many years.

One night when Nikki and Roger were on their way home they spotted him with a woman. Roger laughed and said, *"The old boy is still going strong! He has always had an eye for the women!"*

Nikki wondered why he was not upset that his father was cheating on his mother and said so. She felt like hitting him she was so angry.

Roger said, *"Don't get your dander up, Nikki. After all, it doesn't mean anything. He is still a healthy male who needs a little companionship once in a while!"*

Nikki commented, *"You men are all alike. Your minds are all in the same place no matter what your age is!"* She felt sorry for mom, as she certainly didn't deserve this.

Roger said, *"What do you expect? She leaves him for months at a time. He's still a man!"*

Nikki felt very insecure and she knew now that she would never be able to trust him again with the attitude that he had. She began to wonder what he had done when he was overseas and on the nights that she was in the hospital and decided that he didn't go home to bed, at least not alone. She felt her blood running cold inside of her when she thought of the months they were separated when he was overseas. Up until now, she had never thought of it or even questioned it.

From that night on she decided that given the opportunity, if she and Roger were ever separated at all, she would also take advantage of the situation. She knew that this was not the ideal way of thinking for a healthy marriage, but she would play the same game.

Part Four

Marrakech

Chapter Forty-Three

The beginning of December, Nikki became ill with pneumonia. The doctor said that between her operation and her miscarriage her condition was weak and she was susceptible to illness. She came through it very well. In fact she did not have to go to the hospital, and she would have refused had the doctor wanted to send her. He did tell Roger that he should get her out of the humid climate of Casablanca.

"Why don't you take her to Marrakech as soon as she feels strong enough to travel?"

It was decided that they would leave the day after Xmas and stay through New Years day. Roger said that he would stay with her for a couple of days until she was able to meet some people and then he would return to Casablanca to work and return for the New Year holiday. Nikki was not happy about being left alone, but Roger finally convinced her that she needed to be in the sunshine and breathe in fresh, dry air. He assured her that it would only be for a few days and then he would be back. *"After all,"* he said, *"It is only one hundred and thirty miles away, it's not like you are going to the other end of the world!"*

Monique and Michael decided that they would go for New Years as well, and when Roberta and Antoine found out, they too decided to go. They succeeded in persuading dad to go also and the plans were made.

On the day after Christmas, Roger packed the car and he and Nikki took off for Marrakech. He decided that he would take his clothes for New Years Eve as well and that way he wouldn't have to worry about it when he drove there later with his father. They had all reserved rooms at the Hotel La Mamounia, which was the finest hotel in Marrakech. They felt lucky to get rooms there as late as it was, as the hotel was a very popular place for the holidays and many of the English diplomats stayed there for the holidays. Winston Churchill was also known to stay there on occasion. As they approached the city, Nikki could see the snow covered mountains surrounding it and said, *"I had no idea that it would be like this. It is beautiful!"*

Roger agreed with her and said, *"And again, I say that I am going to show you the world!"* The air was dry and crisp and it felt so good to just breathe it in. Casablanca was so damp that they had to place their leather goods out in the sun to keep them from getting mildewed. Even the paint on the walls would become mildewed. Nikki realized that Marrakech was like the sun valley of Morocco. She was sure that she would become strong and invigorated while visiting this enchanting city. She was completely unprepared when they drove up to the hotel. It was magnificent. When they entered the lobby she saw the glassed in dining room and beyond that the exquisite gardens that seemed to extend as far as she could see. She turned to Roger and said, *"It's more like a park than a garden!"*

There were citrus trees covered with fruit, fountains and lovely green shrubs. It was like being in heaven for all of its beauty, she thought. Roger turned to watch her face and he was enjoying just watching the pleasure that it showed.

Then he said, *"I didn't tell you anything about the hotel because I wanted to see your reaction when you first walked in. You did react exactly as I did the first time that I came here. Have you ever seen anything quite like it?"*

Nikki replied, *"There is no way I could ever describe this place so that anyone could really know how beautiful it is. There are no words in English. I suppose in French it would be "Formidable!"*

Roger smiled and said, *"It is true, the French have words to describe things that we don't have."*

They went to the desk to check in and were ushered to their room. It was on the first floor. Nikki had still another pleasant surprise when they entered the room. It was very large and toward the back of the room were several steps leading to an upper level where there was a table and chairs. Beyond that there was a massive glass sliding door leading to the patio, surrounded by the sumptuous garden.

She was overwhelmed by it all. Roger was smiling as he watched her, because he knew that she was surprised and had not expected anything like this. She had believed that they were going into the interior where it was very primitive, and he had let her believe it as he wanted to surprise her. She glowed with happiness when she realized that it was such modern city with modern facilities. She had even expressed her appreciation that the others were sacrificing their New Years in Casablanca to be with them, but now she realized that they were giving up nothing.

She turned to Roger and said "*You thought of everything. I am so glad that we are on the first floor and we won't have those long walks to the elevator and the waiting for them. We can just step out into the garden.*"

He told her that he had asked for a room in this location. Nikki knew that she would let nothing happen to stop them from being close and having a wonderful time.

Chapter Forty-Four

After hanging up their clothes, they walked out into the garden. They were only a short distance from the main part of the garden that she had seen when they had first arrived. There was a very large patio with the fountain in the middle and surrounding it were tables and chairs and benches. Not only were they on the first floor with a view and an entrance to the garden, but also centrally located.

There were not many people there yet. Most of the guests were coming in towards the end of the week for the New Year celebration. Those who were there were mostly Europeans and an American writer doing research for a book that he was writing.

Nikki had not seen very many Americans since her arrival in Casablanca, as the American bases had been shut down and only the graves registration people were there shipping bodies home. There were some Americans at the Naval Base, but they never had the opportunity to meet them. There were a couple of Americans living in Casablanca who had been stationed there in the service and had married girls from there. These men were doing exceptionally well, as they were the only ones who were allowed to purchase the military supplies when the bases closed. Therefore they had made a fortune, and one couple that they knew had built a mansion that was fit for a king. They had become friendly with them and were frequently invited to their home for parties. The couple that they knew the best had lucked out when it came to making money. He had been asleep one morning when a wealthy Moroccan had awakened him and said,

"I will give you the money to go to the auction and buy the surplus that the American government has for sell. In return, you will become my full partner."

He had literally fallen into a pot of gold, as he would have never had the money to purchase all of the merchandise that was for sale. As a result, he had become a millionaire over night. Roger had been sorry that he had not been there to have that opportunity, but the ones who were there when they closed the bases were the ones who had cleaned up. This had been a thorn in his side, as he felt that he had lived there all of those years and had missed out on the opportunity of a lifetime.

Everyone seemed friendly enough and after they had introduced themselves they ordered something to drink and began talking to them. Nikki looked up and saw a wealthy Arab walking toward them who they had met in Casablanca at a party. She nudged Roger and said, *"That's Monsieur Cabbage who we met at that party in Casablanca. Remember? He told us if we ever came to Marrakech to call him and he would invite us to a feast."*

Roger remembered and said, *"It seems a coincidence that we should run into him so soon."*

He had already spotted them and was walking toward them smiling. He re-introduced himself, asking if they remembered him. They both assured him that they did, but that they had just arrived a short while ago and had not as yet had a chance to call him. He said, *"We are having feasts all this week, as there are many Europeans here and I must call my father and ask his permission to invite you. I will be right back."*

As he walked away, Nikki whispered to Roger, *"It seems peculiar that a man of his age has to have permission from his father, doesn't it?"*

Roger informed her that no matter what age, an Arab son must ask his father's permission for everything he does. He had explained to them the first time they had met him that his real name was not Cabbage that he had taken this name, as the Europeans could not pronounce his Arab name. He had also said, *"Just think of the vegetable in English and you will not forget my name."* He spoke English fluently, as well as many other languages and Nikki assumed that because of his wealth he had had the opportunity to go away to school.

He returned so fast, it seemed that there would not have been time for him to call his father, but evidently he had received permission and asked them if they would like to come. He said, *"Everyone is coming. I just wanted to tell my father that there should be two more places set."*

Then he asked them if they had met Madame and Monsieur Bonet who had with them a young French Countess by the name of Mignon. She is not quite your age, probably about eighteen. He explained that she had no money, but still carried her title, as she had come from a family of royalty. Later on Nikki asked *Madame Bonet* if she was related to the countess and she had said they were only friends. Nikki assumed that the families were friendly and that they had brought the girl with them to Marrakech for the holiday. They too had been invited to the feast, as well as the American writer. Monsieur Cabbage acted like the host of Marrakech. Evidently he came to the hotel every day to meet the guests and would invite them to a feast. It seemed odd that he seemed to prefer being with strangers all the time, as surely, she felt, he must have many friends in Marrakech. He asked them to be in the lobby at eight-thirty and he would have several cars there to pick them up and take them to his home. Roger had told Nikki how delicious the Arab food was and she was looking forward to going to a genuine Arab feast. There were restaurants that offered feasts, but she was sure that it would be much better in a private home.

For the rest of the afternoon they stayed in the garden and soaked up the sunshine. It was cool and crisp, but the sun was warm. However, most everyone wore a suit or dresses with long sleeves or jackets. It was not quite warm enough to be outside without warm clothing.

They had their aperitif, but by this time it was getting too cool in the garden and they all moved inside to the restaurant where they had tables set by the windows for the aperitif hour. After they finished their drink, Roger suggested they go to the room and rest for a while, as he was afraid that Nikki would become over-tired. They had a long evening ahead of them and it had been a long day since they had driven from Casablanca.

After saying their "*A tout a l'heure!*" meaning see you later, they went to their room. Nikki didn't realize how tired she actually was, as she was enjoying all of the new people and atmosphere so much, but as soon as she hit the bed she was out like a light. When she awoke it was dark and for a moment she forgot where she was. She sat up and could see Roger's outline as he looked out the glass door into the garden, as if he were waiting for her to wake up. He told her that she had better start getting dressed, as it was almost seven-thirty. Nikki turned the light on next to the bed and went into the bathroom to run her bath. She said, "*It was a strange feeling when I woke up, I didn't even know where I was!*"

Roger turned to her and said, "*You slept very soundly, as I watched you most of the time.*"

Nikki looked surprised and asked "*Didn't you sleep? It was a long day for you as well and you are the one who drove all the way.*"

Roger looked very pensive and said, "*I guess I had things on my mind and could not sleep.*"

Nikki was wondering what was really on his mind. She wondered if perhaps he was missing Carla and then began to wonder if that affair was truly over. It occurred to her that he just might still be seeing her. She didn't question him, as the hurt was back again. She finally said, "*You are making me nervous pacing the floor and I am sure you don't feel like sitting around waiting for me to get dressed. Why don't you go into the lobby and talk to some people until I am ready. I will be there in plenty of time, I promise.*"

Roger looked relieved and took her up on her offer. After she took her bath she dressed with much care, as she was determined to look her best that night. If Roger did still have his mind on another woman, she thought, and then she would let him know how appealing she could be to other men, if not to him. She still thought of Marcel, but she had tried her best not to, as she knew that it was a hopeless situation and she wished that Roger would feel the same way about Carla. His situation was not quite as hopeless as her's. At least Carla didn't have a husband, but Marcel did have a wife. She decided not to let her thoughts ruin the evening for her. The French Countess was going to show her up tonight. She laughed to herself thinking, here I am, only twenty three, and this girl makes me feel as if I am a middle aged woman. She decided to concentrate on her hair and make-up. She selected her most sensuous dress, which was an off-white silk that was very fitted with a low neckline. When she walked out of her room she looked good. Her face glowed from the sunshine and the color was already returning to her pale face from one afternoon of the Marrakech sunshine. Her long illness had robbed her of her lovely coloring, but now she was beginning to look like her old self again.

As she made her appearance in the lobby she could see that Roger was pleased and proud of her. She made the others look dowdy as she walked in proudly with her long dark hair and brilliant blue eyes. The dress showed off her curves, and she knew that she looked her very best that night. The handsome American writer was watching her as she swept into the lobby and Roger noticed it. He was not too happy about leaving her there alone. He was afraid that he would make a move on her after he left.

The writer complimented Nikki on her appearance and

she thanked him. Roger noted his perfect features as well as the fact that he was over six feet tall and well built. It gave him a complex to even stand next to him, as he had always been self conscious of his size and when he married Nikki he had enjoyed showing her off on his arm as though to say, *"I may not be very big, but look what I have."* He found himself disliking this writer, Bob Mabry, and wondered if he should leave Nikki there alone. However, he felt that because of her attitude about these things, she would not let him get to first base. He hoped that he was right. He still had an odd feeling about the way she had changed since the time he had been with Carla. He hoped that she would not decide to get even with him.

At the same time that he was wondering about Nikki, she was taking in the writer and thinking that she would not mind having a fling with him. She was sure that Roger would not be faithful to her.

Chapter Forty-Five

In a matter of minutes, the cars arrived to take them to the feast. Bob got into the back seat of the car with Nikki and Roger. Roger hoped that it was just because of the fact that they were fellow Americans and that he felt at home with them, and not because he wanted to sit next to Nikki. She was sitting in the middle between them and Roger deliberately made conversation with Bob so that he could watch him all the time. He had to lean around Nikki to talk to him and at the same time he was watching to make sure that he didn't lay a hand on her.

She saw what he was doing and laughed to herself, thinking, "*Good, he's worried!*" She hoped that he would continue to feel that way when he left her there alone. She was aware that he would play around on her again once he had gotten away with it. She also knew that if he did, she would go home and divorce him. She couldn't respect a man whom she couldn't trust, and she no longer trusted him. There had never been a divorce in either of their families and she was not sure how either of them would accept the idea. She still loved Roger, but not as she had before. It was difficult to love someone you could not respect.

When she had married so young, everyone said that it would not last and she wanted to prove them wrong. She wondered if that was the reason she had stayed with him. She knew that she could now be attracted to other men, something she had not felt before his unfaithfulness. Somehow, he had destroyed her values and she resented it. She knew that if he pursued it that she would have an affair with Bob after Roger left and she felt guilty about it, not for Roger, but because of Marcel. She decided that she would have a talk with Marcel when she returned to Casablanca. Their affair had been so intense; she knew that she would never be able to get him out of her system. Many a night when Roger made love to her she had closed her eyes and pretended it was Marcel. She felt guilty about it, but she couldn't help herself. She had read somewhere that when a woman had an affair it usually changed her feelings for her husband and often would break up a marriage, whereas a man could have an affair and forget about it. She was sure that the difference was that a man didn't have to feel any love for a woman to sleep with her and a woman had to feel love or at least a strong physical attraction for a man to sleep with him, unless she was a hooker.

Chapter Forty-Six

They finally arrived at the home of Monsieur Cabbage and Nikki was fascinated with the layout of the place. On the left side there was a large, impressive home, then a garden with mosaic tiles that was groomed to perfection. On the other side of the garden to the right there was another home facing it, which was an exact duplicate. She later found out that the house on the left was for entertaining and the one on the right was for his harem and children. They were never seen by the guests. She wondered how these women could be happy sharing one husband. The wealthy Arabs could have as many wives as they desired, while the middle class could only have as many as they could afford to take care of. It was true that these women had all the luxuries they wanted and many servants to wait on them, but to Nikki this would not be acceptable. She knew that she would not like having to share her husband.

She was wondering what the sleeping arrangements were and as if reading her mind Roger said, "*They usually sleep with the newest and youngest wife, as she becomes the favorite. If he has more than one young wife they are always competing to be the favorite. The others are busy raising the children."*

"Ugh!" thought Nikki, *"What a life!"* She was certainly glad that she had not been born in this country, but she supposed that they didn't know the difference since it was the way of life here. No matter how she looked at it, men all over the world seemed to get the best of the deal. Even as kids, the boys slept with whomever they pleased, but if a girl had done this she would have had a bad reputation.

When they entered the house of Monsieur Cabbage's father, he was relaxed, lying back on several large pillows. He stood up to greet them and then lay back down again. There were four or five round tables, about two feet from the floor with pillows around them to sit on. There was room for six people at each table.

When they sat down, Nikki was advised by the others that only the right hand is used for eating. The other hand was to remain in the lap. Everyone seemed to have been to a feast before except for her. She could not help by wonder what a left handed person would do and thanked her lucky stars that she was right handed.

She noted that Monsieur Cabbage never took a seat and asked why he was not going to eat. It was explained to her that the son was never allowed to sit down and eat in the same room as his father. He directed the traffic of the many servants who started bringing in the courses on large brass trays. The first course was chicken soup and they were given odd shaped spoons and were informed that they had provided flatware for the convenience of the Europeans and

Americans, as the Arabs were accustomed to picking up the bowl and drinking the soup. They never used any utensils.

After the soup, it was fingers only. Next the pigeon pie was served. It was as large as the table and was marked off in portions with powdered sugar for the amount of people at the table.

Roger turned to her and said, "*Stay within your section. If not you will get your fingers chopped off*!"

Nikki laughed, as she knew that he was only teasing her and she knew that she would never be able to eat all of her own portion. She had never tasted anything so delicious. The pastry seemed to have hundreds of layers and was thinner than tissue paper and the meat was well seasoned. When she started eating, she thought that she would not be able to stop, as she found it to be so delicious. Roger nudged her with his elbow and said, "*Don't eat anymore. Save room for the other courses as they get insulted it you don't taste everything.*" It was so good she didn't want to stop, but she did, as she wanted to be able to taste everything if this was a sample of the food.

In a few moments one of the servants came to the table with a basin and pitcher of warm water. Everyone held their hands over the basin as he poured the warm water on them and they were handed clean napkins with which to dry them. This happened between each course. Next came the lamb which had been roasted underground and it was wonderful. The way they tackled that was for two people to serve themselves at once. One would hold it while the other would pull off a piece of meat, then the other one would hold it for the one that had no meat as yet. This went on around the table. When the whole roasted chickens were served the same technique was used.

Then the couscous was served and it too was very delicious.

It was served with a casserole of vegetables consisting of sweet potatoes, yellow squash and carrots and had been baked in the oven with raisins, almonds, brown sugar and butter, which made it very caramel-like and was extremely tasty. By this time Nikki felt that she was going to die of happiness, as it had all been so delicious and she had eaten her share of everything, but she turned to Roger and whispered, "*Why didn't you tell me not to wear a tight dress. I can't breathe!*"

Roger encouraged her by saying, "*We're almost through, if my memory serves me correctly.*"

They had served excellent champagne with the meal, something that they also never used themselves, as it was against their religion to drink alcoholic beverages and they served it only when there were Europeans and Americans there as a courtesy. For dessert they had small cakes with the same kind of pastry as the pigeon pie, filled with almonds and sweetened with honey. Hot tea was served out of a beautiful, large tea urn that Nikki had never seen and it was flavored with mint. She was happy to know that this was the end of the meal, and was not even sure that she would be able to get up from the table, she was so stuffed. Some of the other guests were explaining to her that when the female children were very small, some of them learned to make the pastry and that was all they did their whole lives. Nikki realized that it would be difficult to make this and she would never attempt it.

When the feast was over, the guests began to mingle and talk. Nikki asked, "*What do you suppose they do with all of the leftovers? So much food was taken back to the kitchen.*"

It was explained to her that after the guests ate, the

sons ate, then the wives and children and last the servants. Whatever was left after that went to the beggars who came to the back door. She kept thinking that the wives were not treated very well. They had to eat the food after everyone else's hands had been in it.

After they relaxed a while, to her surprise, many of the guests got up and performed while the old man lay back on his pillows and smiled contentedly. The Countess sang like a canary with someone playing the piano to accompany her. She had a lovely voice and was the best one there. When the guests finished, they brought in the Arabian dancers. Nikki had always seen them in their sheer, sensuous garments in the movies, but here in Morocco this was not the case. They wore thick, heavy robes and sang as they danced. They had weird sounding instruments and their voices seemed to come from their stomachs. After a few minutes it began to get on her nerves and she was glad when it was finally over.

When they finally got back to the hotel it was late and Nikki was exhausted.

Roger took one look at her and could see how drawn her face was and immediately asked the others to excuse them. He apologized and said, "*My wife has not been well, and she is here to get her strength back.*" He took her her by the arm, and very protectively steered her toward their room.

"*You get right to bed,*" he commanded her in a very concerned voice. "*I want you to enjoy this vacation and get well. I can see that you are very tired.*"

It was the first time Nikki had been up that late since her illness and she obediently got into bed. She was grateful for Roger's concern and was asleep immediately.

Chapter Forty-Seven

The next morning Nikki woke up early. Normally she was a late sleeper, but she supposed that she was too eager to see more of Marrakech and could not sleep late. Roger was still asleep and she thought of dressing and going out into the gardens, but was sure that he wouldn't be happy about it.

She found that she was hungry and could not understand why after the enormous meal they had consumed the night before. She decided to order room service. She took the phone as far from the bed as possible so as not to wake Roger and ordered breakfast for both of them. She felt that he could sleep until their breakfast came which would give him at least another forty-five minutes to sleep, as the people here did not rush things. By now she was speaking French well enough and had the confidence to order their meal without Roger's help. A couple of months before that she would not have dared.

She slipped on her robe and slippers and walked out into the garden, not intending to be seen. However, their room was so close to the main patio area that suddenly she realized everyone was already outside soaking in the morning sunshine. She was spotted immediately and was embarrassed as she had not even combed her hair. She waved, not to seem unfriendly and quickly ducked back into the room. She decided to take her bath and start putting on her make-up, as she knew there was still plenty of time before room service would arrive. She quietly closed the door so that Roger would not be disturbed and ran the water for her bath. She had just finished with her make-up and hair when there was a knock at the door.

She put on her robe and went to the door to have the food brought in. Roger began stirring and she knew that he would wake up at any time, so she leaned over him and gave him a kiss and said, "*Breakfast is ready!*"

He opened his eyes and smiled. He pulled her down on the bed and she slipped off her robe and climbed in with him and as they embraced he said, "*I wanted you so badly last night, but you were so tired I didn't have the heart. I suppose I'll just have to grab you when I can!*"

She laughed and said, "*Anytime you want to wake me, feel free! You know that I am always ready.*"

He laughed and said, "*I think that I married a nympho!*"

With that Nikki replied, "*If I don't give you enough homework, you may look for it elsewhere!*" Roger frowned as he knew that the wounds had not yet healed since he had his affair with Carla.

After they made love, Nikki said, "*I'm famished. Let's eat before our breakfast gets cold.*"

Roger was pleased and said, "*Now I know you are feeling*

better. Your appetite has finally come back and it makes me happy to see you this way. I think that one day here has done marvels for you!"

Nikki replied, "*Well then, you had better hurry as I want to get out there and absorb some more of that Marrakech sunshine.*"

Roger was bathed and dressed by the time Nikki had decided what to wear and had finished dressing. They went out through the sliding glass door to the garden and up to the patio where their new friends were. Nikki smiled sheepishly and said, "*I think I goofed this morning. I forgot how close we were to the main patio and wandered outside looking like a wreck!*"

Immediately Bob said, "*You couldn't look bad if you tried. I believe that you are the only woman I have ever seen that looks good with no make-up on and your hair uncombed!*"

Nikki found herself blushing as usual and at the same time noticed the puzzled look on Roger's face. Then she told him what had happened.

She could tell that he was jealous of this man and didn't appreciate the way he was flattering her. She was enjoying it, as after all, she had done nothing wrong and had not flirted with him or encouraged him. It was obvious that he had fallen for her and she was glad to see that Roger noticed it. She also knew that he was becoming a little uncomfortable about leaving her there alone.

Madame Bonet said, "*We must have made a big hit last night as we have all been invited back again tonight.*"

Nikki moaned and said, "*I can see myself now, rolling home, as I will surely gain at least ten pounds on this trip!*"

Bob replied, "*You could use a little more meat on those bones, Nikki, it won't hurt you.*" Roger agreed, but Nikki could see that he resented Bob's comments.

She really did enjoy talking with him. He was so well traveled and she loved hearing about his experiences in the different countries. He had several successful books published and evidently was making good money. He was always trying to pick up everyone's check and even though they would tell him no, he would do it anyway and they would let him. His clothes were very well made with very fine fabrics and they screamed money. No one seemed to resent him picking up the tab except for Roger. She realized that she would have to be careful; she didn't want to fight with him on this trip. She wanted to have a good time.

In the afternoon Monsieur Cabbage came to the hotel. He informed Roger that the Pasha Glaoui had asked to meet him and is wife. Roger seemed surprised and asked, "*Why us?*"

Monsieur Cabbage answered that he usually likes to meet the Americans when they come to this city. He wondered why he didn't ask to meet Bob, when he suddenly turned to Bob and said "*He wants to meet you as well.*" *I am supposed to bring you all to the golf club.*" The golf club seemed to be the place in Marrakech where only the elite were permitted to go. He informed them that he would be back in an hour to collect them.

Roger remarked, "*I think that we are all just a little too casual to meet the great Pasha!*" When they went to their room to change, Nikki was full of questions. Roger explained to her who he was. He told her, "*Morocco had been ruled by the*

French and the Spanish for many years, which is why there are so many of them living here and why the French language is spoken by everyone. We live in French Morocco, but when we drove to Tangier that time, if you will remember, we went through Spanish Morocco. That is why we had to go through both French and Spanish customs. The only place that is international is Tangier. The Sultan Muhammad Ben Yusef wanted to get rid of the Protectorate, as did the Nationalists, but the Pasha Glaoui wanted to remain on good terms with them, as he had acquired many special privileges and an enormous fortune and he stood to lose all of this if the Sultan put an end to the Protectorate. Therefore, the Sultan, who is the King, was exiled and was replaced by another Sultan, his uncle, Mouley Ben Arafat, who did not have any desire to rule the country. He was just a puppet Sultan so to speak. At that time, the Pasha became the most powerful man in French Morocco as he is the one that rules the country now." He added, *"If the Nationalists ever take over, they will bring the Sultan back and the Pasha will lose everything."*

When he finished explaining all of this to Nikki she had an expression of awe on her face. She couldn't believe that this powerful man had really asked to meet them. To her, it was like meeting the King or the President of a country and she realized that they were being honored with his request. She finally said, *"He must keep track of everyone who comes here!"*

"He evidently has his spies around the hotel and everywhere else." Roger replied. *"I wouldn't be at all surprised if our friend Monsieur Cabbage isn't one of them. At that party in Casablanca, I was told that he was very close with the Pasha Glaoui."*

Nikki had not realized up until now how important a man he was and felt they were lucky to have met him. She was always looking for new things to write home about and this would certainly make interesting news.

In an hour Monsieur Cabbage was there to collect them and they left for the golf club. They were taken to the greens where the Pasha was playing golf.

Monsieur Cabbage introduced them and it seemed to Nikki and Roger that he barely looked at them. He was a very tall, black man with piercing eyes. He looked as if he was at least six feet, six inches tall or more, as he even towered over Bob. He spoke very good English and said that he was happy that they had chosen to visit his city. Nikki was wondering if she was supposed to curtsey or something, but she was sure that Monsieur Cabbage would have told her if it was necessary.

They thanked him and were ushered back to the car. They went back to the hotel and picked up the Countess and Monsieur Cabbage took them to his house where he brought out clothes for Nikki and the Countess, typical clothes that the wealthy Arab women wore and told them to put them on and they would take pictures. He gave Bob and Roger each a Jellaba as he was wearing. Nikki's crown was larger than that of the Countess and he explained it was because Nikki was married and the Countess was not. He had the servants bring out a large tea urn and they took pictures of Nikki serving tea Arab style. They were sitting in the center of the mosaic tile in the garden, and Roger took some pictures of them and then Monsieur Cabbage took some of them all together. Nikki was sure that her family would get a kick out of them when they sent copies home and could not wait to get their reaction.

When they arrived back at the Hotel, the Countess announced that she should let Madam and Monsieur Bonet know that she was back; she definitely let it be known that she had to check in with them.

When she left, Roger, Bob and Nikki talked about the strange meeting with the Pasha. They could not figure out why he had asked to meet them as outside of the few words that he did say, he never stopped playing golf to have any other conversation with them while they were there. Bob was in serious thought and said, *"I was here for about ten days before you people arrived and he never asked to meet me! Then all of a sudden we were told that he always likes to meet the Americans."*

Roger thought for a moment and said, *"They must have looked at the reservations for the holidays and found that there would be other Americans coming and decided to take us there all at once."*

"That's possible," Bob mused.

That night was like a reproduction of the night before, except for a few minor changes in the menu and Nikki announced later that she would like to rest her stomach for a couple of days and didn't want to go to any more feasts for a while. Roger agreed with her, saying, *"Well, I am leaving in the morning anyway and I think it would be better if you stay around the hotel."*

Nikki was sure that he assumed that Bob would be going back and he didn't want her to be with him.

Chapter Forty-Eight

As planned, Roger left early the next morning to go back to Casablanca. Nikki hated the idea of being alone, but she had made friends and she knew it would be just a matter of a few days when he would be back, as would Dad and all of their friends. He had never mentioned to anyone that he was leaving and when Nikki went out to the patio they were all surprised to see her alone. Everyone was there except for Madame and Monsieur Bonet and the Countess. She told them that he had returned to Casablanca, but would be back in a few days for New Years Eve with some of their good friends and his father.

She closed her eyes and threw her head back to enjoy the sunshine when she was suddenly startled by Bob who was asking her if she would like to take a walk around the gardens. She said, "*That would be nice. I would love to see them, as I have not yet checked them out. I had not been well when we arrived here and have been resting most of the time, trying to get my strength back.*"

Bob said, "*I wondered why Roger was so worried about you all of the time. Just let me know when you are tired. I don't want you to be sick when your husband gets back. He will surely blame me for it."*

Nikki laughed and said "*No, but he will be furious with me!*"

As they walked away from the others Bob remarked, "*I have noticed that you have a very jealous husband. He did not like it at all when you and I talked together.*"

Nikki lied, "*I think that you are imagining things.*" Of course she knew that he was right. She told him that it was a pleasure to have someone who she could speak English with besides Roger. "*Although many people here do speak it, I have to speak slowly to them or they don't understand me, especially with my Texas accent. Besides, if I don't speak French I will never learn it well.*"

Bob remarked that he thought she was doing very well. He added, "*Even your accent is good. Though I speak French, my accent is very poor as I learned it in school and they don't teach it with the proper accent there.*"

Nikki told him how she had learned to speak as well as she did, adding that she had a long way to go before she could say that she spoke it fluently.

"*It must have been terrible to be so ill and not be able to talk to anyone!*" He said sympathetically.

Nikki explained to him how the doctor and nurses had all spoken English and didn't let her know about it.

He looked astonished and said, "*That was cruel!*"

"*No*" Nikki replied, "*I did come out of there speaking French. They really did me a favor. It was the doctor's idea and he was right. If you are going to live in a country you should make every effort to learn the language.*"

Bob nodded and agreed that it was thoughtful of the

doctor to think of that. Nikki stopped and picked an orange. As she did so she said, "*I hope this isn't against the law here, but I don't see any signs.*"

Bob took her hand with the orange and said, "*Don't eat it! They are bitter as gall!*"

Nikki asked "*What do they do with them?*"

His answer was, "*They make marmalade and candy.*"

Nikki realized that marmalade was very popular in Morocco, although she had never really cared for it, but now she knew why. For the rest of the walk they didn't talk. Nikki was enjoying the scenery, but found that she was getting tired and Bob led her back to the patio. As she fell into the chair she said, "*You'd think I was an old woman, I'm so tired from that walk!*" One of the other women had noted how protective Roger was with her and asked her what was wrong with her. Nikki didn't like the image she was giving of herself and began to explain, "*I had pneumonia and the doctor sent me here to get away from the humidity in Casablanca and to rest. Normally I am a very active person and I belong to a tennis club and play tennis almost every day. I hate for people to get the impression that I am some kind of an invalid. I really feel fine now, it's just that the doctor said that it would take time for me to get my strength back, but I am getting better every day.*" She realized that she was babbling on and probably doing too much explaining and stopped.

Bob looked at her and said, "*It's a shame that you can't play tennis now. I am a tennis buff and have been looking for a partner ever since I got here!*"

Nikki replied, "*I wouldn't be here if it were not for the fact that I was ill. So you still wouldn't have a tennis partner.*" Everyone laughed when she said it.

Chapter Forty-Nine

That night Nikki ate dinner at the hotel restaurant for the first time since she had arrived in Marrakech. She had eaten lunch there, but never dinner. She found that the food was excellent, and was pleased that she didn't have to eat some of everything on the menu. It was very good for a change, as she was tired of Moroccan food. It was a beautiful dining room. With the gardens all lit up it created an indoor-outdoor atmosphere that was quite romantic. She had taken a small table and had just started her appetizer when Bob walked in.

He came toward her and asked *"Do you mind if I share your table?"*

"You are very welcome, I am not fond of eating alone and I would enjoy your company very much." No one else that they knew was around. The few guests who were in the restaurant had evidently arrived that day as she didn't recognize any of them. She assumed that the others had gone back to Monsieur Cabbage's for another feast and wondered how they could stand it for three nights in a row.

When she asked Bob about it he said, "*They went to a popular Moroccan restaurant tonight that I recommended to them. They asked me to join them, but I informed them that I have had enough Moroccan food for a while. It is very good food, but I have been here for a while and will continue to be here after you leave. Besides, I didn't want to leave you here all alone for the evening. I felt that you might get lonely and I also thought I would enjoy being with you.*"

Nikki was not quite sure what to say. She was not sure if he was just being friendly of if he was interested in her for other reasons. She finally said, "*Thank you, I really do appreciate it.*" When dinner was over he insisted on paying for her meal.

"*No,*" she argued, "*I will just charge it to my room.*" Bob insisted that he wanted to buy her dinner and she wondered what he had on his mind next.

They walked into the lobby to the lounge area and started talking while they sipped on their after-dinner drinks. Nikki asked, "*Do you know Madame Bonet very well?*"

Bob said, "*No, I have only talked to her in the garden with the others. However, she must be very well known around here, as most of our invitations to the feasts have come through her. In fact, I had never met Monsieur Cabbage when she invited me.*"

Nikki said, "*It seems strange that they should have that young girl with them. From what I understand, they are not related in any way. I hear her singing all the time. Their room is just above ours. She has a beautiful voice.*"

Bob replied, "*I too have wondered about it. It seems that whenever the subject has come up about their relationship the answer was cut short, and it is very suspicious to me. Sometimes she acts as if she does not hear you.*"

Nikki found herself thinking of her as the *mystery woman*. Her husband had very little to offer to a conversation; she was the aggressive one. They both mused over the strange situation and Nikki could tell that Bob was just as puzzled as she was.

Bob started telling her about his experience in Egypt and several other countries he had been to and the evening went by so fast that before she knew it, she looked at her watch and it was two o'clock in the morning. None of the others had come back to the hotel. The lobby was empty except for the two of them.

She stood up and said, *"I had no idea how late it was! Roger would have a fit if he knew that I was up this late. I don't even feel tired. I think that walk did me a world of good today and I am getting my strength back. I have really enjoyed the evening with you, but I guess I had better go to my room now."*

Bob walked her to her room and as she opened the door he just stood there as if he were waiting to be asked in.

Finally she said, *"We have some brandy here in the room, would you like a night cap?"*

Bob did not hesitate to accept her offer. He said, *"I hope that I am not tiring you out too much."*

She shook her head; "I *am not tired at all.*" She poured two glasses of brandy and they sat at the table looking out into the gardens. Most of the lights had been turned off, but there were a few soft ones that were left on all night. Nikki noticed that Bob was looking at her and she knew that he was sizing her up and wondering if she was interested in him. She was very intrigued by him and she realized that she did want him. Besides, she was sure that Roger was not being faithful to her after the things that he had said when they had seen his father with another woman. She figured that he was probably with Carla or some other woman tonight.

She then thought about Marcel and knew that she could not be unfaithful to him. She really was in love with him. She said "*I'm sorry Bob, but I do not cheat on my husband.*" and he could see that she meant it.

At eight in the morning the phone rang. Nikki grabbed it and in a very sleepy voice said "*Hello.*" It was Roger.

He asked, "*Were you still asleep?*"

Nikki answered, "*Yes, I was still asleep. I had a hard time falling asleep last night and probably didn't get to sleep until around four o'clock.*"

Roger was upset and Nikki could tell. "*You are supposed to be out in the sun! I guess you were with that writer all evening!*"

Nikki wasn't sure if he was asking or telling and she finally said, "*As a matter of fact, we did sit in the lobby and talk until around two o'clock. Roger, everyone else had left the hotel and Bob was telling me about his travels and it was so interesting that I lost all track of time. When I realized how late it was I went to my room, but I just couldn't get to sleep. I forgot to bring a book. If I could have read, I guess I would have fallen asleep, but I just wasn't very tired. I guess I have been resting too much!*" Then she added, "*I miss you, honey. I found it very lonely without you.*"

His voice softened and he said, "*I miss you too. Now, get yourself dressed and get out in the sun. I'll call you later on tonight.*"

Nikki ran her bath. She was feeling better than she had in a long while. Just as she was about to get into the tub the phone rang. Thinking that it was Bob, she ran to answer it and was surprised to hear Madame Bonet's voice at the other end of the line. "*Nicole, the Pasha Glaoui has invited you to a feast at his palace tonight. He has asked me to call and invite you.*"

Nikki could not believe her ears. She asked Madame Bonet if anyone else had been invited and the answer was, "*Only you, my husband, the Countess and myself. You see, we really rate!*"

Nikki was disappointed that Bob had not been invited and thought it peculiar, since the Pasha had asked to meet him as well. She decided to accept the invitation, as after all, it was an honor and then she took her bath.

When she had finished, she put in a call to Roger. When she finally reached him at his office she excitedly told him the news.

Roger asked "*Was Bob invited?*" Nikki repeated what Madame Bonet had told her.

She heard Roger take a deep breath and said, "*Don't go Nikki!*" She could tell by the sound of his voice that something was wrong.

She asked, "*Why Not? After all it is quite an honor and I have never been in a palace before!*"

Roger was very serious when he said, "*Nikki, listen to me! Don't you understand why you were invited?*"

She answered, "*I have no idea. All I know is that Madame Bonet called me and told me that he had invited me.*"

Roger said, "*Now listen to me carefully. I have lived over here most of my life and I know the kind of intrigue that goes on here. The day we were invited to meet the Pasha, it was because he wanted to take a look at you. The only reason that Bob and I were invited was to keep it from looking suspicious. The rich Arabs are always looking for new, young women for their harems. He probably has his eye on the Countess also. Don't go Nikki!"*

She could tell that he was upset and more so than she had ever known him to be. She asked, *"What shall I tell them, I have already accepted?"*

"Tell Madame Bonet that you are not feeling well. Tell her your stomach is upset and that you are not up to a feast. They all know that you have been sick." By this time Nikki was frightened and Roger said, *"He is the most powerful man in Morocco and if he keeps you, you will never get out. There would be nothing I could do to help you. He will offer you jewels and treat you like royalty, but you will never leave that palace again!"*

Nikki answered, *"I won't go, Roger, but I am afraid to be here alone."*

Roger suggested, *"Find Bob and tell him what has happened and ask him to stay by you today and tonight. At least you will have protection."*

"As soon as I get dressed I will go and look for him." She was terrified at this point.

Roger suggested, *"If you have to sit up with him in the lobby all night, don't stay alone!"* Then he added, *"I will come back as soon as possible and remember, I love you very much."*

When Nikki hung up she was beside herself with fright. She called Bob's room and there was no answer. She hurriedly finished dressing and headed for the restaurant. Bob was waiting for her and she had never been so happy to see anyone in her whole life. She said, *"When you finish eating I have to talk to you!"*

He could see that something was wrong and asked, "*What is it?*"

She said, "*Let's go to my room. We can't talk here. In fact, maybe we should go to your room.*" She wondered if she was going out of her mind, but suddenly it occurred to her that they might have bugged her room, as they seemed to know when Roger was leaving.

Bob stood up and said, "*Let's go. We can order something in my room.*"

She didn't argue with him and was trembling so badly that she could hardly manage to put one foot in front of the other to walk.

When they finally reached his room he said, "*Now, tell me what this is all about. What could have happened in the short period of time since I left you to upset you so much?*"

Nikki began to relate what had happened and told him what Roger had said. Bob agreed. "*Roger is right. I have learned a lot about these people since I have been here and you have just given me the information that I need for my book. I have been waiting for something like this to happen.*"

Nikki looked at him with disbelief and asked, "*Do these things really occur?*"

Bob's replied, "*This is one of the things I have been researching here and have been trying to find out how they do it.*"

Nikki suddenly said, "*Madame Bonet!*" Then she stopped, thinking it wrong to say what she was thinking without proof.

Nikki said, "*It is not right to accuse people when you don't know for sure, but ever since we came here I have been curious about their relationship with that young Countess. She is a pretty, young girl and they are not related to her. I have mentioned to*

Roger that I felt that something was not right. Do you think that she is finding young women for the rich Arabs here in Marrakech? They could be paying her for her services. It would be something like white slavery! I can't help but be suspicious, as most of the invitations have come through her and especially the one from the Pasha. It's true that we knew Monsieur Cabbage, as we met him in Casablanca, but since then, most of the contacts have come through Madame Bonet."

Bob looked worried and said, "*You could be right. We are going to have to investigate this Madame Bonet.*"

Nikki asked, "*How can we do that?*"

Bob answered , "*I have my ways. When you travel and write as I do, you have contacts. I was told to stay here, as this is where it all happens. Nikki, I don't want you out of my sight today. Call Madame Bonet as Roger told you to do and tell her that you are not feeling well and cannot go. We will see what happens after that. I feel that another attempt will be made.*"

Nikki thought of the Countess and said, "*We have to warn that poor girl, I am afraid for her.*"

Bob warned her, "*Stay out of it. If you warn her she may say something to Madame Bonet, whom she evidently trusts and God only knows what will happen. You must not let them know that you suspect anything!*"

Nikki said, "*But the poor girl, she probably doesn't suspect anything!*" She has gone to several feasts and probably thinks this will be just another one, only more elaborate. I know that's how I felt when I got my invitation."

Bob repeated, "*Stay out of it Nikki, you cannot let them know you are on to them. Just call them and tell them that you are not feeling up to a feast tonight and let it go at that.*"

She immediately put in a call to Madame Bonet. When she answered the phone she said, *"Madame Bonet, this is Nicole. As you know, I came to Marrakech on doctor's orders to rest and I think I have overdone it. I am feeling very tired today and cannot go the feast. Maybe he will ask me another time. I really feel that I should rest."*

Madame Bonet sounded irritated when she replied, *"That is a shame Nicole, I am sure the Pasha will understand. Perhaps you are tired from your long night with that handsome American writer!"*

Nikki felt her heart stop. *"We did stay up and talk until two this morning and I suppose that was just too much for me."*

Madame Bonet laughed and said, *""Don't worry Nicole, I will not tell Roger about it!*

Nikki replied, *"Roger knows about it as I told him this morning."*

Madame Bonet laughed and said, *"I am sorry that you are not well. Be sure and get some rest."* It was obvious that she knew everything that happened last night.

When she hung up she turned to Bob and said, *"They do have my room bugged and it is going directly to Madame Bonet's room."*

"Roger instructed you to stay close to me and so you will. In fact, we will stay here in my room tonight. In the meantime, let's go see if your room really is bugged or if you are only imagining it. We will have to be very quiet."

They headed for Nikki's room, being careful not to be seen. Bob began looking behind pictures, under the scattered Persian rugs, under the bed and everywhere that he thought it could be. All of a sudden he checked a lamp on the other side of the room and there it was. He carefully pulled it out and held it up for Nikki to see. He then put his finger over his lips as a sign for her not to say anything. She was stunned, as they quietly left her room. *"I tried to turn that lamp on one night and it didn't work."* She added, *"I have been involved in an intrigue and didn't even know it!"*

Chapter Fifty

They decided to have dinner early that night, before the dinner crowd came in and while everyone was dressing to go out. They felt that the fewer people that saw them, the better off Nikki would be. They had just sat down to eat when the door of the restaurant opened and Roger came flying in. He looked relieved when he saw them. He kissed Nikki and then turned to Bob and thanked him for looking after her.

Bob told him about the room being bugged. When Roger asked why they thought to look for it, Bob spoke up, *"I just had this feeling that they might be bugging your room since they had an eye out for her. I have been here for a while and I know how these people think. In fact, that must be how they knew that you were leaving yesterday, as you never mentioned that you were planning to leave Nikki here alone when we were all together. However, I'll have to admit that this is the first time I have run into this sort of thing since I have arrived and I guarantee you it will be in my book."*

Roger commented that he didn't blame him. After all,

this was why he was here in the first place. The only thing that Roger didn't like about it was that Nikki could have been the victim and he was relieved that she had called him. They decided to order dinner. Roger was hungry, as he had jumped into his car and headed back to Marrakech in a hurry. The realization of Nikki's danger hit him as he talked to her. He had not stopped to eat all day and was ready for a good meal. He ordered a drink and sat back to enjoy it and relax. He said, *"Nikki, thank God you called me this morning after Madame Bonet invited you. In a matter of a few hours you could have been lost to me forever."*

Nikki smiled and said, *"At least I know that you care."* She glanced sideways at Bob for his reaction and she could see that he probably cared as much as Roger did.

They decided to spend the rest of the evening at the hotel. Roger was very tired from his hurried trip and all the tension that went along with it; and all he wanted to do was relax and have a few drinks. They walked out of the dining room to go to the lounge area when they saw Renee and Antoine checking in. Nikki ran up to them and asked,

"Aren't you a little early? You were not due until tomorrow evening"

"We were so excited about getting away that we decided not to wait until tomorrow. We would have been here yesterday, but Antoine had some business to finish up before he could leave." She then turned to Roger and said, *"It looks like you are early too."* At the same time her eyes fell on Bob and she realized why Roger had chosen to come back sooner.

When she questioned Roger about it he said, *"We'll talk about that later." Let's get you settled in your room."* They too were on the first floor, but on the other side of the patio area. Their room was the reversed version of Nikki and Roger's room.

Roger said, "*We have some very important things to discuss and I think it would be best if we stay in your room. Besides, I want Nikki to rest, as she has had a very bad day.*" He turned to Bob, who was standing at the door and invited him in.

It suddenly occurred to Nikki that he had not brought his father with him. "*How will dad get here?*" she asked.

Roger said that when he left so suddenly, he told his father that he should come down with Monique and Michael, as he had not yet packed. He was glad that he had brought his clothes down on the first trip so that he didn't have to worry about it. "*I just knew that I had to get here as fast as I could.*"

Nikki felt a twinge of guilt, seeing how concerned he was about her. Maybe she was wrong about him, there was no doubt in her mind now that he loved her; he was too upset over the events of the day. She knew that he had been jealous when Bob had paid so much attention to her, but when he became so worried about her welfare, he suddenly had not even thought of that angle.

Roger said, "*We have plenty of brandy in our room, I'll go get it and bring it here where we can talk without being heard.*" By this time, Renee and Antoine were both looking very bewildered, wondering what was going on. Roger turned to them and said, "*We will explain everything in a few moments, but right now I want to go and get that brandy, as I know that I need it and I think we all will when we tell you what has been happening around here.*"

He asked Bob if he would go with him and Bob answered, "*I was just going to suggest it, as I want to show you what I found.*"

When they entered the room Bob immediately gave him the sign to be quiet as he walked toward the lamp. He pulled the mike out and showed it to Roger. Roger picked up two bottles of brandy and they left the room without saying a word. When they were outside of the room Bob remarked, "*I'm almost certain that your room is wired directly into the Bonet's room. Aren't they just above you?*" Roger nodded and agreed.

When they got back to Antoine's room he finally said, "*Will you two detectives please tell us what is going on here? What is this big mystery all about?*"

Nikki, Roger and Bob all started talking at once. Finally they all stopped and Roger said, "*Since it is Nikki's story, why don't we let her tell it.*"

Nikki said, "*I wish it was not my story, as I have been scared out of my wits. I feel safe now that I have Roger back and all of my good friends around me.*" She then related what had happened and Renee and Antoine both sat with their mouths gaping open. They couldn't believe it. Then Nikki said, "*Roger, I wanted to warn the Countess, as I told Bob that I think that Madame Bonet has a racket going for her with the wealthy Arabs. You know how we wondered about them. Bob told me to stay out of it, that it was better that they don't find out that I am on to them. However, I am sincerely worried about that girl. I am anxious to see if she will return to the hotel after the feast.*"

"*Bob was right,*" Roger replied, "*I hope that your thinking is wrong, but if it is correct, she could be sold to the Pasha.*"

Nikki asked, *"Do you think they would do it right away? After all, they know that we have all met her. If she doesn't return with them, we would surely suspect something." "Besides"* she added, *"If they were listening to my end of the conversation with you this morning, I am sure that they knew that you were warning me not to go and why."*

They finally decided that they would go and enjoy their vacation and would act as if they were unaware of what was going on. They also decided that they would accept no more invitations to feasts. Renee looked disappointed and said, *"Just our luck! We have to miss out on the feasts, and talking about feasts, I am famished!"* Nikki had not thought about the fact that they had not eaten and suggested that they go into the dining room. Antoine said, *"No, we will all stay here. I will call room service and order dinner in the room tonight. Is anyone else hungry?"*

When they informed him that they had just had dinner, he went to the phone, asking Renee what she would like. She looked at the menu on the dresser and gave her order. Antoine selected his dinner from the menu and picked up the phone to order.

After that, they started making plans for the couple of days until New Years Eve. Monique and Michael and dad would be arriving the next day and Bob was the first to speak. *"I have been to some excellent restaurants here in Marrakech, so I can suggest those to you."* They all seemed pleased with that and asked him if he would like to take in the sights with them. He accepted without hesitation, looking relieved. *"There are not any other people my age here besides you. They are all older and I really appreciate being asked to join you. It becomes lonely when you travel alone all of the time."* They seemed pleased that he had accepted, including Roger, as he felt that he owed him that much for helping with Nikki until he got back.

Nikki was the first to speak. *"I want to go up into the Atlas Mountains and have a snow ball fight!"*

They all laughed and said they would put that at the top of the list. Roger was glad to see that she was not showing the signs of her illness any longer. They decided that they would wait for the others to arrive so that they would not miss out on any of the fun.

Chapter Fifty-One

When the rest of their party arrived the next day, they were informed of everything that had happened and what their plans were. Monique and Michael seemed pleased with the plans, but shocked at what had almost happened to Nikki. They had excluded that information from dad, as they were sure he would want to turn around and take Nikki home. They felt that as long as she was constantly surrounded by her family and friends and not left alone, there would be no danger.

Instead of going to the mountains that first day, they decided to go to the market square. They had decided that it would be better to go into the mountains in the early morning when they would have plenty of time to come back down before dark. When they went into the old section of the city to see the market, Nikki was fascinated with the snake charmer who was in front of the market. She had always been afraid of snakes and spiders and she couldn't believe that she was standing so close watching the performance.

Several times she felt a chill go up her spine and though she was enjoying it, she was relieved to finally walk away.

They got back to the hotel and noticed that the Countess was there, and decided that perhaps they had been letting their imaginations run away with them. Yet, Nikki knew that they had been keeping tabs on her because of her room being wired. She whispered to Roger "*Maybe they had to bring her back, as everyone would wonder what happened to her.*" They all knew that she had gone with them to the Pasha's feast. They were being careful of what they said in their room, as they didn't disconnect the wires on the lamp because they didn't want them to know that they knew about it. They only talked about things in general.

As they sat in the lobby, they watched the English diplomats come in, but there was no sign of Churchill. Finally Roger went over to the desk and asked if he was expected. They told him that he had not made reservations for this year. Nikki was disappointed, as she had hoped to see him. The English women were wearing exquisite furs and jewelry. Nikki remarked to Roger that she would look underdressed compared to them and he replied, "*With all of their wealth and jewels and furs, I assure you that they would change places with you in a moment.*"

The second day they drove up the narrow, icy road into the mountains. Nikki was afraid to look down. She had no idea that it would be so dangerous. There was a sheer drop off and if they had missed a turn it could have meant their lives. When they finally stopped at a lodge for lunch, she was relieved that they were safe. The view was absolutely marvelous. Without saying a word, Nikki sneaked around to the side of the lodge and formed a snowball. As she came around the corner of the lodge she threw it right in Roger's face. He looked surprised and then started laughing so hard that he couldn't gather enough strength to throw one back, but in a few minutes, like a bunch of kids, they were having a snowball fight. They were having so much fun that all of the worries of the Pasha were forgotten and they acted as if they didn't have a worry in the world. As it got late in the afternoon, they decided that they had better start back down the mountain before it got dark, as then it would be too dangerous. Nikki seemed to be the only one who was nervous about the mountains coming up, but now they all felt that it would be safer to go down before dark.

When they got back to the hotel, dad was waiting for them. He had elected not to go with them. They went to a Moroccan restaurant that night and it was very good, but nothing like the feasts they had been to. When Nikki and Bob told them about the feasts they had had at Monsieur Cabbage's home, they were sorry that they had missed them.

They decided to get a good night's sleep so that they could enjoy the next night which was New Years Eve. Nikki was looking forward to the big event.

The next morning Nikki, Monique and Renee went to the beauty shop to have their hair done. When they came out of the beauty parlor, they went to Nikki's room and she recombed everyone's hair as they had done a terrible job and they were mad that they had spent the money. They called room service and ordered raw eggs as they wanted to give themselves facials. They laughed, as they were sure they would think they were crazy. In fact they even called back to make sure that it was raw eggs that they wanted. After spreading the egg whites on their faces, they lay on the bed with their feet up on the headboard to relax. As the masks hardened, they had a difficult time trying to keep from laughing and ruining their masks.

The rest of the day they lounged around so that they would be in good shape for the evening ahead. They finally went to their rooms to get ready for the big night. Nikki was happy as she put on her ball gown. She could feel the excitement in the air. She knew that this was one New Years Eve she would never forget.

Chapter Fifty-Two

They had made plans to meet in the lobby at nine-thirty. Nikki turned to Roger when she finished dressing and said, *"I can always feel it when I look my best and tonight I think I do."*

Roger agreed with her. *"Those English women cannot hold a candle to you, even with all of their fine jewels,"* he said. He reached in his pocket and handed her a small box.

She was surprised and he seemed delighted to have thought of it. *"What is it?"* she asked.

Roger said, *"It is my New Years gift to you. Open it; I think you will want to wear it tonight."*

Nikki said, *"But I don't have anything for you. Since when do we exchange gifts for New Years?"*

Roger smiled and said, *"I saw it and couldn't resist it. I knew what you were wearing tonight and I thought it would go nicely with it."* Nikki opened the box and was surprised to see a beautiful pair of diamond earrings. She looked at Roger and said, *"They are beautiful!"* She kissed him and thanked him. He could see the delight on her face when she put them on and wondered if he should tell her the story about them.

Finally he said, *"Nikki they are not real diamonds. There is a jewelry store in Paris that sets imitation stones in gold so that they look real. They are actually semi-precious stones, called zircons. A friend of mine just came back from Paris and had bought some things and he asked me if I wanted to buy something for you. I thought they were very pretty and they look real. Some day I hope that I can replace them with diamonds, but in the meantime, no one has to know that they are not. Only a jeweler can really tell."*

Nikki said, *"Well, I still love them." They were long dangling earrings and they showed up well with her long hair.*

When they made their entrance, all eyes were on her. The women looked annoyed as the men were all staring at her and being very obvious. Roger whispered, *"See, I was right!"* He was proud to be the man whose arm she was holding onto that night.

They were seated at a long table. Dad was beaming when he looked at Nikki. He said, *"I have a beautiful daughter!"* She was embarrassed, as he said it loud enough for everyone around them to hear. They had a long table as there were eight of them. There were three baskets made of toffee and they were filled with French pastries.

Nikki had never seen anything as unusual as this and asked, *"Are we supposed to eat the basket also?"* They decided that each couple would have a basket to take with them. Bob had been asked to join their table and he could not take his eyes off of Nikki, although he was trying hard not to make it obvious. This evening she was lovelier than he had ever seen her. She was absolutely ravishing, he thought. He envied Roger at this moment. It was true that he loved his freedom to travel and write, but tonight he was sure that he would have given it up in a moment to be married to her. He was wishing he had met her before she had married. He was sorry that the Pasha thing had happened, as it had brought Roger back two days sooner than he had planned, and he had never had another chance to try again to be together. He decided at that moment that he would definitely go to Casablanca when he finished his work in Marrakech. He would find something there of interest to research. He was sure of that. Maybe with a little more time to work on Nikki he could have had her, at least for a night.

Nikki was watching Bob from the corner of her eye. Suddenly she looked around and saw Madame and Monsieur Bonet come in. The Countess was not with them. She was sitting between Roger and Bob and said in a whisper, "*The Countess is not there!*" They both looked around at the same time and Madame and Monsieur Bonet saw them. When dad saw that they were upset he asked what was wrong and they told him they would explain later. He had no idea of what was going on, but Nikki realized that tomorrow they would have to tell him. As long as she was surrounded by people at all times Roger felt that she was safe.

Madame Bonet was coming toward their table wearing one of her fake smiles and said, "*Bonne Annee!*" Then she said, "*Isn't it a shame, Mignon had to fly home as her mother has become ill? She is missing the best night of all and was looking forward to it so much.*" She then turned to Nikki and said, "*I'm glad to see you are feeling better my dear. You look ravishing tonight!*" They acted as if they believed her and told her that they were so sorry to hear it.

Bob turned to Nikki and Roger and whispered, "*I am going to stay in Marrakech until I can find out what really did happen to the countess!*" They were both glad that he had made that decision.

When dinner was over, the band started playing and everyone got up to dance. Roger took Nikki out on the dance floor and they did the one thing that they could do together perfectly. They danced so well together that others stopped dancing to watch them. From the first night when they had danced together at the USO they had found that they were perfect dancing partners and through the years they had learned all of the fancy steps that had become popular as well as a lot of steps that they had made up. Roger found that no matter what he did, Nikki followed with ease. She was easy to lead and she had good rhythm. When they finished dancing everyone stood around them and applauded. They continued to dance every dance in the set and when they sat down they were thirsty. The champagne flowed that night and they were all tipsy by the end of the gala. Once Bob had asked Nikki to dance and as he did, he was saying, "*There is no way I can compete with Roger, but I would like to have the next dance with you.*" Roger seemed flattered by his comment and never suspected that he wanted to get her out on the dance floor where he could talk to her alone.

He said, "*Nikki, I have to stay in Marrakech and find out what is going on. I know I will have great success with my book if I can uncover some of the things that are happening here. Besides that, my curiosity has gotten the best of me. I plan to come to Casablanca when I finish here.*"

Nikki agreed with him and said, "*We would love to show*

you around Casablanca and I can go with you during the day when Roger is working."

He ushered her back to the table and said to Roger, "*I cannot compete with you, my friend. I could tell that Nikki was completely bored dancing with me. You have spoiled her!*"

Roger was flattered and thought, "*He really isn't a bad guy. He is just being friendly and my suspicions were wrong.*"

At midnight the lights went off and magnificent fireworks went off in the garden. When the lights came on, the band started playing a march and the waiters marched in, in perfect unison, each carrying a miniature orange tree. They branched out to all of the tables and placed the trees along the tables. When they opened the oranges, they were filled with sherbet to have with the French pastries. It was a very unusual presentation and they were all enjoying every moment of it. None of them had ever been there for New Year's Eve before and they thanked Nikki for getting pneumonia so that they had an excuse to go there. They were all as surprised and impressed as she was. By the time they went to bed it was four in the morning. They all agreed they would sleep late in the morning and meet in the garden when they awoke.

When they got to the room, Nikki very quietly went to the lamp where the bug had been planted. When she reached for it, it was gone. She turned to Roger and said, "*Now that Mignon is gone, they have taken the bug out of here. I am sure that we will find out in the morning that Madame and Monsieur have left. We have to go and look for her. I know she is at the Pasha's with his other wives. I feel so terrible for her. I know that they are lying about her going home. I don't have any idea how, but I am going to find her and get her out of there.*"

Roger became enraged when he replied, "*Are you crazy? Why don't we wait and see if Bob can find her. Nikki, I don't want to take any chances of losing you to these people! You would probably not be able to find out anyway.*"

Nikki was very upset when she said, "*I have to know if she is alright and if there is a way we can get to her.*"

Roger said, "*Why don't we let Bob do the detective work for us. He is here for this kind of thing and if anyone can find out, I am sure that he can. We will ask him in the morning after we check and see if the Bonet's are gone.*"

With that, Nikki was ready to go to sleep.

Chapter Fifty-Three

Nikki and Roger were the last ones to arrive. Everyone they knew were already there, including the people they had just met before the New Year crowd had come in. There was only one couple missing, Monsieur and Madame Bonet. Bob had inquired about them already. He knew that he was taking a chance, but he had to know if they had checked out. He was told that they had checked out shortly after the gala had ended.

When they saw Nikki and Roger they informed them about what had happened. They were all trying to figure out what had actually happened to the Countess. Roger told them to forget it, as he was sure that they had their spies out around the hotel and was afraid that they would be overheard. Then he said, *"Bob, you said that you were told to stay at this hotel, right?"* Bob nodded. Roger continued, *"If we start making too many inquiries, no telling what will happen. I am sure that it will get back to the ones that we don't want to know about it. There has to be someone, or maybe more than one person, who are working at the hotel and getting all the information they want. Someone had to have a key to get into our room and wire it. Let's act as if we have no idea about anything that is going on here. It could put Bob in danger after we leave."*

Nikki asked, *"Are you just going to let it go? I am really concerned about that poor girl!"*

Bob said, *"You are all leaving tomorrow. Why don't you let me look into it and I will let you know what I find out. I am here for this kind of information and it is better that you leave it to me. I have my ways, but it is far too dangerous for you people who are living in this country."*

They promised that they would stay out of it if he would come to Casablanca and let them know what he found out. He agreed that when he finished his business there he would come to Casablanca.

They spent the rest of the day lounging around. They were all tired from the night before and some were really hung over. After lunch, the women decided they would get their packing over with and then they would not have to worry about it. When Nikki went to her room to pack she was thinking that it was certain that the wiring had lead to Madame Bonet's room just above her and now that they were gone, someone had removed it. She was sure that someone in the hotel had to be involved. They seemed to be able to enter the room easily enough and they would have to have a pass key. Nothing was missing and she was sure that all they wanted was to remove the bug from their lamp. She made a mental note to tell Bob that there was an inside party involved.

Someone knocked at her door about the time she was thinking of all this and she found she was nervous and jumpy. She asked who was there and the answer was, "*Its dad, open up!*" He came in and said, "*Nikki, there is something going on around here that no one had told me about and I want to know what it is. I have seen you all whispering to each other and I feel that you are trying to keep something from me. I was told a little bit of it this morning, but I still do not know what has happened.*"

Nikki said, "*Before now, I would not have been able to tell you anything in this room, as it was bugged since the first day we got here. However, I see that it has now been removed and we can talk freely.*" Dad looked dumbfounded. She told him about everything that had happened from the day they had been invited to the golf club to meet the Pasha, including the disappearance of the Countess and now the Bonets suddenly checking out in the wee hours of the morning so that no one could question them. Dad was devastated. He loved Nikki as if she was his own daughter and he could not bear to think of anything so appalling happening to her. When he finally managed to get his voice he said, "*Nikki, it could have been you!*" Nikki tried to calm him down and said, "*I don't know, the Countess is only eighteen and he would probably have preferred her.*" Dad remarked, "*He could have taken both of you! He can afford fifty of you! I am sure that if he asked to meet you, he wanted you as well.*"

Nikki was thoughtful and stated, "*I feel lucky, because if I had not called Roger that morning, I would have gone to that feast. He had already called me earlier and I am not sure that I would have heard from him again that day. They knew exactly when he planned to leave for Casablanca, as they were listening to our conversation the whole time we were here. After we realized what was going on we no longer said anything that included our plans. We were with our group of friends after that and it would have been difficult for them to get to me. I guess they gave up and settled for the Countess. I am positive that Madame Bonet heard my end of the conversation with Roger when he was telling me not to go to the Pasha's feast. I was arguing with him at first, until I realized that what he was saying was serious and then I was so frightened, I never said another word in this room. I ran to look for Bob and found him in the dining room. He stayed with me all day until Roger got back."* Nikki could see that he was shaken by what she had told him. She assured him, *"Don't worry, we are leaving tomorrow and, I don't think we will make plans to come back here. It's a shame, as I have enjoyed it so much and would love to come back and go skiing. Now it is out of the question"*

You will have to be careful. I do not want you going about alone when we get back. They could pick you up there just as easily!"

Nikki had not thought of that, nor had Roger. She wondered if she would have to live in fear from now on. She finally said, *"For the first time in my life, I wish I was ugly!"*

Dad smiled and said, *"The only thing you have to your advantage is that you will grow older. They are not looking for older women; they want the young ones who can give them children."*

Nikki said, *"I guess I'll have to start lying about my age and telling everyone that I am in my thirties."*

Dad laughed at her and said, *"They would never believe*

you, my dear. You are very young and you look it. Maybe if you became pregnant they would lose interest in you."

Nikki answered, "*I didn't think of that.*" Suddenly she saw the humor of what they were saying. Here she was with her father-in-law, making plans to get pregnant. She was sure that Roger would find it amusing also.

Part Five

Casablanca

Chapter Fifty-Four

After an early breakfast, everyone piled into their cars to drive back to Casablanca. Bob was there to see them off and promised that they would be hearing from him as soon as he knew what was going on.

Nikki looked at Roger and said, "*Well, I guess I have a lot to write home about now, but I don't dare. The family will be worried about me. I guess this experience will have to wait until after I get home. At least I'll have something left to tell them.*"

It was nineteen forty-nine now and they discussed the fact that it would be two years in May since they left the states. Time had flown, yet so much had happened. Nikki had definitely grown up and she was no longer the naïve girl who had first come to Morocco.

A few days after they returned, Roger came home and said, "*Start packing, we are moving!*"

Nikki was quite surprised and asked him where they were moving to.

He said, "*I found a wonderful two story apartment, right*

across the street from the Park Lyautey." The tennis club was there and Nikki loved the idea of living so close to it. When Roger described the apartment to her she was excited. The only thing she didn't like was the fact that she would no longer be a neighbor to Fabia and Monique. True, she knew that she would see Monique and Renee at the tennis club and therefore would not be that far away from them. However, Fabia did not play tennis and she decided that they would have to make arrangements to get together. As of lately, Fabia had been very tied down as she was pregnant with her second child.

Their new apartment was very sophisticated. The living room, dining room and kitchen were downstairs. There was a bar built in to the corner of the living room. It had a brass rail that went around and formed the banister going up the staircase. The master bedroom had opaque glass doors that opened onto the balcony looking down into the living room. Further down the balcony was the bathroom and on the other side was a sun room which they made into another bedroom. There was a large terrace off of the living room and though they were only on the third floor, it was much higher up, since the apartments below them were also two stories.

They started entertaining at home more often now. They would always invite Marcel and Juanita, but they never came. Occasionally Marcel would drop by, but he would never stay for very long. It was obvious that Roger had new friends.

Nikki could still not get Marcel off of her mind. She longed for him, longed for him more and more. Roger seemed to be behaving, but she could not help herself. Now that Roger and Marcel were not as close as they had been in the past, she felt that maybe Marcel would consider seeing her again. Dad had decided to go back to the states. Again, Nikki and Roger were alone. She waited for him to stray again, but he seemed to be keeping it very discrete if he was doing anything wrong. However, she did notice that his desire for sex was declining and wondered what he was doing in the afternoons, as he would call her and make excuses not to come home for tea.

One morning she got up the courage to call Marcel. She had wanted to do so many times before, but couldn't get up the nerve. When he answered the phone, he sounded pleased and surprised to hear her voice. He asked her what was going on and she said, *"I want to see you alone again. I miss you so much!"*

There was silence on Marcel's end of the line and then he asked, *"Is Roger coming home for lunch?"* Nikki said that he was, but Marcel could come over after he left at two o'clock.

Marcel said, *"Nicole, it is too dangerous for me to come there during the day when the servants are there. Let me call you back. I have a plan."*

Chapter Fifty-Five

When Marcel hung up the phone his hands were shaking. He wanted to see Nikki more than anything in the world. He called a bachelor friend of his and asked him if he would be at home that afternoon. He made arrangements to pick up a key from him and decided that finally, he and Nicole would have a place to meet. He knew that they could tell no one about it and when his friend asked him who he was taking there he said, "*You don't know her.*"

His friend laughed and said, "*So, she is married!*"

Marcel only laughed and hung up. He picked up the key and called Nicole. When she answered the phone he said, "*Nicole, I have a place for us to meet. It is safe. We will not be disturbed, I promise you. If you are careful when you come here, we will not be found out!*"

He was excited when he heard her asking how often they could use it and when they could start meeting. He realized that she was just as eager as he by the tone of her voice. He gave her the address and apartment number and said, "*I am going to be there at two o'clock. Take a cocher and meet me there as soon as Roger leaves."* When she agreed, he hung up and found he was happier than he had been in a very long time. He had missed her, this he knew, and he had not hung around them very much. He was afraid of giving himself away to Roger. He also felt that he and Roger were not as close as they had been before and did not feel as guilty as he had felt before. He knew that Roger had slept with other women when he had the opportunity, even for the one night that Nicole was left alone in Marrakech. He also knew why his free time had been cut short and he had had to return to Marrakech in a hurry when Nicole's security had been threatened. This had shaken Marcel up as well, and he would have offered to go with Roger, but was afraid that Roger would suspect something. He had been relieved when Roger called him and told him that she was safe. He had told Roger before he left, *"You should go there as soon as possible. If the Pasha gets her, you will never see her again."* He knew that they would not touch her if she had friends around her. He was also wondering about the American writer that Roger had spoken about and wondered what had happened between him and Nicole, as they seemed to be close during that time. Roger had remarked that he had told Nicole to stay close to him for protection, but he mentioned that he was not too happy about it, as the American was a handsome man and definitely interested in her. He assumed that was why Roger had that affair with the Hungarian dancer.

Roger had said, *"I don't think Nikki would do anything wrong, as she was raised to think that way."*

Marcel had managed to keep a straight face and knew

that once Nicole had had an affair she might do it again. He found himself thinking about it and was feeling jealous, though he knew he had no right to feel this way, but he had wondered about it quite often. In a way, he would not have blamed her, as he had not tried to make contact with her at all and now he realized that he had been a fool not to tell her about the Hungarian girl.

Chapter Fifty-Six

Roger was noticing that Nikki had been restless lately and wondered why. He was somewhat sorry that they had moved, as he felt that she might miss her friends. Then he realized that she was seeing them at the tennis club every afternoon and decided that she might be a little homesick.

He was wondering too, what had happened between her and Bob while he was gone from Marrakech. He could not help but notice a look on her face when she was around him. Then he would shake it off and tell himself that it was his imagination. He was certain that Nikki was not the type of girl to do anything like that. He noticed that she had seemed different ever since his affair with Carla. She seemed to have more self confidence and was not depending on him every minute as she had before. He assumed that it was because she was now speaking French rather well and didn't need him as much as before. Also, she had grown up as well.

Now that his father had left, he was able to have some afternoon affairs. The dancer worked at night and was at home in her apartment during the day. After lunch and siesta he would often stop by and see her. He didn't go as often as he would have liked to, since he would have to have something left for Nikki, or she would suspect something. The dancer didn't mean a thing to him; it was just a little variety to keep from getting bored. He realized that he had been foolish when he had his affair with Carla, because if he had used the afternoons as he was doing now, Nikki would have never known that anything was going on and she would still feel the same about him. He was certain that she didn't love him as she had when they had first arrived in Casablanca.

He knew that it would only be a matter of a short time that he would tire of the Hungarian girl. She was good in bed, but he wanted to have more variety. As long as he was playing around, he decided that he would like to try different girls and planned to stop seeing this one shortly. He was already bored with her. He wondered if there was something wrong with him, as he could not get into an affair as he had had with Carla; then he would figure it was because he was trying to live in the past. He realized that the only reason he was playing around was that he was taking advantage of his freedom while his father was gone. Nikki had not been too enthused about sex lately either. He wondered if it was because they had been married so long that it had become less enchanting to her and felt that it did happen to other couples. When they had been in Paris she had cooperated much more than now. He realized that he was now thirty years old and wondered if that made a difference. All of his friends were having affairs and seemed to be enjoying them, or at least they said they were. He never admitted to anyone that he was bored with it. He was afraid that they would poke fun at him.

He suddenly realized that he had not seen Marcel very much lately and decided to go by his office one morning. Marcel was very busy, but stopped to talk to him. He finally asked him if he was having any affairs at the present time and he shook his head. Roger was surprised and asked, "*What is wrong? It isn't like you, Marcel. I have never known you when you have not had some other woman on the side.*"

Marcel answered, "*Let's face it Roger, we are getting older and I suppose the novelty has worn off. I am home every night with Juanita. You can ask her if you don't believe me.*"

Roger told him about his own dilemma and said that he was wondering why he was feeling as he did. "*Maybe the novelty has worn off for me too. However, Nikki doesn't seem too eager lately, and I feel that I have to find someone to take her place as long as she is acting this way. I am sure she has lost her faith in me, as she acts different now and I can tell that she is not in love with me anymore. Sometimes I wonder where I am heading. She is a wonderful woman and I spoiled our marriage.*"

He was desolate, Marcel could tell. Then Roger mused, "*I wonder if she did have an affair with that writer the night I left Marrakech.*"

Marcel answered, "*Well, you shouldn't have any complaints. You were with the Hungarian girl that night. I imagine that Nicole is on to you and assumes that you did cheat on her.*"

Roger looked at Marcel and asked, "*You say this, but how would you feel if you thought that Juanita was cheating on you? Wouldn't it bother you?*"

Marcel admitted that his vanity would be hurt, but he

added, *"I can't seem to get it on with her anymore. I guess that is the price you pay when you run around as much as I have all of these years. I have to find a new woman now to get me excited."* He could see that Roger was not happy about his predicament, but he did not feel guilty for some reason, as he had felt the first time he had his affair with Nicole. He and Roger were no longer close as they had been and they had more of a strained relationship now. He doubted that they could ever be that close again.

Roger noticed that Marcel was not too sympathetic and realized that their relationship had waned. He suddenly got up and said, *"Well, I had better let you get your work done. I have plenty to catch up on myself, as since the old man has left, I have not been spending the afternoons in the office. Come by and see me sometime. We really should try and get together."*

Marcel answered, "Call me and we will try and resume our friendship. Let's face it Roger, we haven't been close for the last year. I was hurt in the beginning, but then I realized that you do live a different kind of life than I do. I don't like going to the fancy balls and all of that nonsense."

Roger said, *"Well, I am not too fond of those things either, but I have to keep Nikki happy. She loves to dress up and go to the fancy affairs. American women are different, I guess. That's about all we have in common any more. We dance well together and we both enjoy it."* As he walked out of Marcel's office, he was depressed and when he thought about the deterioration of their friendship, he felt bad. He was still trying to live the same life that he had lived before the war, but he knew now that it was impossible. He had lost his friend and also the love of his wife. Suddenly it occurred to him that he had probably changed also.

Chapter Fifty-Seven

After Nikki hung up the phone she called Monique and told her that she would not be able to meet her at the club. She said, *"I will explain later, but if Roger should ask, tell him that we have been playing together every day. I doubt that I will be playing for some time, so you had better find another partner."*

Monique asked, *"What is going on Nicole? I am sure that something must be happening in your life!"*

Nikki knew that she suspected something and finally said, *"If you want to know if I am having an affair, I am!"* Nikki informed her that this was not the first time. *"Monique, I have made up my mind that two can play the same game and I find that I love playing that game!"*

Monique was still laughing when she said, *"Don't worry Nicole, I will cover for you. We will have to tell Renee though, as she might say something in front of Roger when we are all out together."*

Nikki was worried and asked, *"Can we trust her?"*

Monique assured her that she could. *"Renee is no angel,*

Nicole. She has had her affairs. There is no one now, but she has had them. I know you can trust her."

Nikki was stunned as she hung up the phone. At home her friends would be calling her a slut. In this part of the world it was considered normal. Then she remembered the night that Roger had gotten in the fight at the club with that man and his wife had acted so indignant, and then not even a week later they had seen her with another man. Suddenly she realized that this was accepted over here, however, she knew that she could never flaunt it as so many of them did.

She finally finished her bath and was dressed. She put on her tennis skirt, as that way if Roger should arrive home ahead of her, he would naturally think that she had been playing tennis.

She left the apartment, hailed a cocher and gave him the address that Marcel had given her. She felt the excitement mounting as she got closer to the street. She was finally going to be in the arms of the man she so desperately loved. When she arrived, Marcel was waiting for her. He said, *"I stopped and had a duplicate made of the key. That way, if you ever get here before I do, you won't have to wait outside where someone might see you."*

Nikki put it in her racket case, as she knew that Roger would never look in there. *"I will let Roger think that I am still playing tennis every day. Monique is covering for me."*

Marcel smiled and said, *"Good girl. Did you tell her who you were meeting?"*

Nikki shook her head, *"She didn't ask and I didn't tell her. Besides, the less they know the better. There can always be a slip of the lip."*

He seemed pleased with her decision and also very

pleased to see her. He said, "*That is enough talk for now. It is time we get down to what we came here for!*"

Nikki smiled and said, "*You don't know how I have dreamed of this moment. It has been torture staying away from you.*" He started undressing her and she let him. She liked to have a man undress her. Roger had never done that. As he took off her bra, he kissed her breasts and she was already so excited she couldn't wait. She finally said, "*Hurry up, you are tormenting me!*"

Marcel laughed and finally got her clothes off, kissing her every time he bared another area of her body. She started undressing him and saw that he already had an erection. She did the same to him as he had done to her. He finally picked her up and carried her to the bedroom. She was in ecstasy, it had been so long, much too long, she thought. She was glad that they had finally figured out a way to be together. She was also wondering if she would want Roger to make love to her anymore.

As if reading her mind, Marcel said, "*When you are with Roger, you must act eager, Nicole, or he will suspect something. I think that he is very jealous of you.*"

Nikki said, "*You will find out what a marvelous actress I can be.*"

Marcel repeated what Roger had told him, that she didn't seem eager for sex anymore. "*However,*" he added, "*He thinks it's because of his affair with Carla, and that you have never forgiven him.*" Finally he said, "*That's enough talking for now, Mon Cherie. We have business to take care of.*"

They embraced, and as their bodies made contact, Nikki knew that this was the only man she ever wanted. The electricity that went through their bodies was so powerful and they knew they did truly belong together. They made love and lay in each others arms until five thirty. Finally Marcel said, "*We must stop for today, I have to get back to the office and close up before going to the café.*"

Nikki replied, "*If only Roger wouldn't come home for lunch we could have more time together.*"

Marcel laughed and said, "*You are a greedy little thing, aren't you?*"

Nikki laughed and said, "*I am greedy when it comes to you. I don't think I can ever get enough of you. It's like I want to crawl inside of you and be a part of you. I'm so happy that we are together again.*"

Marcel kissed her and said, "*You are always with me. I have waited for us to be together again and I hope it will be forever.* He kissed her goodbye and said, "*Until tomorrow.*" Then he was gone.

Nikki put on her clothes and left the apartment. She found a *cocher* as soon as she walked out on the street and was glad that she didn't have to stand around and wait. She had him drive her to the tennis club. When she arrived, Monique was about ready to leave.

She said, "*So, Nicole, how did it go?*" She could tell by her face that it went well.

"*I am in love, Monique.*" Nikki said happily.

Monique answered, "*That is good. Nicole, I don't want you to get love and lust mixed up. It is very easy for a woman to do that.*"

Nikki answered, "*I could not sleep with a man if I didn't love him.*"

The nights that Roger wanted sex were the worst times for her. She found that he was nothing in comparison to Marcel. However, she did notice that he didn't want her as often as usual and assumed that he was seeing someone else. His father was gone and she knew that he didn't have to explain to anyone where he had been. Suddenly she realized that she didn't care anymore and also that she didn't love him any more. She couldn't understand what she had seen in him other than that they danced well together. She thought, *"You can't dance through life together."* He could be sweet when he wanted to, but lately he had taken her for granted, and she did not like that. She suddenly decided that she was glad she was seeing Marcel and she didn't care about anything else. She felt that she had become hardened, because she didn't even feel guilty about what she was doing, as she had in the past. In fact, she was happier now than she had ever been in her life.

Chapter Fifty-Eight

Roger came home for lunch one day to inform Nikki that Bob had called him. He said, *"Bob will on be here for about a week and he has found out a lot of things and wants to get all of us together tonight."*

Nikki had been so wrapped up in her romance with Marcel that she had forgotten about the Marrakech incident, and wondered how she could put it out of her mind so completely. However, she was curious to know what he had found out. Finally, after giving it some thought she said, *"We can't talk in a restaurant. Why don't I fix dinner here and we'll invite the others over as well."*

Roger was delighted. *"Good idea!"* They had not entertained at home in a long while and the idea appealed to him. He told Nikki that he was meeting Bob after lunch and that he would not stay for the two hour siesta. Nikki said, *"As soon as the market opens I will go and get some food to prepare."*

They ate a light lunch, which they that gotten in the habit

of doing since dad had left, as most every night they went out and had a large dinner.

Roger gave her a quick peck on the cheek and said, *"I'll see you later. Invite them for eight o'clock so that we can have a few drinks and talk before dinner."* Nikki agreed and he left.

She went to the phone and called Marcel. He had put a private phone in his office so that she didn't have to go through his secretary anymore. He was afraid that she would suspect something with Nikki calling. That way, she could call him whenever she pleased without anyone getting wise to the fact that they were in constant touch with each other. They both knew that their affair would have to be kept a secret from everyone. When he answered she could tell that he was eating. She said, *"I hope I haven't interrupted your lunch, but I have to talk to you."*

He said, *"I ordered something in the office. In fact, I have been doing this so that I can get my work done. Seeing you every afternoon has thrown me behind."*

Nikki laughed and said, *"Well, Mon Cherie, it looks like you will be able to catch up on your work this week."*

Marcel sounded disappointed when he asked what was going on. Nikki told him that the writer was in town and that he was coming to dinner along with the others to tell them what he had found out about the Countess. She said, *"While he is here this week, I guess I will have the duty of showing him around while Roger is working. It would not look right if I didn't and he wants me to play tennis with him, as he told me that he expected it when he came here."*

Marcel frowned to himself and said, *"Be sure that tennis is all that you play with him!"*

Nikki laughed and said, "*We will be at the club with Monique and Renee, playing doubles. I don't go in for orgies, you know!*"

Marcel joked, "*Don't knock it until you have tried it!*" Then he very gently said, "*Nicole, I know I can trust you. I will admit that at one time I wondered if anything did happen between you two when he was protecting you in Marrakech!*"

Nikki replied, "*As frightened as I was at the time, sex was the farthest thing from my mind! Besides, Roger did come right back when he found out what was happening.*"

Marcel felt that she was doing a little too much explaining, and wondered if something had happened between them. He became slightly irritated and asked, "*Nicole, when can we start seeing each other again?*"

She explained, "*He plans to be here for a week, but hopefully I can push him off on Monique. She has a weakness for Americans and she just might like the idea of entertaining him. As soon as I can fix things up, I'll let you know, but in the meantime, I will call you every day until we can start meeting again.*"

Marcel said," *I'll miss you,* Cherie."

Her answer was, "*Not as much as I will miss you my darling. Let's hope that I can get Monique interested in him and she can take over. She mentioned that he was good looking when we were in Marrakech.*" They said goodbye and Nikki called Monique and Renee and they all agreed to meet at her apartment at eight. They were all very curious to learn what Bob had to say about the Countess.

Nikki took a *cocher* and went to the market. She decided that it would have to be a simple dinner, without a lot of fuss. She loved preparing gourmet dinners, as she prided herself on her cooking, but there definitely wouldn't be time to do it. She was certain that by now Bob was ready for a good American meal of steak, potatoes and salad. She rushed to make her purchases, being careful to select tender filet mignons, fresh lettuce and mushrooms. She had plenty of potatoes at home. As she was leaving the market, she decided that she would make a pineapple upside down cake and bought a can of sliced pineapples. When she got home, she started the cake immediately so that it would have time to cool. She then scrubbed the potatoes and put them in the oven to bake. She then scooped them out and mashed them with butter, a small amount of milk and grated cheddar cheese. After she restuffed the halves she topped them with more cheese and breadcrumbs and dotted them with butter, ready to be popped back into the oven when she began her steaks.

By the time she was bathed and dressed it was almost time for Roger and Bob to come home. She thought about Marcel and realized how much she missed him that one day. She hoped that Monique would take Bob off of her back and had a plan on how to do it.

When Roger and Bob arrived, Roger started fixing drinks. He turned to Bob and said, "*We may as well wait for the others before you start telling your story, as you will only have to repeat it again.*"

Bob looked at Nikki and thought she even looked good in a simple apron. She was still the loveliest woman he had ever known and he envied Roger. He noticed that there was a coolness between them and wondered if things were going well between them. He was anxious to get Nikki alone and try and talk her into having an affair while he was there.

His thoughts were interrupted when the doorbell rang and Roger went to open it and let the others in. He fixed them all a drink and Nikki put out some appetizers, as they all pulled their chairs around to face Bob as he began to relate his story.

He began, "*I was afraid that I would have to leave Marrakech without knowing anything. I had to be careful not to reveal the fact that I was suspicious of anything. Also, I had to find the right person whom I could trust to help me. I made friends with an Arab after all of you left. He was a nice fellow and seemed to be not quite as wealthy as the others we had met, although he was not exactly poor either. I asked him some questions, such as how the rich Arabs managed to find such beautiful, young girls for their harems and he volunteered a lot of information. Of course many of the women are honored to be in the harem of a wealthy Arab, as they come from families without much money and they are actually bettering themselves. However, you were right about Madame Bonet, as she is their biggest source in supplying European girls for them. The rich ones can afford variety and they want it. Therefore, they pay very well for it. He told me that she has to be a very wealthy woman, as they pay her a lot of money for the girls she brings to them and it seems that she has brought many girls throughout the years. I realized then that I could trust him and told him about what had happened when we were all there together. Nikki, you are very lucky. They were definitely after you. It is rare that they get a lovely American girl in their harem and they think it to be prestigious. When the Pasha was told about you, he wanted to see you. This man told me that there had been an American girl that he had heard about and the way he described her, it was definitely you. He had been told that they could not get to her because she was never left alone. I asked him about the Pasha and he said that when the Pasha asks to meet someone he is definitely interested. He does it in a way that no one suspects what he is after. Roger that is why you and I were invited. He had Madame Bonet invite Nikki to the feast after you left, as he intended to keep her there. He felt that she was alone and would not be missed right away and by the time she was missed, no one would have any idea what happened to her. That is why Madame Bonet called you after you had already talked to Roger. She didn't expect you to call him back again and felt like they had it made. She would have made a lot of money off of you. He didn't keep the Countess the night of the feast as they were afraid that all of us would become suspicious, since Nikki knew that she had gone there. Before I discovered that your room was bugged, they evidently listened to all of Nikki's conversations on the phone with Roger and when she called him that morning to inform him that she had been invited to the Pasha's for a feast, by her answers and the fact that she cancelled out, they realized that he had told her not to go and why. The poor Countess was unsuspecting, as evidently she totally trusted the Bonets and thought nothing of it. It seems they went there for another feast and that is when he kept her.*

I asked this man if he knew how it would be possible for me to see the girl. I wanted to get her out of there, but I did not have the slightest idea of how I could do it. I thought that if I could accidentally see her someplace, I could signal her and get her out. He told me that the only place the Pasha's wives ever went was to a small park near the palace where they walk and get their exercise. I went to the park and hid and waited, but I had to be very careful, as there were men guarding them. They were all dressed in Arab robes and their faces were covered so that they all looked pretty much alike. However, as you know, all Arab women in Morocco are tattooed on their forehead. When I saw the one without the tattoo, I looked at her eyes and realized that it was the Countess. If you remember, she has green eyes. I know it was her. Also, I know that she saw me, but she acted like she did not recognize me. Then I realized that she had been drugged, as there was funny glaze in her eyes. I think I could have gotten her in the car and taken off with her if she would have cooperated, but she was so far out of it, she didn't even see me. It was as if she didn't care. I said her name and she completely ignored me. I know she has been doped up and brain washed. She does not even know what happened. When I decided it was hopeless, I went back to the hotel, packed and headed for Casablanca. I have never cleared out of a place so fast in my life. One of the guards who was with the Pasha the day we met him was there, and I was afraid he might have seen me. I knew that if the Pasha found out that I was snooping around, he would have had me killed. I got the information for my book and the information that you wanted and got the hell out of that place. It is hopeless; there is nothing anyone can do for her. They are guarded at all times and it is impossible."

Everyone was looking at him in disbelief. Finally Nikki broke the silence and said, "*There by the grace of God go me.*" When she realized how close she had come to being in the same situation she began trembling. They all saw how shaken she was and Roger quickly refilled her drink. She started sobbing, saying, "*I wanted to warn her. It is my entire fault. I should have warned her!*" She was uncontrollable by this time and everyone was trying to tell her that she would have put her own life in danger had she opened her mouth. Then she started yelling, "*What if he comes here!" They will come for me, I know they will.*" She was in complete hysterics by this time and Roger managed to get a straight shot of whiskey into her to calm her down.

He said, "*Nikki, you don't have to worry. No one can hurt you now.*"

Monique suddenly said, "*What is to keep them from coming here to find her?*"

This time everyone was nervous as no one had even given it a thought. They were still living in this country. Nikki remembered dad talking about it, but she never really took him seriously.

Then Bob said, "*You are all getting paranoid for nothing. That is not the way they operate. They do not touch a girl until she is already in Marrakech. I asked the man if it was possible, because I did think about it too. He told me that they just don't do it that way.*"

Roger asked, "*What is to keep them from kidnapping Nikki from here and taking her to Marrakech?*"

Bob answered "*They can't afford to take chances like that. It would be way too obvious. Don't think I didn't ask the man all of these questions, as it was the first thing I thought of.*"

Everyone hoped that he was right. Nikki still did not feel secure and finally said, "*Roger, I want to go back to the States. I don't feel safe here now. I am afraid to be alone now.*"

Roger said, "*Don't panic Nikki; no one is going to bother you here. There are many women in Casablanca from all over the world and it has never happened yet. Casablanca is a melding pot for all of the countries and it has always been safe here. We will just have to stay away from Marrakech.*"

Nikki replied, *"You could not drag me there for all the money in the world!"*

Finally they decided that it was time to eat and Nikki got busy preparing the steaks. She at least got her mind off of it, as Monique and Renee had come into the kitchen with her to help her get the dinner on the table. As she cooked the steaks and heated the potatoes, she sautéed the mushroom to serve with the steak and Monique watched to see that they did not burn. As Renee put the French bread on the table, Roger opened the wine and they all sat down to eat. Bob commented on how good it was to have a home cooked meal, and Roger laughingly said, *"Come to think of it, it is nice. We rarely eat at home. We go out every night. Of course we do have lunch here, but we have gotten into the habit of eating a light lunch since my parents went back to the States."*

Monique and Renee both said that they wished they could say the same and Michael and Antoine both said that they were not to be spoiled like American women are. It was all in fun, in a kidding way, and Nikki was sure it was to get her mind off of what she had heard. They knew she was very frightened. After dinner they thought of playing bridge, but there were only seven people, so instead they decided to go to the club.

Chapter Fifty-Nine

When they got to the club, Nikki was surprised to see Marcel there with some of his friends and his brother. He walked over to greet them and said, *"Since your trip, I have seen very little of you Roger. Are you keeping Nicole to yourself?"*

Roger said, *"I think it is you who is staying away. We go out all the time, but we never see you anywhere."*

Marcel remarked, *"Well, I think I deserve a dance with Nicole."* He took her arm and led her to the dance floor. They were playing slow music and he whispered to her, *"I want you to call me tomorrow and let me know what your friend has found out."* Nikki agreed that she would. Then Marcel said, *"I had a feeling that you would be here tonight, that is why I came. I want you to know that I missed you terribly today. By the way, that American is a handsome bastard; don't get any ideas about him!"*

Nikki replied, *"I don't need him, I've got you!"*

Then Marcel said, *"I am surprised that Roger is not jealous of him. I could see the way he was looking at you and I am sure that Roger did as well."*

Marcel was being very flippant and was trying to get a rise out of her, but she was determined to keep her cool and not let him get anything out of her.

Finally she said, "*Yes, he tried to get to me in Marrakech, but he is not my type*!"

Marcel asked, "*What is your type?*" With that,

Nikki answered,

"*If you don't know by now you never will!*"

Marcel laughed and when the set ended he took her back to the table. Roger asked him to join them and introduced him to Bob. Marcel refused, saying that he was with another party and Nikki was relieved, as she was afraid to be around him for fear of giving herself away. Just at the sight of him she felt an electric spark that she had never known before and as their affair had progressed, it had gotten stronger and she was sure by now that she truly was in love with him.

When she sat down, Bob asked Roger if he minded if he danced with her. Roger was not too happy about it, as it was a rumba and he liked to dance the Latin dances with her, but he found it difficult to refuse. Bob could see that he was reluctant and promised to bring her back as soon as they had one dance. From the corner of her eye she could see Marcel watching them and when Bob tried to dance close she pulled away and said, "*You are not supposed to dance close to the Rumba.*" She pulled away from him and made sure that their bodies did not touch.

Bob looked at her and said, "*I noticed you were dancing very close with that Frenchman, why are you so afraid to dance close with me?*"

She replied, "*Because that Frenchman happens to be Roger's best friend and he knows that he would not try anything with me."* Then she added, *"He was very jealous of you in Marrakech in case you didn't notice and I don't want him to think that anything happened between us. In fact, when we go back to the table, I hope you will ask one of the other women to dance."* Bob said that he would.

Nikki said, *"Why don't you work on Monique? She likes American men. Roger watches me too closely and I am afraid to do anything. We are very well known here in Casablanca."* Roger asked Renee to dance and the rest of the evening they joked and talked. Nikki made it a point not to make conversation with Bob.

Chapter Sixty

Around ten thirty the next morning the phone rang. Roger had just left about fifteen minutes before and Nikki found herself being lazy, as they had been out late and she was still tired. She answered the phone, dreading the thought that it was probably Bob, but it was Monique, much to her relief. She asked, "*What is up this early in the morning? Roger has just left for the office.*"

Monique answered, "*Nicole, I have been covering for you for a long time, now it is your turn to cover for me. I won't be at the tennis club for the rest of this week. I just thought I would let you know.*"

Nikki laughed and said, "*So it is Bob! I saw the two of you in serious conversation last night when you were dancing and I know that you have a soft spot for American men!*" Nikki knew that she was being pushy, as she had never told Monique who she was seeing, and Monique had never asked, but she had to know if it was Bob, as that way she could be with Marcel. She felt as if it had been a month since they had been together, but it was actually one day. Nikki said, "*Well, you can have the Americans, I'll take a Frenchman any time!*"

Monique laughed and said, "*As the old saying goes, the grass is always greener on the other side!*"

They both laughed and then Nikki said, "*This is great, this means I won't have to entertain Bob anymore! We will have to tell Renee to cover for both of us.*" Nikki was feeling sorry for Renee and asked, "*Poor Renee, when does her turn come?*"

Monique replied, "*Give her time; she will get involved with someone. We will be covering for her before it is over with.*"

They laughed and hung up. Nikki was thinking how different it was here than in the States. Maybe some women did these things, but they wouldn't discuss them as she and Monique were doing. She decided that she liked it better this way, at least you could tell someone and not feel like a whore. She was now involved in the game and decided that she liked it. However, she knew that she would never be able to play the game if she were still in love with Roger. It would have never occurred to her if he had not hurt her the way he had.

Nikki immediately called Marcel and told him to meet her at the apartment. He was delighted and asked what happened to the American. She said, "*He was trying to make time with me when we were dancing and I told him that I didn't play that game. I told him that Monique liked his type and that he should go work on her if that is what he wanted.*"

Marcel laughed and said, "*Well, you managed to get rid of him anyway and I like that. I will meet you at the regular time and I will be anxious to see you. I also want to hear what happened in Marrakech.*"

Nikki told him she would be there with bells on and

he asked, "*What are these bells?*" She laughed and said, "*Just another crazy American saying that doesn't work in French. It means that I will be looking forward to it.*"

Marcel laughed and said, "*You Americans with your expressions!*"

Monique called Renee and said, "*I need a favor from you. Will you cover for me this week? I won't be coming to the club and neither will Nicole.*"

Renee laughed and said, "*I can't cover for anyone!*"

Monique was surprised and said, "*You are seeing someone also?*"

Renee answered, "*If I cover for Nicole, her husband will know.*"

Monique was stunned when it hit her. "*You mean it is Roger?*" she asked.

Renee pleaded, "*Please don't say anything to Nicole. I do love her, but let's face it, if it's not me it would be someone else. Nicole couldn't care anyway, as she is so wrapped up in Marcel!*"

Monique was in shock. "*How do you know it is Marcel? Nicole as never told me who it is.*"

Renee answered, "*His secretary got wind of it and it's all over town.*"

Monique became worried for Nicole and decided to call her back. When she told what she had learned, Nicole said, "*If Roger finds out I will never admit it is true. I can always say that I called him to give messages to Juanita for me. After all, they don't have a phone at home. Who is Renee seeing?*"

There was a dead silence on the line and then Nikki said, "*I know, I'd bet my last franc that it's Roger.*

Monique answered, "*You said it, and I didn't. I don't think they have been together before. I think the arrangements must have been made last night.*"

Nikki thought for a moment and said, "*Oh hell! I'd rather it be Renee than one of those dancing girls. At least I won't have to worry about him bringing home a disease to me.*"

Monique said, "*I never even thought of that.*" It was odd, as she had wanted to have an affair with Roger from the time they that they had met and she never responded to his passes. He had tried and she knew that Nicole had seen it. One night when they had all been drunk they had gone to the beach and gone swimming in their panties and bras and the men in their skivvies, Roger had grabbed her and Nicole had seen it, but she had pulled away from him. She was glad that Nikki was getting even with him and especially that it was with his best friend. Now that they were all in the same boat, no one really had to cover for anyone, as they would all be playing the same game and it would not be tennis.

Chapter Sixty-One

When Nikki met Marcel that afternoon, she informed him that their affair was all over town, via his secretary. She also told him of her plan, that if Roger should find out she would say she was sending messages to Juanita. Marcel said, "*Good thinking. I will start delivering messages to her immediately. That way, if he checks she will tell him that I have.*"

She then told him about Bob's story and what had happened in Marrakech. When she told him that she had definitely been on the Pasha's list, Marcel put his arms around her and said, "*Thank God you had the good sense not to accept that invitation!*"

He grabbed her and they embraced. He said, "*That one day that we were apart felt like a month. I missed you. I could not get any work done just thinking about you and to be even more honest, I was sure that the two of you had something going in Marrakech when Roger was here in Casablanca. Now I realize that I was wrong. Excuse me for doubting you, Mon Cherie.*"

As he led her towards the bedroom there was the sound

of a key in the door. Nikki ran out on the veranda and hid in the corner. It was the owner of the apartment and he warned Marcel to be careful. He said that Roger had asked him to use his apartment and that he had told him that someone else was already using it. "*In case he decides to investigate one day, maybe you should find another place. Roger was sure that it was you, as he said that is your way of doing things. He asked who was using it and when he did not get an answer he knew it was you.*" Then he added, "*Marcel, we have been good friends for a long time, and I have to tell you that it is all over town that you are having an affair with Nicole. I am truly worried for you that it will finally reach Roger's ears. That's why I think you should look for another place.*" Marcel thanked him, not admitting or denying anything. He knew that he could trust him and was not worried.

When he left, Nikki came into the room and asked, "*What will we do?*"

"*We will have to find another place now.*" Marcel replied, "*I will just have to rent my own apartment.*" He told her that small apartments were easier to find and not to worry.

Nikki then told him that Roger was presently having an affair with Renee. "*I just hope that she doesn't let it slip about you and me.*"

Marcel looked surprised and asked, "*Did you tell her about us?*"

Nikki explained, "*I told you that it was all over town. Your secretary caught on before you got your private phone. Even Monique didn't know who I was meeting, but Renee is the one that told her this morning.*"

Marcel looked worried and said, "*I just hope that this*

thing doesn't come to a head, because if it does, we are in for big troubles!"

Nikki remarked, "*As long as Roger is playing around, it shouldn't make any difference to him. At least he wouldn't have to play act with me anymore. I have known for a long time that he is pretending that he wants sex when he really doesn't and half the time he has a difficult time getting it on. I am no dumbbell, after all, he is only thirty years old and I know there has to be another woman in his life. I know about the Hungarian girl. He has just been more discrete this time, just as we have been. I wonder if he has heard anything about us.*"

Marcel was very pensive when he said, "*I hope not, as I still think of him as a friend. Even if our friendship is not the same as it was, we do go back a long way.*"

Nikki was becoming haughty when she said, "*Well, I really don't care one way or the other. As long as he is being unfaithful, there is no reason why I should not be.*"

Then Marcel made a statement that infuriated her. He said, "*Men are different, Nicole. When they find out that their wife is playing around it hurts their pride. They don't like to be laughed at and they feel that it hurts their image.*"

She was becoming more irritated by the second and said, "*Well, don't you think it hurts a woman's pride?*"

Marcel answered, "*But a man is different, he is afraid that people will think that he is inadequate. A man takes pride in his ability to satisfy a woman!*" *Nikki was talking louder than usual as she became more and more infuriated.* "*Women have feelings too you know! I can't believe that you men think that you are the only ones who should expect faithfulness!*" Marcel began to laugh and said, "*This is the first time I have ever seen you mad. You are a real little spit-fire! I really like a woman with fire in her!"*

Nikki was so angry by then that she didn't answer him. She finally said, *"I guess we had better cancel out today. When you find your apartment, let me know!"* With that, she picked up her belongings and walked out.

Marcel was so stunned that he just stood there, not believing that she had walked out on him. Then he became angry with her and decided that he just might not even bother to look for an apartment.

When a week went by and Nikki had not heard from him, she was beginning to think that he was through with her. She had decided that she would not sit around the house and wait for him to call her and started going to the tennis club. She and Monique were playing together again, as Bob had left. What really got to her was that Roger had ruined the whole thing and he was still having his affair with Renee in someone's apartment, she was sure. She wondered when he would tire of her, as she did not seem like his type and didn't seem to be the most passionate woman in the world, as she had always seemed to be on the cool side in Nikki's eyes. Monique was upset that Bob had not extended his visit, but he had told her that he was way behind schedule and had a lot of territory to cover. He had left for Tangier.

Chapter Sixty-Two

Roger was wondering if the rumors were true about Nikki and Marcel. Marcel had not called him for a while, in fact he had not heard from him since that night at the club. He was trying to figure out how long it had been. He had not believed it when someone told him about it because he felt that even though they were not as close as before, Marcel was still like a brother to him and would not move in on his territory. He also knew that Nikki was too fond of Juanita to sleep with her husband, even if she did want another man. But deep inside, he felt that she was not the type to carry on an affair with anyone. It was below her standards and she had always been a very out-spoken, honest person. He just did not believe it and was sure there had to be an explanation for the rumors that were going around. People had a tendency to exaggerate things, and he was sure that it was a misunderstanding. He didn't know if he should approach her on the subject or not. He felt that he actually didn't have the right to ask her about it, since he was doing as he pleased and she had never questioned him, though she certainly had the right. He had not been a very good bed partner to her in recent weeks and he was sure that she suspected that he was up to something, but he felt that she didn't want to know. He had hurt her before and she probably didn't want to be hurt again. It did bother him that this ridiculous rumor was going around; however, he finally decided to ask Nikki in a nonchalant way what she thought might have started it.

When he came home for lunch that day, he said, "*Nikki, I want to talk to you.*"

She was busy getting the food on the table and asked, "*Can't it wait until we sit down?*" He decided that her answer was enough. If she was worried, she would have asked him immediately what he wanted to talk about. When they sat down, Nikki was scared to death of what he was going to talk about, as she was sure that he had heard the rumor. However, she knew that she had to play it cool and act as if she had no idea of what he wanted to talk about. Her answers were ready and she would not have to stumble on her words. She very innocently asked, "*What is it you want to talk to me about?*"

Roger hesitated and finally said, "*There is a stupid rumor going around this town that you and Marcel are having an affair. Is there any truth to it?*"

Nikki looked him straight in the eye and said, "*I heard about the rumors also. I don't know how they got started and therefore I was not worried about it. The only thing that I can think of is that I called him a few times at the office to give Juanita messages. We hardly ever see them anymore and they don't have a phone at home. I assume that his secretary thought that I was calling him for other things. It annoys me that gossip travels like it does and then people get the wrong impression of you. I was very upset when I heard it and figured you would also hear it, but there is nothing to it. You know how Marcel feels about you and you know how I feel about Juanita. It is the most ridiculous thing I have ever heard!"*

Roger was relieved, as her answer did make sense. He said, *"I was sure that it was something like that and I never believed it, but I had to ask you and let you tell me the truth. His secretary should be fired. Please excuse me for even questioning you about it."*

Nikki had not acted the least bit flustered and she could see that he did believe her. She decided that she deserved an Academy Award. Finally she said, *"If I didn't love Juanita, who knows what would have happened. He does appeal to me, you know. After all, it was no secret that you have had an affair with that Hungarian dancer and are now having one with Renee."*

Roger was stunned. He had thought he was playing it cool and had no idea that she knew about it. Especially Renee, as it had just started and he wondered if she had told Nikki about it herself. However, he doubted that she would do such a stupid thing, as she would be afraid that Nikki would tell Antoine. He had no idea that she knew about the Hungarian girl either and finally asked her, *"Where do you get all of your information from Nikki?"*

She replied, *"You have lived in Casablanca a hell of a lot longer than I have, and you ought to know by now that you can't keep secrets in this town. Besides, you have not been the greatest lover these days. Before I heard about it, I was sure that you were with someone else, as you seldom want anything from me anymore. At age thirty, that is not normal. What's the matter?*

Isn't my blood hot enough for you anymore? Have you tired of me in these few years that we are married? Before this it was Carla and you promised me you would never do anything to hurt me again. Your promises are not worth much, I can tell you that. Now that it is out, you can sleep in the other bedroom from now on. I don't want to catch any diseases from you that you may happen to pick up. If I were to have an affair with Marcel or anyone else, you would have no right to say anything about it. I am not as stupid as you seem to think I am. It is true, you have not run around and left me at home alone at night, but now that your father isn't here anymore, who cares whether you show up to work or not. I am glad that this has come out, because now I don't have to pretend that I love you anymore. You have the whole afternoon to do as you please and you don't even have tea with me anymore. Tell me, where do you take Renee? Surely she wouldn't take the chance of letting you come to her apartment!"

Roger finally decided to get a word in, "*As a matter of fact, you have the whole afternoon free as well as I do. How do I know that the rumor about you is not true?*"

He was striking back, but Nikki was too quick for him. "*You know that I go to the tennis club every day. You can ask Monique if you don't believe me. Why don't you ask Renee while you are fucking her today?*" She was becoming sarcastic and angry and Roger didn't know how to handle her when she became this way. Then she asked, "*And who can I ask about you? Have you told your office people that if I should call that you have been there? I know that I called you several times and you were not in.*"

Roger was becoming more and more upset with himself for having started this whole conversation. Now that Nikki had opened up on him, his defenses were down. He had not been prepared for this and there was no use denying anything, because it was obvious that someone was keeping her posted on what he was doing. Now he knew that their relationship had reached rock bottom and he was sure that Nikki would not put up with it for long.

He still believed her story about not having an affair with Marcel. Maybe it was because he didn't want to believe that Marcel would do this sort of thing to him. He still liked to think of him as his best friend. He was sorry that they had come to Casablanca, because if they had remained in the States he was sure that all of this would not have happened. He suddenly realized that he was just trying to show the other guys that he could get away with the things that they were doing, even though he was married to an American. He knew that he was actually bored with the affairs that he had been having lately, and that it had been much better when he and Nikki had been together and she had truly loved him. If only he could go back and start over again. Nikki no longer loved and trusted him. In fact, she had no use for him at all. He had tried to hide it from himself that Nikki had not been as affectionate as she used to be in the old days. They had enjoyed the same things and had so much in common. Now there was no respect or love left on her part and he realized that he still loved her as much as he could ever love anyone, but his way of showing it had not been the best. He was sure that she would now decide to go home and divorce him. He had really made a mistake when he married her, as he had lived in this country most of his life where these things were accepted and an American girl would never accept it. He also knew that he would never put up with Nikki cheating on him as Renee was doing now. He was far too jealous to put up with it. He was chauvinistic and he knew it, but he could not accept it because of his jealous nature. Of all of their friends, Michael was the only one who was faithful. He was too much in love with Monique and would not give her the opportunity to leave him. He knew the story about her great love affair during the war when Michael was away. He had never mentioned it to Nikki as he didn't want her to lose respect for her. They were very close friends and he was sure that was why Monique had rejected his advances on the beach. If she had told Nikki about it, Nikki had never revealed her confidence. That was one good think about her, when she was your friend, she was a faithful one.

His heart ached when he remembered how naïve she had been when he married her. He had taught her everything and she had enjoyed having him teach her the facts of life. He had always been proud of her and enjoyed the fact that all of the other men were envious of him. Now he was aware of the fact that he had lost her love. His father had warned him to treat her well and he was sorry that he had not taken his advice. She was now cool and indifferent and he knew that she was through with him. If she would at least show some anger or hate, he would feel that there might be something left, but it was complete indifference. Because of this, he knew that there was not a chance for him to make it up to her.

She had acted as if she had forgiven him after his affair with Carla and they had enjoyed their trips to Paris, Tangier and Marrakech since then, but he assumed that his recent actions had turned her off completely.

When he thought of their trip to Tangier, he remembered how Nikki had enjoyed that city. She was in awe, as they stood and looked across the water and could see the Rock of Gibraltar on that clear day. She loved the flamenco dancers and the Spanish food, but she had mentioned to him that though she loved the city and found it to be a very romantic place, the thought that he had been there with Carla was still on her mind and she couldn't help but wonder if they had gone to the same places as he and Carla had gone. Though she had tried to forgive him, she knew that she could never forget the pain he caused her, and she mentioned that she wondered if she ever would be able to.

He knew that his parents would be furious with him when they returned, as this time, he as sure that she would tell them. He hoped that they would remain in the States for a while, as he was not ready to face them. He still hoped that they could patch things up before they came back. He suddenly realized why Nikki had not asked to go home; she wanted to be there to tell them when they got back. He made a vow with himself to try and win back her confidence.

Chapter Sixty-Three

Marcel had been angry with Nicole the day she walked out of the apartment. He had decided to punish her and had not tried to contact her for a week. He missed her so badly that he finally decided to look for an apartment. He found one in an area where he knew they would not have to worry about being recognized. Most of the people that had settled there were the ones who had drifted in from other countries during and after the war. They kept pretty much to themselves and didn't try to make friends with the local people. He assumed it was because they didn't know who had sympathized with the Nazis and Vichy French and who had not. You didn't need a passport to get into Morocco and these people were considered the ones without a country. They could not leave once they came there, as they didn't have passports.

He had heard many tales about the terrible things that had happened to them in the Nazi prison camps and he supposed that they had found that they had so much in common and didn't bother to mingle with others unless it was business.

Most of them were Jews and had tattoos on their arms. It had been bad enough in Casablanca with the Vichy French, as the Jews had been tortured by them as well. He felt sorry for these people and couldn't blame them for not trusting other people. Some of them had managed to keep enough of their belongings to be able to go into business in Casablanca. He was certain that the ones who had nothing left were being helped by those who did. He remembered the days when they had been forbidden to even listen to the radio in Casablanca. They would put it on very low and put their ear up to it so that in case they had a neighbor who was a spy for the enemy, they would not hear the radio and report it. That had been their only means of getting any news of what was happening, as most of the news in the papers was all propaganda. It had been a tough time for everyone in Casablanca as there had been a terrible food shortage as well.

He picked up the phone and called Nicole, but there was no answer. He assumed that she was back at the tennis club every day playing tennis or bridge. He finally reached her three days later. She was on her way out and seemed cool when she heard his voice. He wondered if he had waited too long to call her and felt an ache inside of him. He said, *"Nicole, I have been trying to reach you for days. It took me a while to find an apartment. I know I was upset when you walked out on me that day, but you will have to admit that I had good reason."*

Nikki's reply was short and curt. *"I knew that you were mad, but you could have called! I didn't go the club the first few days, I sat around and waited to hear from you and finally decided that never again will I wait for any man!"*

Marcel knew he would have to go easy, as he did not want to lose her. He finally said, "*There was no reason to take the chance of calling until I found the right apartment for us. Nicole, please, I need you.*" The tone of her voice changed and he knew that she believed him.

She said, "*I need you too, Marcel. I need you more than I ever have before. Roger and I are on the outs completely and we don't even share the same bed anymore. What is the address?*"

He gave it to her and told her that he would have to get some furniture. She insisted that they could meet there even though there was no furniture and they both decided to leave for the apartment at once. He knew that he would get there first, as the *cochers* were much slower than his car.

Nikki pulled out an old comforter and managed to shove it into her grocery basket. She then left the apartment and took a *cocher* to the apartment. Marcel was waiting for her and she melted when she saw him. How could she stay mad at him? She realized how much these meetings meant to her, although she was sure that it would lead to no permanent thing, as eventually she would have to go back to the States. Now that things were so bad between her and Roger, she knew that it was only a matter of time that she would go home and get a divorce. She had decided to wait for his parents to come back and tell them what had happened and ask them for the money to get her home.

In the meantime, she would take advantage of every minute she possibly could to be with Marcel. She knew that she would never share a bed with Roger again and when his parents came back she would have to leave, as there was not an extra bedroom.

She threw herself into Marcel's waiting arms and they embraced and kissed. She then spread the quilt on the floor. "*You think of everything, Nicole.*"

Nikki laughed and replied, "*I didn't think that I would enjoy lying on the cold marble floor!*" All of the floors in Casablanca were marble. It was the cheapest material to use since there were so many marble quarries there. She knew that at home it would cost a small fortune and only the very wealthy homes had it.

After they made love, Nikki finally told him what had happened between Roger and her. "*I know it is just a matter of time that the folks will be back and they will know that something is wrong when I refuse to sleep with Roger. He can just sleep on the couch until I leave. However, I also know that it is inevitable that I will have to go home and divorce him. He had the nerve to question me, when he has been screwing around with every whore in Casablanca.*" Nikki was furious when she thought about it.

Marcel said, "*There goes that hot little temper of yours again!*" Then he took her in his arms and said, "*Do you realize that when you leave here that it will be the end of us? Why can't Roger sleep on the couch? Nicole, I love you.*"

Nikki replied, "*It would only be a matter of time that you would be cheating on me, as all of the men here do. I don't want any part of it. It is true that a lot of men at home run around on their wives, but not like this!*"

Marcel said, "*Don't you realize that you are cheating on Roger too?*"

She answered, "*It never would have happened if he had behaved himself. Sure, I knew that I wanted you the first day I saw you, but I do have my principles and willpower, you know.*

It was not until he started having his affair with Carla that I did anything about it and then, it probably would never have happened had you not come to the apartment that night. If Roger had not put me into that position, I doubt that you would have come over to begin with. I am sure that you knew that I was starved for love, that I had no willpower. Besides, I have not had affairs with every man that has come along and don't think they haven't tried. I have slept with no one but you. I do love you, you know." She then added, *"It's true you were his best friend, and he would have been upset to know that there was anything going on between us, but then he has been having an affair with one of my friends. I really don't feel guilty anymore. I don't care if he does find out. I would love to flaunt it in his face, but because of Juanita, I can't. He would have had Monique long ago, but she valued my friendship and rejected his advances. She doesn't love her husband, but she didn't get involved with Roger because of me. She has a weakness for Americans anyway."*

Marcel laughed and said, *"Yes, I remember her with her American major. She was with him constantly when her husband was in England."*

Nikki said, *"When Roger was overseas I never even looked at anyone else and I never thought that he did, but now that I know him better, I am sure that he had someone then. How long can a woman be expected to put up with this kind of thing? Maybe here they have to, but in the States a woman would have filed for divorce a long time ago. I know that if I do go home, I am heading for an attorney and I plan to file for divorce as soon as my residence has been established."*

Marcel was upset at the thought of her going home. He knew that he would never see her again. Then he asked her,

"Why do you have to leave? Stay here and we will keep on seeing each other. I don't want to be without you."

Nikki insisted, *"When Roger's parents come back, I will have to leave. I will never let Roger back in my room and there is not enough room in that apartment for all of us if we live separately. Besides, I cannot go on living a lie."*

Marcel tried to soothe her and said, *"We will have to make the best of the time we have left, Nicole. I want to see you every day."*

Nikki agreed that it was fine with her. *"When I denied that there was anything going on between us I did it for you as you are good friends."*

"Were good friends," he corrected her. *"We are never together anymore. He has made all of his new friends and doesn't call me anymore. I think that you have lost a husband and I have lost a friend!"*

"That's not true," Nikki argued. *"I know that Roger still considers you his best friend. It's just that we have been running around with married couples and you never have wanted to take Juanita out, which makes it sort of awkward."*

Marcel admitted that it was true. Nikki said, *"I just wish that there was some way that you and I could spend some time together away from here before I go home. I would love to be able to stay with you day and night, never having to say goodbye for a while. I would like for it to be forever, but I know that is quite impossible."*

Chapter Sixty-Four

Roger was unhappy, as he knew that Nikki was going to leave him. He didn't like having to sleep in the other bedroom and wished that he could get her to make up with him. He tried his best, but she was cold and did not respond to anything he tried to say or do. He could not believe that there was no hope. He finally decided to see Marcel and see if he had any ideas about it. After all, Marcel did know how to keep Juanita in line and he might have a few pointers for him. However, he did realize that Nikki and Juanita were from two different worlds. Any advice at all would help.

When he went to Marcel's office he was not there. The secretary told him that he would find him there more in the mornings, that he had not been working in the afternoons lately. Roger was trying to figure out why, as he knew that Marcel could stay out all night and get away with it. He tried to tell himself that Marcel was messing around with one of the dancers, as they worked at night, but deep inside he felt that the rumors about him and Nikki could be true.

At one time he would never have believed it, but he had not been close to Marcel the past few months or longer. Their friendship of the old days was gone and they were now more like strangers with each other.

He did realize that he and Nikki had been running with other married couples and Marcel acted as if he was a single man, as he was never went out with his wife. Even though he himself had played around, he had still taken Nikki out at night, except for the time when he was seeing Carla, and it was obvious that he was a married man.

As he thought of all of this, he decided that he would just drop into the tennis club that afternoon and see if Nikki was there playing tennis. Since he had stopped seeing Renee, he didn't particularly want to run into her, as he was not in the mood for explanations. He decided that he would find some excuse to talk to Nikki. Around three o'clock he found himself heading towards the club.

When he arrived he found Monique and Renee out on the tennis court. He asked them where Nikki was and Monique said, *"She hasn't gotten here yet. I talked to her this morning and she said that she would be here, so I guess she is running late."* She tried to be as nonchalant as possible and was sure that she had not given any sign that she did not expect Nicole.

He noticed that Renee was ignoring him and never said a word. Roger studied Monique for a moment and then asked, *"Are you covering up for her?"*

Monique asked very innocently, *"Covering up what?"* Roger looked at her and said, *"I think you girls have something going on and are covering up for each other."*

She laughed and said, "*I don't know what you are talking about. When Nicole gets here I will tell her to call you.*"

Roger answered, "*Never mind. I'll talk to her tonight.*" With that he turned and walked away. It was the first time that he really did suspect that there was something fishy going on. Monique had been a little too cocky and though she lied well, he knew that she had not told the truth.

As he drove off, he suddenly remembered asking his friend for the use of his apartment and being told that someone else was using it. He was certain that it was Nikki and Marcel. He drove over to the apartment and parked his car up the street. He was prepared to wait until he saw them come out. He could be patient and then when he did see them, he would let Marcel have one on the jaw. He stayed there until dark, but there was not a sign of them.

When he got home he found Nikki all dressed up and waiting to go out. She acted irritated when she asked, "*Where in the hell have you been? We are invited to a party tonight, remember? When I went to get my hair done, I called the club to tell Monique that I wouldn't be there and she said that you were looking for me. What did you want?*" Roger remembered that they had been invited to the anniversary party for Fabia and Pasqual. He told her that he had gotten tied up in a deal and suddenly he felt like a fool. He had spent the entire afternoon spying on her and she had been at the beauty parlor. Nikki knew that his affair with Renee was over, as Monique had told her when she called her to tell her that Roger had been at the club looking for her and asking questions. Nikki had run out for a *cocher* and gone to get her hair done so that she would have a good excuse.

When Roger realized that she had had her hair done, he no longer thought that she had been with Marcel, though she had been earlier.

He said, "*I was beginning to believe that the rumors about you and Marcel were true. I knew he had been using a friend's apartment and when you were not at the club I went there and waited for you to come out.*"

She almost laughed in his face. She wanted to tell him that they had their own apartment now, and would have loved to have seen the look on his face. When she asked him what he had wanted, he said, "*It was not important.*"

"Well", she said, "*If it was not important, you sure went to a lot of trouble to find me*!" He acted like a beaten man as he went in to take his bath and dress.

Chapter Sixty-Five

The next morning Nikki couldn't wait until Roger left so that she could call Marcel and tell him what had happened. She decided that it would be a good idea for her to go to the club for a few days in case Roger checked again.

Marcel laughed when she told him that Roger had waited outside of the wrong apartment. He said, "*In the meantime I will get a bed for us and a couple of chairs and table.*"

Nikki replied, "*Don't spend a lot of money unless you intend to keep that apartment after I am gone.*"

Marcel said, "*I wish you would change your mind about leaving, Nicole. I don't know what I will do when you leave. I have grown to love you very much and the thought of not seeing you again makes me feel very sick inside.*"

"*It is inevitable,*" Nikki replied, "*I will have to go home when Roger's parents come back. I will not share a bed or a room with him ever again.*" Marcel was unhappy, but he said that he did understand.

Nikki was very unhappy when she thought of having to

leave Marcel, but she knew it would have to happen sooner or later. She again mentioned the fact that she wished they could have some time alone together before she departed for the States.

"I was thinking," she stated, *"that perhaps I could tell Roger that I need to get away alone to think about things. However, if you and I were gone at the same time, I am afraid that both Roger and Juanita would become suspicious. I really don't care at this point, as I have told you before, but I would have to face his parents when they returned. As it is now, I know they will sympathize with me and help me."* Marcel frowned and said, *"I can't believe that you would sacrifice our being together just for what they will think of you. Nicole, don't you realize that once you leave Roger, you will never see them again?"* Nikki didn't answer at first, as she was thinking now. Finally she said, *"They could not possibly hold it against me after the things that Roger has done. He has always been the black sheep of the family."*

Marcel was puzzled and asked, *"What is this black sheep?"* She laughed and said, *"There I go again! It's another American expression."* She explained to him what a black sheep was.

Then Marcel decided, *"Let me think about it. I am sure that I can come up with an idea."*

When they hung up, he sat at his desk for a long time and tried to figure out a way. He knew they would be taking a chance, as it was a small world. Even if they went to Paris they could run into someone they knew. He thought about how much he would love to go to Paris with Nicole. He wondered how it would be to go to sleep with her in his arms and wake up the same way. They really did need some time together and maybe with a lot of talking, he could change her mind about leaving. He really wished that he could marry her, but was sure that it would be difficult for him to get a divorce.

He had a sleepless night, trying to figure out a plan, and finally came up with a solution. He called Nicole the next day when he knew that Roger would be gone and said, *"I have a plan."* She could tell that he was excited and she became excited even before hearing what it was.

She asked, *"Yes? What is it?"*

He went on to say, *"When you leave to go back to the States, you will have to go through Paris, right?"*

Nikki replied, *"I suppose so, as I sure don't want to go back on another freighter. I shall insist on a French Liner, as a matter of fact!"*

Marcel explained, *"About a week before you leave, I will leave for Paris, as it is just about time for me to go on my buying trip. I go twice a year, so no one will think anything of it. In fact, I will go ahead and take care of my business before you get there. When you arrive, you will take a cab to the hotel where I tell you to go. We can stay together for a week or ten days."*

Nikki asked, *"What about the ship? I am sure that I will have reservations on one of the liners."*

Marcel insisted, *"I can take care of that also. When I arrive in Paris, I will cancel your reservation and make a new one on the same ship, but it will be about ten to twelve days later. It takes five days for the ship to get to New York and five more to return. I think they stay in port for a day to clean the ship before they take on new passengers. So we will actually have twelve wonderful days and nights together. You can even say that you wish to spend a few days in Paris to shop for gifts before you leave and that would give us two weeks together.*" Nikki was beginning to love the idea of being in Paris with Marcel. When she told him she would do it he said, "*I don't want you to go home, but at least we can have that time until I can think of a way that we can be together permanently. I will go with you on the boat train to the ship in Marseilles.*"

Nikki liked the plan more and more, but was wondering what he meant when he said "*together permanently,*" but decided not to question him about it now. She was sure that he would tell her what he meant when they were together. Once she left Casablanca, she knew that Roger would not be able to check on her, as he could not call the States from there. At any rate, she knew also that once she left, he would probably forget about it, as he would know that it was over. She and Marcel decided to go on as they had before, as she wouldn't be able to make her plans until Roger's parents got back and she was not sure when that would be.

Chapter Sixty-Six

Roger was sure now that when his parents returned that Nikki would be leaving. He knew that she had washed her hands of him and there was not enough room in the apartment for them to sleep separately once his parents did return. He thought of sending her on before his folks got back so that she would not be able to tell them what he had been doing. He felt that this was the best plan. He could always tell them that they were not getting along, but his father knew him like a book and would see through him. He could easily make a few inquiries and find out. It was true that his father had had a few affairs himself, but that was different. He was so proud of Nikki and he really did love her. He knew that he was in for a bad time and dreaded their return.

He was behaving himself now and he couldn't understand why. Nikki would not let him come near her. They had been living under the same roof, but not as man and wife. He had no desire to start an affair with anyone else. He just wanted Nikki back, but he could not make her budge. He had it coming to him, he realized, but he had hoped that she would change her mind. She was a strong willed woman, that was for sure, and once she decided something it was hard to stop her. He felt like it was too late to try and salvage their marriage. He had a letter from his father saying that they would be returning at the end of the month. It was already April of nineteen forty-nine and he knew that time was running out. He had even thought of looking for a three bedroom apartment and maybe Nikki would not leave. When he asked her about it she said, "*Why should I stay here? I have no husband anymore! I want to go home to my family and be with people who really care about me. Who knows? I might meet someone else and remarry.*"

It hurt him when she said it, but he was sure that she would. She was almost to the point of being cruel to him. He didn't blame her, as he knew that if he had acted like a husband to her this would not be happening now. It would be ridiculous for them to go on as they were, as there was nothing left between them. It was almost two years since they had left the States and it was obvious that she was anxious to go back. When he asked her if she had any forgiveness left in her she said, "*A person can only forgive so much!*" She told him that she did not intend to go through life worrying about being dumped when she got older and lost her looks. She was adamant about the fact that she wanted her freedom.

Now he was trying to keep busy and didn't even go home for lunch anymore. He knew that Nikki wanted no part of him and she had begrudgingly thrown his food at him when he had come home. He had a lump inside that wouldn't go away. "*Damn,*" he thought, "*I love that girl!*" As time went on, things got worse when they were together. He longed to put is arms around her and be close to her, but she let it be known that he was not to touch her. She said, "*I do not belong to you any longer. Go find yourself some whore!*" It was pure torture to be around her and see her act so cold to him. She was a far cry from the girl he had brought with him to Casablanca.

One day, when things were really bad between them, he asked her, "*How would you like to go home now. There are freighters leaving for the States every day now.*" He was not prepared for what happened next.

Nikki became furious. He had never seen her so angry in all the years they had been married. He had no idea that she had such a raging temper until now. Her face turned red and she said, "*There is no way you will ever put me on a freighter again! I will not have two weeks of that. It was bad enough when we were together and cared about each other. I am going to Paris and take the boat train to Marseilles and sail on a French liner! I know that your parents will give me the money if you won't!*"

He said, "*Okay, if that is what you want, I will do it.*"

Nikki could not believe her ears. She looked at him and asked, "*Why are you doing this, Roger? Is it because you don't want your parents to know what you have been up to?*"

He answered her question with a look of despair. Finally he said, "*It is difficult to live in the same house with the woman I love and not be able to touch her. I still love you, Nikki, and it hurts. I can't eat, I can't sleep and I am going out of my mind. Maybe if I don't see you every day it will be easier. You know, it's funny, since you and I have become estranged, I haven't even wanted another woman.*"

For the first time, Nikki felt sorry for him. She finally

said, "*How do you think I felt those nights that you stayed out until four-thirty in the morning. Do you think I ate or slept? If only you would have realized that you truly did love me before our marriage became such a farce, we could have worked things out, but now I could never love you again and I could never trust you. You can't have one without the other. You brought me to a strange country and took advantage of the situation. Don't you realize what you have done? I loved you Roger! I would have done anything in the world for you, anything at all! Then you mistreated me and turned my love into hate. In fact, I don't even hate you. I just feel sorry for you. I wouldn't give a damn now if you went out and fucked every whore in this city!*" She then added, "*If you think that I have been enjoying this, you are really crazy. I haven't been eating or sleeping very well either!*"

Roger could see that she was thin again, and could see that she was not happy. She said, "*What started out to be a beautiful, happy marriage has turned into a nightmare. You think because you are a man you can do as you please, but it doesn't work that way with me. I wasn't raised in a country where the women take a back seat and let their husbands do as they please. The trouble with you is that you are too European in your way of thinking. You may call yourself an American, but you have lived over here too long, and at heart you are not. In the beginning, everything was glamorous to me and I was naïve, but I have finally grown up. I am no longer eighteen. I don't intend to wait until I am too old to find a good, faithful husband who will give me security and a family. Thank God I lost your baby!*"

She could see that Roger believed that she meant what she said. Finally, after quietly thinking it over, he said, "*I guess the best thing I can do for you is to let you go. I don't want to hurt your anymore than I already have. I never did want to hurt you, Nikki. I know that it is hard for you to believe this, but I still love you very much. I really don't blame you if you don't want to give me another chance. You already did that and I just screwed up again. I will make arrangements for you to leave on a French liner."*

Nikki felt sorry for him, but she was not about to turn down his offer. "*Give me a chance to get my things packed. I will need about ten days.*" she said. She had brought with her all of her silver and china that she had inherited from her mother. She and Nora had each taken half and she had no intentions of leaving all of her earthly belongings behind, though she was anxious to get away from Roger and Casablanca. She decided that she would ship most of the things home from Paris before she left, as she knew that she could not handle large baggage by herself. Roger looked as if he was about to cry when he saw that she was happily making her plans to leave. Deep down, he hoped that she would change her mind, but he could see there was no hope whatsoever. He left the apartment, because if he did break down, he didn't want Nikki to see him. He didn't want her pity and he certainly didn't want her to stay with him for that reason alone.

Chapter Sixty-Seven

In the morning Nikki wrote a letter to her Aunt Emma. She told her that she was sending everything home and tried to explain as best as she could what had happened. She told her that she had no idea when she would be leaving or arriving, and therefore would call her from New York.

She explained that she and Roger had not been getting along for a long time and that she was planning on getting a divorce. She asked that the family forgive her, as she was well aware that there had never been a divorce in the family, but said that under the circumstances, she could no longer live with him. She asked her to keep her things until she returned and to please let Nora read the letter as she was very busy and didn't have time to write to both of them. She knew that she would be in Paris for at least a couple of weeks, and decided not to say anything about the estimated time of her arrival.

When she finished her letter, she stamped it and took it to the mail box on the corner. She realized that she was excited about seeing her family again as she had missed them more than she knew. Two years was a long time to be away from her loved ones. She had already decided not to call Roger's family when she got to New York. She would let Roger be the one to give them the news. She felt badly about not being able to say goodbye to them, also Eileen and Bill, but decided that the sooner she broke off the ties, the better off they would all be. She wondered if she would be happy living at home again, as she knew that she had outgrown that kind of life.

After she mailed the letter she took her bath and got dressed. She had been meeting Marcel earlier now that Roger was no longer coming home for lunch. She was anxious to tell him the news, as now that she knew when she would be leaving, he could make his own arrangements.

When she got to his apartment he already knew. Roger had been to see him the first thing in the morning, after he left home. He had gone to his house before he left for his office. He had cried when he told Marcel that Nikki was leaving. Marcel still loved Roger and could not help but feel sorry for him. He said, "*Roger, if you wanted to live this kind of life, you should have known better than to marry an American girl. The American women do not understand our way of life here and cannot accept the fact that their husband has to have other women. Nicole confided in me a long time ago when you were still with Carla. You have a beautiful wife that most men would give an eye for. You have acted foolishly and now you must pay for it. I am sorry for you, but I am sorry for Nicole as well. She cannot accept infidelity and you should have realized that before you got yourself into this mess. You know American women better than I do, or at least you should. I am sorry if I seem to be lecturing to you, as I know that you don't want that now. It is too late to do anything about it anymore, but I hope that this has taught you a lesson and that you won't let yourself get hurt again."* He then asked, *"Do you think that there is anything I can do to change her mind?"*

Roger replied, *"I don't think so. I have done the damage and I will have to pay for it for the rest of my life. If you think that you can persuade her to stay, go ahead and talk to her. I am sure that she no longer loves me and I don't want to see you waste your time."* He seemed pathetic to Marcel and he felt sorry for him, as he knew that his friend was losing a woman that he would never be able to replace.

He then asked, *"When does she plan to leave?"*

Roger answered, *"In about ten days. I am going now to make arrangements for her to leave before my parents return. I know they will be here in a couple of weeks, as they plan to fly back."*

After Roger left, Marcel left for his office and called Air France to make his reservation for a week before Nikki would leave. He then called the company in Paris that he did business with and told them to reserve a suite for him at the George V Hotel. When he had made all of his arrangements, he called Roger and said, *"I will be in Paris on my buying trip when Nicole gets there. If you like, I will be happy to meet her plane and see that she gets on the boat train without any problems. That is, if you wish me to do this for her."*

Roger thanked him and said he appreciated it. He didn't seem to be the least bit suspicious and Marcel was glad. In fact, he said, *"You know Marcel; I was foolish enough to believe the rumors about you and Nikki. In fact one day I waited for the two of you to come out of Albert's apartment, as I was sure you had been using it. I have become a very stupid person to think that my best friend would do this to me."*

For the first time in many months, Marcel felt guilty, but he knew that Nicole was through with him anyway and there was nothing he or anyone else could do about it.

He called the Paris office again and told them to make it for three days in Paris and to let him have one of their villas at the Riviera for ten days. He asked for the one with the best view of Monte Carlo. They owned several elaborate villas that they used for their best customers when they wished to go there. He decided not to tell Nicole about it, as he wanted to surprise her. Everything was set. He and Nicole would have their time together before she left for the States, but he wondered what he would do after she was gone, as he knew that he loved her more than life itself.

Marcel took Nicole's face in his hand that afternoon and said, *"Mon Cherie, we will have our time together. We can even stay longer if you wish, as Roger will not be checking on you once you are gone, as he cannot call the states. He will know that he has lost you forever and I am sure he will never know when you leave Paris. The day you arrive in Paris I will wire him, saying that I have sent you off on the boat train. If I am gone longer than usual, I can find many excuses for remaining longer in Paris. After all, I have my business associates there and I can invent many problems.*

He then said, *"I am sure that Juanita will want to have you to dinner before you leave. She adores you, Nicole, and she will want to tell you goodbye."*

Nikki nodded and said, *"I could never leave without seeing her and telling her goodbye. I also want to see your mother."*

She knew that Madame Beret had loved her because of Roger, but wondered if she would approve of the idea that she was leaving him. She would probably scold Roger for not behaving. She did not have to return the ruby, as when dad had taken it to have it mounted for her, they had appraised it for insurance and he had found out that it was paste. He informed her of the fact, as he didn't want her to think that they had to be beholden to her for the generous gift. When she took her other jewels in, she found that her husband had sold her jewels after having copies made of them. He was also a woman chaser, but as he had gotten older, he had found out that he had to pay a lot of money for his pleasures. Most of the women in Casablanca kept their expensive jewels in the bank and wore the paste jewelry when they went out, as they thought of it as an investment and didn't want them laying around the house, as the servants were not honest. Now she found that she had nothing left in her old age, but she knew that her sons would be good to her and they were, as she had not had to change her style of living. Although Marcel and Juanita and their children had moved to their own villa, he was still contributing to her livelihood, as well as Jon, who was still living with her. Jon and Theresa had not had any children as yet and she would say, "*Theresa is not a good wife to Jon. She is bad for him. She is not a real woman, as she cannot give him a child.*" She wanted sons, as she wanted the family name to be carried on. She would talk about it in front of Theresa and Nikki felt sorry for her.

One time when she was rattling on about it, Nikki said, "*I have not had a son for Roger yet either. Does that make me not a real woman?*"

Madame Beret said, "*It is different. You come from another background and I know that American woman do not produce as many children as we do. You are not Catholic and that also makes a difference.*"

They had all been silent through dinner on this last night that Nikki would be there and it was a very gloomy atmosphere. They knew that Roger was heart broken that she was leaving him and they were sorry that she would not stay and give him another chance. The only one who was on Nikki's side was Juanita. She had taken her aside and said, "*You do not have to have this kind of life, and I am glad that you are leaving him. Even though I will miss you, I hope that when you go home you will meet a good man who will be kind to you.*"

Nikki felt guilty and wondered what Juanita would have said had she known about the plans that she and Marcel had. She thought that she would react as she herself had when she found out about Roger and Renee. Juanita and Madame Beret both cried when they told her goodbye. It turned out to be a very emotional evening. Nikki realized that they knew they were living in different worlds. She embraced them both as well as the children whom she had grown to love, and Theresa and Jon. The children were too young to even know the meaning of divorce, as it seldom happened in Casablanca.

Nikki was remembering her first night with these people when she had arrived in Casablanca and it seemed to long ago. So much had happened since then. She had been so innocent and happy in those days. She realized that although the ending was not what she had hoped for, she had learned a lot from these people.

The last night was with Monique and Michael. Fabia joined them, but her husband stayed with the babies, as the youngest was too small to be left with servants and Fabia's mother was not well. They went to their favorite restaurant in Casablanca for dinner. Nikki drank a lot of wine and ate very little. She was drunk when they got back to their apartment. She missed Marcel and was looking forward to seeing him when she reached Paris and was so excited that she couldn't swallow her food. It seemed to be what she was living for at the time. Only Monique knew what her plans were and she had said, "*I admire you for doing what you truly want to do. I realize now, how foolish I was not to have divorced Michael and gone to my American lover. Now I see how much courage you have, don't be surprised to hear from me when I get to America, as I have decided to go through with a divorce and go there and marry him. He is still single and is waiting for me. If I don't do something soon, I know he will be lost to me forever.*"

"*I hope that you will find someone who will be good to you, as you deserve it. I remember our talks when we were first friends, and I know you deserve the best.*"

Nikki promised her that they would keep in touch. She said, "*However, I will write to you at your sister's house, as I don't want Michael to see my letters and tell Roger where I am. I don't want him to know where I am.*"

When they got home that night, Roger looked around at all of her packed bags. She had a separate bag for Paris, as she did not want to open all of the other ones until she needed them. Roger had still not accepted the fact that she was leaving him and that he would never see her again.

She slept very little that night. She was dreaming of the

next couple of weeks with Marcel and she also feared that Roger would try and come to her room as he had quite a bit to drink and she never knew what he would do when he got drunk. As it was, he had stayed in the living room and had kept on drinking until he finally passed out.

Part Six

Paris and Monte Carlo

Chapter Sixty Eight

The next morning everyone was at the plane to see her off. She was glad that she didn't have to be alone with Roger. She could not wait to be on the plane and on her way to Marcel. After that, she would worry about facing the music with her family and making a new life for herself. Roger was very melancholy as he remarked, *"I remember my other Nikki who would not get on a plane."*

She said, *"Your other Nikki has been gone for a long time."*

He realized that this beautiful, self-confident woman was nothing like the clinging vine that he had brought here with him and it saddened him. He found her to be even lovelier as she had matured from a girl into a woman. He also admired the new Nikki, but missed the old one. He knew that she was fading from his life forever.

Nikki's only regret was that she could not tell Roger's parents goodbye and knew that they would be heartbroken when they returned to Casablanca and found her gone. She decided that she would call them when she got back to the States. She did hope that one day she would see them again. As she got on the plane she waved goodbye to everyone, and softly told Roger, "*Now you can fuck every whore in Casablanca and not have to worry about me!*"

When they announced that the plane would be landing in a few moments, Nikki realized that she had slept most of the way. She was completely drained from all of the emotional problems with Roger and had not slept well for weeks. She had refused lunch when it was served, put her seat in the reclining position, and fell into a sound sleep. She realized how relieved she was that it was all over. She powdered her nose and put on fresh lipstick.

As she went through customs she smiled at the men and they passed her through without checking her luggage. She had learned to do this since her arrival in Casablanca. She knew that it would not work when she arrived in the States as a pretty face was not a passport to special privileges at home.

When she came out of customs Marcel was waiting for her with a big grin on his face. She ran into his arms and they stood there kissing and embracing for a long time. At least they were at an airport. People thought nothing of it, as this was always happening. They were either crying or embracing. She felt that it had been a year since he had left Casablanca. Then he said, "*Come, the company has loaned me a beautiful car.*" He told the sky caps to load her luggage into the car, as he opened the front door of the Rolls Royce for her. She was impressed, as she had never been in a car such as this in her life. He drove to the George V Hotel. Again she was impressed when she entered the lobby. It was a magnificent, old hotel. They took the elevator to their suite, which was filled with roses and there was champagne and cheese and fruit on the coffee table. "*What elegance!*" she exclaimed. She could not help but show her surprise and happiness. She reacted exactly as Marcel had hoped she would. She hugged him and kissed him and said, "*Thank you, my darling, you have thought of everything. This past week has seemed like a year to me, but now I know that it was worth it not having you for a week to be able to be with you now.*" Mentally, she was comparing this to the hotel where she had stayed with Roger and there was no comparison. She realized that from now on she would have to put him out of her mind and forget him. Why compare?

Marcel broke into her thoughts with, "*We will have three glorious days here and then I have a wonderful surprise for you!*"

Nikki replied, "*What could possibly be more wonderful than this?*"

Marcel laughed and said, "*You haven't seen anything yet! But now, I am sure that you are tired and hungry.*"

Nikki said, "*Come to think of it I am hungry, as I slept the whole way here and didn't have lunch. I am not tired, but I am excited and I don't want to waste too much time sleeping on this trip. I want to be with you every moment I can. I will have plenty of time to sleep when I get home.*"

Marcel said, "*I will draw you a bath and then we will have some snacks and I will open the champagne and we will drink a toast to our time together. Then we will go out and have the best food in Paris. The tourists do not know of this place. We will go where the Parisians go and we will not run into anyone we know from Casablanca.*"

It was the first time Nikki remembered that they would have to be careful. She had felt so free once the plane took off. She knew that for Marcel's sake they would have to be careful, as he had to go back to Casablanca and live there, whereas she really didn't give a damn who knew about her anymore. She did realize that until Roger signed the divorce papers she would have to play it cool.

"So, tell me, how was the big sendoff? Was Roger still in a bad state?"

Nikki told him about all of her friends coming to the plane to see her off and what a relief it was that she had not had to be alone with Roger.

Marcel said, *"I do feel sorry for him, but I do have to say that it is his entire fault. I could see when you first arrived in Casablanca that you were madly in love with your husband. I envied him, that he had a wife like you. When I first laid eyes on you, I fell for you immediately. I never even hoped that we would be together as we have been. I warned Roger to behave himself, as he has a woman that all the men would envy him for. I knew that I would never have tried to do anything about my feelings for you if Roger had not treated you as he did. I could see the unhappiness on your face and it broke my heart, as I loved you then, but secretly.*

When I realized that he did not deserve you, I decided that I would have you, as I had longed to do from the beginning."

Nikki admitted, *"I was attracted to you from the beginning as well, but I never dreamed that we would end up like this. Had Roger remained faithful to me, I would have been a faithful wife to him. It's true that I might have missed something more than what Roger had to offer me, as I had never been with a man before, except to go out to parties or to a show. I am sure that I would have been curious about what another man would be like, but I could never have cheated on him and been able to look at myself in the mirror if he had remained faithful to me. I suppose it is only natural to be curious about these things, but I never would have dreamed of going to bed with any other man in the beginning of our marriage."*

Chapter Sixty-Nine

When Nikki walked into the bathroom she was in for another surprise. The bath was exquisitely scented and there was a beautiful gown and matching negligee hanging on the door. She realized that he had spent a lot of time planning for her arrival and she loved him even more. She did not know how she would ever be able to leave him. He made her feel so desired and wanted that she almost felt like crying.

After she luxuriated in the bath for a while she heard the door open and Marcel came in. When he climbed into the tub with her, she squealed with delight. It was the first time she had ever made love in the bathtub. When she finally dried herself off, she put on the gown that he had bought for her. When she reached for the negligee he said, "No that is only for when you have to open the door for room service!" She laughed and hung it back up. They went into the bedroom and climbed into the luscious, oversized bed. She had never seen anything like it before. They lay down and made love for the rest of the afternoon. They finally fell asleep in each other's arms and when they woke up it was already dark. Nikki panicked when she realized that she had not unpacked her suitcases and hung up her dresses. She said, "I am so foolish! I am sure that everything will be wrinkled and need pressing!" She opened the bag and started unpacking. When she opened the closet door to hang them up, to her surprise and delight there was a complete Paris wardrobe hanging there. She was overwhelmed with happiness as she said, "Marcel, you are too good to me! I don't feel that I deserve all of this!"

Marcel asked, "Haven't you known me too long to even say this? These have been the happiest days of my life. I finally have a chance to show you how much I really do love you and how much I care."

"But this must have cost you a fortune, darling. I know that you can't afford all of this!" Nikki insisted.

Marcel smiled at her and said, *"You let me worry about that, Mon Cherie!"*

Later on when she started to comb her hair and put on her make-up, she noticed that Marcel was getting into his clothes for the evening and she realized that he had bought some beautiful clothes for himself as well. He had never seemed to have been that fond of good clothes, but she realized that he wanted to look his best when he escorted her around Paris.

She commented on his good looking suit and he said, *"I have to look good when I am with the most desirable woman in Paris, don't I?"*

Nikki laughed and said, *"Do you realize that this will be the first time that we will be able to go out in public alone? We have never even had a meal by ourselves. It is true that we all went out together, but even that has been a long time ago. When I think of you and me, all alone, going where we want to go and doing what we want to do, it really makes me feel wonderful inside. I can't believe that all of this is happening!*

Marcel replied, *"I too have dreamed of this ever since we made our plans. We shall take advantage of all of the times that we could not do it."* He added, *"I only wish that it would not have to end, Nichole."* He was very serious when he said this. He told her that he planned to go with her on the boat train and see her on board the ship.

Nikki got a sick feeling inside of her when she thought of the day they would inevitably have to say goodbye. She finally said, *"Let's not talk about that now; I don't want to think about it. As Scarlet O'Hara always said, "I'll think about that tomorrow."*

Marcel looked puzzled and asked, *"Who is Scarlet O'Hara?*

Nikki laughed and asked, *"Didn't they ever show "Gone with the Wind" over here?"*

Marcel said, *"You know that I never go to movies."*

Nikki was thinking to herself, one thing about Roger and her, they had both loved the same type of movies and they had both loved to dance. They had had a lot in common, but she now wondered if she would ever meet anyone in the future who would be as compatible. Here she was with Marcel, happier than she had ever been, but he was not fond of dancing and he did not like shows or movies. Then she said, *"It's a good thing that I saw all of the club shows when I was here before."*

Marcel insisted, *"I'll take you anyplace you want to go. However, we would be taking a chance of running into people from Casablanca, as they all come to Paris to do these things. When I said that I never go to shows, it was because I never had anyone that I wanted to go with before. I want you to be happy Nichole and I will do whatever you want."*

She smiled at him and said, *"You don't have to worry about that, darling. I don't want to waste our precious time with shows anyway. I just want us to be together and alone as much as possible. That is all I care about."*

He looked pleased as he pulled her up and kissed her. *"I was hoping that was how you felt, as I feel the same way, Mon Cherie."*

In a few minutes they were dressed and Nikki had on one the exciting dresses that Marcel had bought for her. He let out a whistle and said, *"You look even lovelier than I imagined. The dress was not as attractive on the model as it is on you. I know your figure pretty well, as it fits to perfection!"* He looked pleased with himself and Nikki thought that sometimes he looked like a little boy when he was so happy.

She asked, *"How did you do it?"*

He is answer was that he would look at a model about her size and say, *"A little more up there."* They were both laughing as they walked down the hall to the elevator. As they went through the lobby, many admiring glances came their way. Marcel said *"You see? They are all looking at you!"*

Nikki answered that the women were looking at him as well. Marcel proudly replied, *"We are both beautiful!"* Nikki loved his carefree way. She had never seen him like this, as in Casablanca they had not been able to be themselves and were not as relaxed as they walked along arm in arm. He asked, "*Do you want to take a taxi or walk? It is not very far from here.* They decided to walk. When they arrived at the restaurant she saw that it was small, but elegant. The maitre'd met them at the door and seated them at a table. He evidently knew Marcel, as he had not given his name. He told Nikki that he ate here always when in Paris, because the food was always excellent and it was never full of tourists. Nikki was soon to find out that he had not exaggerated. Everything they put in their mouths was delicious, but she only ate a small portion of each course. Marcel, noticing this, asked, "*Are you not happy? You eat like a bird!*" Nikki explained that she was too excited to eat very much and also that she had been eating so little as of late that she had shrunk her stomach. Marcel was concerned about her as he knew that she had not eaten all day. Finally he said, "*When we go back to the hotel, I will order something to put in the refrigerator in our suite in case you get hungry. You are getting very thin again Nicole. I don't want you to look as you did when you came out of the hospital. You have to have small amounts at a time so that you can get your stomach back to normal.*" Nikki smiled and said, "*Don't worry darling, I will get my appetite back, you will see. In fact you will be sorry as it will cost you a lot of money to feed me.*"

He laughed and said, "*We'll come back another night when we have stretched your stomach a little bit. It is so delicious I cannot bear to see you not be able to eat it.*"

Nikki remembered how frugal the French were when it came to using up food and asked him to forgive her. She promised she would try and do better the next time.

When they left the restaurant they went to a small café

where they had a typical French orchestra. Nikki loved French music. They used accordions and violins and it was so beautiful. The French songs were either very happy or very sad. There was no in-between. They danced to a couple of slow pieces and Nikki found herself cuddling up to Marcel as she had done so many times in Casablanca. He said, *"If you keep this up we will have to go back to the hotel!"*

He had so much sex drive. He could go four or five times in one day and she had been shocked when she had realized this. Roger had never been able to do it more than twice a day, even when they had first married. She supposed it was true what they said about the French, that they were over-sexed. She was smiling as she thought about it and Marcel asked her, *"What are you smiling about. What's going on in that pretty little head of yours?"*

She told him what she had been thinking about and she spoke in English so that the others would not understand her, as the music was loud and she had to speak louder than she wanted to. He held her close and they finished the dance. When they got back to the table he ordered some brandy and then asked for the check. He turned to her and said, *"Nicole, I am going to show you what this Frenchman can do!"* He had a look of happiness on his face that she had ever seen before. He was radiant and she knew that she was also.

When they came out of the café, Marcel ordered a taxi. When they got in, he told the driver to take them back to the hotel. This was the first time he had not asked Nikki what she wanted to do. When they got to their suite he commanded, *"Get undressed."* That night, he made love to her in a way that she had never had it before. He used every trick he knew and they were both in such ecstasy that they would not have known if the hotel had been swallowed up into the earth. She knew that she would never find an American that would be able to please her as he did and she felt that she didn't want anyone if she couldn't have him. When they finally fell exhausted into each others arms she asked, "*Why have you waited so long to show me how a Frenchman makes love?*" He replied, "*Because I was afraid that I would frighten you. I have wanted to do this ever since we first started seeing each other, but I didn't know how you would react.*"

"*My God, I have never known anything like this in my life. It was wonderful. I hope that you will not be afraid to show me new things now.*"

Marcel laughed and said, "*I have shown you everything tonight. What more could there be?*"

She agreed that she could not think of anything. They fell asleep in each other's arms and woke up the same way in the morning. Nikki went to the bathroom and used the bidet. She certainly had learned by now what it was for and how to use it. She realized that the Americans were missing a very convenient bathroom fixture. When she came back into bed, Marcel rolled over and they made love again. She felt like she had died and gone to heaven and told this to Marcel.

He said, "*Heaven will never be like this. Nothing could be as wonderful. It is so good to be with the person you truly love. Do you realize that you are the only woman I have ever been in love with in my whole life? Nicole, I don't know what I will do when you leave.*"

They ordered breakfast up to the suite and Nikki realized that she was famished. She wanted a large breakfast, not a continental one as they usually had. When she got through giving her order to Marcel, he started laughing until the tears rolled down his face. Then he said, *"Now I know how to give you an appetite!"*

Nikki started laughing with him and they were both crying, as they laughed so hard. It was not that it was so funny, but they both realized that they were so happy and could not seem to handle it. They were doing what they had both dreamed of doing from the day they had met, two years ago. They were not missing out on a moment of their time together, except for the few hours that they slept and even then, they were always in each others' arms.

The breakfast finally arrived. Nikki could hardly wait until the waiter left so that she could dive into the food. As she ate she said, *"They have to be so perfect! A person could starve to death before they get through!"*

Marcel watched as she ate heartily and was pleased to see that she had regained her appetite. She had ordered a typical American breakfast, but in the place of toast were the heavenly croissants. Marcel had ordered a continental breakfast, as he was not accustomed to eating very much in the morning. Nikki had gotten out of the habit of eating a large breakfast since she had arrived in Casablanca, as they always had a big lunch at noon. However, this morning she was famished, and she was having it all. She ate until she thought she would explode and begged Marcel to eat some of it.

He said, *"No, you have to eat all of it. You are the one who ordered it."*

She looked at him and asked, "*Can I just rest for a while?*"

He laughed and said, "*You always take me seriously. Don't you know when I am joking?*" With that she pushed herself away from the table.

They lounged around for a while and finally decided to get dressed and go to the park, as it was a beautiful day. Here she was, in Paris, and it was spring again. She supposed that she was just lucky, as she had certainly not planned it this way. She thought of the first time she had come here and how excited she had been. She had thought that she would never enjoy it again as much as the first time, as it had been so exciting and she had had such a fantastic time, but she was finding out that it was more exciting now, as she was with Marcel. When she had been there with Roger, she was still feeling the hurt of his affair with Carla and though she had tried to tell herself that she had forgiven him, she knew deep down that she would never be able to do so. Also, she had thought about Marcel at the time and had secretly wished that she was with him. Now her dreams had come true and she realized that she had loved Marcel so much even then, that there would have been no hope for her to love Roger as she had before.

Nikki looked at Marcel and suddenly said, "*We forgot to celebrate our anniversary!*"

Marcel looked puzzled and asked, "*What are you talking about?*"

She explained to him that it was well over a year since they had started seeing each other. Marcel said, "*Well, it is never too late!*"

She laughed as she put on one of her daytime frocks that he had bought for her. She looked at herself in the mirror and was pleased with the way she filled it in. Marcel was watching her and said, *"You will have to let me pick out your clothes from now on, Nicole."*

She said that she wished that he could. As she began to think about the time when they would have to say goodbye she got a pained look on her face. When Marcel saw it, he knew what she was thinking and said, *"You will worry about that tomorrow, Cherie!"*

She laughed and said, *"You catch on fast, don't you?"* They both laughed, trying to cover up the feelings that they were sharing at that time. They were determined not to let it ruin their time together.

Chapter Seventy

They walked to the park and decided to take a ride in the horse and buggy. Afterwards they sat and watched a marionette show that they played for the children. The puppets were very cleverly made and they were both laughing as they sat and enjoyed it. Suddenly Nikki realized that Marcel was actually enjoying the silly thing and she teased him about it. He said, "I enjoy everything when I am with you, Nicole." No matter where they went or what they did, they were having a wonderful time. Every day Nikki put on one of her new outfits that Marcel had bought for her. She could see that he had so carefully selected them and he was so delighted with her reactions. When they would get back to the hotel they would be exhausted, but not so much so that they could not make love.

On the third day, Marcel said, "*Get dressed, we are going shopping.*"

"*Shopping for what?*" *Nikki asked.*

Marcel said, *"I want to buy you something special that you will always remember me by while we are apart."*

She asked, *"Do you think that I need something to remember you by?" I would like it if we could have our picture taken together. I will always have that. I want that more than anything as you do realize that I have no picture of you."*

He agreed, *"It is true that I have none of you either, although I could never forget your lovely face if twenty years went by, but I would like to have one also. The only one that I have is one that Roger sent of the two of you after you were married and I don't think I will want to look at that one.*

When they finished dressing they went to the portrait studio and had their picture made. Marcel asked the photographer if they could have a rush job on it. The photographer was insulted said, *"My work is a work of art! I cannot rush it and do it well."* Marcel then asked how long it would take and he answered, *"It will be at least a month before it is ready."* Marcel slipped his hand in his pocket and took out fifty thousand francs. Nikki figured that it was five hundred francs to the dollar and he was giving the man a hundred dollars. He asked the photographer if that would help rush it a little and the photographer grinned from ear to ear and asked, *"When do you want it?"*

Marcel answered, *"Tomorrow!"*

"I will stay up all night and finish this for you," the photographer lied. *"You may pick it up at two o'clock."*

Marcel and Nikki left the shop and he hailed a cab. She was not sure where they were going, but Marcel seemed determined to take her to wherever it was. They pulled up in front of a very expensive looking jewelry store. Nikki asked, "*Why are we going here?*"

Marcel said, "*Because I want to buy you something very special.*"

She said "*You have already spent a fortune on me and we still have over a week to go!*"

Marcel complained, "*You just won't let me spoil you, will you!*" It was more like a statement than a question.

Nikki said, "*You have already spoiled me!" You have spoiled me for any other man. I will never marry again, as if I can't have you, I don't want anyone. I love you with all my heart and you don't have to buy my love!*"

Marcel smiled and didn't answer. When they entered the store he turned to Nikki and said, "*I want you to pick out something magnificent and I want you to promise me that you will never take it off!*"

She was afraid to argue with him, as he was speaking in a commanding voice again. It was an impressive store and Nikki looked at the less expensive things. Marcel took her arm and led her to the display of diamond jewelry. She said, "*Marcel, I can't let you do this.*"

He argued, "*If I didn't want to do this, I wouldn't!*" He asked the jeweler to pull out a tray of diamond bracelets. He picked one up that was exquisite. The diamonds were set completely around it and they started from large ones on the top, tapering to smaller ones as they went around the back. The smallest diamond had to be at least one carat and the largest one had to be at least five or six carats. Nikki could not believe her eyes.

She said, "*Marcel, it will cost you a fortune.*"

He asked, "*What I want to know is, do you like it?*"

Nikki answered, "*Who wouldn't like it?*"

Marcel told the jeweler that he wanted it engraved and that they would wait for it. He told him to engrave it, "*To my future wife, Nicole from Marcel.*" When the jeweler walked away, Nikki said, "*You know that is not possible, Marcel.*"

He looked at her and said, "*Everything is possible, Cherie.*"

The rest of the day and night, Nikki was so busy looking at her bracelet, she hardly noticed anything else. Marcel finally said, "*If I had known it would turn your attention away from me, I would have waited until just before you left before I gave it to you!*" She promised that she would not look at it except when he was not in the room.

That night they went back to the small restaurant where they had eaten the first night. This time Nikki ate everything they put in front of her. She was determined to please him. They drank to everything that they could think of and Marcel informed her that this would be their last night in Paris. She looked sad when he said it, but he smiled and said, "*There are other places in France besides Paris, Nicole. The best is yet to come!*" She looked at him and could not imagine anyplace more wonderful than Paris. "*We will leave tomorrow at three forty-five. I have reserved our place on the plane. I had planned to drive, but I decided I did not want take that much time. I want you in my arms every moment that we are together.* Besides, we will have a car when we get there."

"*Where are we going?" Nikki asked. "I cannot stand the suspense!*" He didn't say anything and she decided not to insist on his telling her, as she knew that he wanted to surprise her.

Besides, she knew that once they got to the airport she would know where they were going. They decided to go back to the hotel early.

"You will have to get up early tomorrow, as you will have to pack. "I will go and pick up the portraits while you are packing." Marcel had not forgotten anything. Nikki liked that about him. She felt that he was the most thoughtful man she had ever met, but she had not known any other man intimately before she had married Roger.

Chapter Seventy-One

The next morning they were awakened by the hotel, as they had left a call. Nikki got up and decided to take her bath first. "Do you want to take your bath now, or shall I?" She asked. "We will both take our bath." Marcel laughed. "We will leave Paris as we arrived!" Nikki laughed and went in to run the bath. She poured in the scent that Marcel had bought as they got into the tub together, laughing playfully. He bathed her and she bathed him. They finally finished and got out of the tub to dry off. "That tub will never have such a good time again," he laughed. "I know it will miss us!" Nikki agreed. She began to pack and suddenly she realized that there was no way she could ever get her wardrobe into her bags. Marcel had been waiting for this moment and as he watched her struggle for a while he finally broke down and started laughing as he went to his closet and brought out the new set of luggage he had purchased for her at the same time he had bought her wardrobe. Nikki was amazed, "You think of everything!" She again realized how thoughtful he was.

She had never had a complete set of luggage, only odds and ends, and she was thrilled to have a full matching set, besides all of her lovely new clothes to fill them up. "Now I will travel in style." She exclaimed. She threw her arms around him and began kissing him. Marcel was enjoying her reactions to everything he had done and said, "Well, we don't want the servants to think that we are poor, do we?" She looked at him and asked, "What servants?" Marcel realized that he had almost given his surprise away and finally told her that they were going to Monte Carlo where he had a villa reserved with a car and servants. "Now we can play house, we won't have to leave the villa if we don't want to. We will have a chef, who is supposed to be one of the finest in the area." Nikki was elated and said, "We can pretend that we are married." Marcel answered, "The servants think that we are on our honeymoon, as that is what the office told them when they informed them that we were coming."

Marcel left to get the portraits and Nikki was hoping that the man would have them ready. She was anxious to see how they came out. He had made one for each of them. She wondered where Marcel would keep his, without someone seeing it, but decided not to ask him as she didn't want to ruin the pleasure he was deriving from it. She continued to pack and decided to leave her old luggage behind, as everything fit into the eight pieces of luggage that Marcel had bought for her. It was really beautiful luggage and she was proud of it and could not believe that it really belonged to her. She decided to leave one open for the portraits, as Marcel had already finished packing.

Nikki was thinking seriously now and wondering to

herself if she would ever really marry Marcel. She knew that she loved him with all her heart, but she also was afraid of getting hurt again. She had never felt this way about Roger, as she was so young when she married him and probably didn't really know what true love was. When she left Roger, she had made a vow to herself that no one would ever hurt her again. She was also trying to decide what to do with her life. She knew that she would have to go home and get her divorce, but didn't know if she would want to remain there permanently, as she felt that she had outgrown her home town. She did not like the thought of burying herself there, as she would never go back to the small circle of women who did nothing much with their lives except gossip. She was sure that the city had grown and the people had grown with it, but it was still a far cry from what she had become accustomed to. She was seriously thinking of going to New York and trying to become a model, as it had always appealed to her, but she had been twenty when she had been offered the job and now she was twenty-four. She wondered if she stood a chance, but with her new stylish Paris wardrobe, she decided that she could at least give it a try. She felt that it might impress the designers if they saw that she was well dressed in her Paris creations. If all else failed, she knew that she could always go back to secretarial work, although she had never really liked doing that type of work. She was confused when she thought about what she would do, but decided to worry about that when she got home. She did not want to think of anything that would mar her happiness while she was with Marcel.

When Marcel got back with the portraits, she was delighted with the way they had turned out. The man had really flattered both of them and truly was an artist. When she said this to Marcel he said, "You are a beautiful woman and so is your portrait." He refused to believe that it had flattered either of them. She laughed when he insisted that they both looked as good, if not better than the portrait.

Chapter Seventy-Two

When they boarded the plane she was anxiously looking forward to their next adventure. She was going someplace new and Marcel and only Marcel would be the one to show it to her. She loved the idea. When she mentioned it to him he said, *"I am also happy about it, as I want to take you someplace that will belong to you and me alone." I have never been able to do this before and I am looking forward to it as much, if not more, that you are."*

Everything they did was first class. She had never realized that Marcel was so wealthy. He lived very modestly and dressed that way as well. His home was very modest. He was very low key and she doubted that anyone, including Roger, really knew how wealthy he was. Most of the people in Casablanca who were wealthy built mansions and flaunted their wealth. No one knew that Marcel had money. She knew that Roger would be surprised if he found out. Finally she said, *"I would never have known that you are as wealthy as you are, you never let on to anyone that you have this kind of money."*

Marcel smiled and said, "*Well, at least I know that you love me for me and not my money.*" Then he said seriously, "*Why spend it when there is no one you want to share it with. I was waiting until I met the right woman so that I could spoil her.*"

Nikki could not help but feel sorry for Juanita, as she lived so frugally. She had no jewelry except for a simple wedding band and she made all of her own clothes. That was the only thing that went against Nikki's grain. It seemed so unfair, as she had given him three children. She had always heard that the mistresses were the ones who lived the most lavishly in this country and was finding out that it was true. She decided not to mention it to him, as she didn't want to make him angry and spoil their last days together.

When she became quiet, Marcel must have realized that she was thinking and he was the one that brought it up. "*Nicole, you must know that I have never loved Juanita. It is true that I married her, but it was to give my children a name and to keep me out of the service so that I could provide for them. There were many others who slept with her before I came along, and I have never had the respect for her that a man should have for his wife. I have provided for her and will continue to do so as long as I live, but when I die, my money will go to my children, unless I can obtain a divorce and marry you.*"

Nikki didn't say anything and he assumed that it was because she had her doubts about marrying him. "*Nicole that is why I was so angry with Roger when he treated you as he did. You didn't deserve that kind of treatment. I would never have treated my wife as I did Juanita, had she been like you. We would not have to live in Casablanca.*" He added, "*I could just as well open a plant in Paris. You would never have to go back there at all.*"

Nikki replied, *"I would have to think about this for a while Marcel. I want a husband who would be faithful to me and in this country there is no such thing. It is true that in America many men do run around on their wives, but as a rule, if they are compatible and happy, they are faithful to them. I don't want to be hurt again. I love you with all my heart; but if you were to cheat on me, I think it would kill me. I never loved Roger as I do you. I was too young to know the meaning of love when I married him. I wanted to love him, because I was not happy with my life as a child and I wanted to get away. You are the kind of man that women chase and sooner or later you would not be able to resist them. You would find the younger women more appealing.*

Marcel was upset when she said that and he asked her, *"Did you forget that I will get older too? My birthday is the day after Roger's, we are the same age."* He was pleading with her now, *"Nicole, I could never tire of you, I love you too much. Please let us not speak of it anymore. We can both get our divorces and I will establish my business in Paris. Meanwhile when we are apart, we will write to each other and you will have time to decide what you want to do. I could never hurt you, Nicole, that I promise with my life!"*

Nikki agreed that she would have ample time to decide what she wanted to do. She could see that Marcel was unhappy and she said, *"I don't want to say anything that will spoil our time together. I know that we love each other and that is enough for now. By the way, how long can you stay away from Casablanca?"*

Marcel answered that he could stay as long as she wanted him to. He had attended to his business in Paris before she arrived and the materials were being shipped to Casablanca.

He had a good man there who could run things for him for a while. He asked *"How long do you think that you can stay?"*

Nikki thought for a few moments and said that her family had no idea when she was coming, as she had told them she didn't know. *"Roger can't call the United States from Casablanca so he won't have any idea when I arrive. I can stay longer than the two weeks we planned. Do you think that we will be able to keep the villa?"*

Marcel nodded and said, *"I can keep it as long as I want."*

Nikki was happy, as she decided that she was going to live her life to the fullest and was going to enjoy every day she could, as she knew that when she got home it would be boring, at least compared to what she was doing now. The only thing that she didn't like was that it would delay her residency of six months before she could file for divorce and it would be another month before her divorce would become final if Roger didn't give her any trouble about signing the papers. That had worried her, but he had told her that he would give her a divorce and she just hoped that he would keep his word.

She looked out of the window just as they were circling over Monaco. She caught her breath as she looked at the Mediterranean Sea. Marcel explained that Monaco lies along the Cote d'Azur, a short distance west of Italy. He informed her that it is surrounded on three sides by France and the fourth side by the Mediterranean Sea. He told her that it was a principality of its own and ruled by the Prince. *"Monte Carlo is to the North of Monaco. I have asked for a villa with the best possible view, so we will be up in the high area where the Palace is located."*

Nikki had heard of Monte Carlo and also about the casinos. She wondered if they would go there, but decided not to ask. This was Marcel's show, and she would let him make the suggestions. The seat belt sign came on and they were about to land.

Chapter Seventy-Three

On their arrival they were met by their chauffer. He had a beautiful Rolls Royce Limousine waiting for them. He loaded the luggage into the car and they drove to the villa. The scenery was magnificent. Nikki didn't think about being nervous as they drove up the mountain. She felt light-headed as they went higher. Normally she would have been a wreck, as when they had driven into the Atlas Mountains in Marrakech she had been in a cold sweat. She felt so safe with Marcel, as if he could protect her.

When they approached the villa she was in for still another surprise. It was a mansion, with terraces overlooking the beautiful city and the Mediterranean. As they walked into the villa, it was as if they were entering a scene in a movie. Marcel had never been to this villa and he was just as elated as she was. She turned to him and said, "*This must have cost you a fortune!*"

Marcel explained that it belonged to one of the large companies that he did most of his business with and it was not costing him a single franc. "Some of the large companies in Paris keep villas staffed at all times for their better clients. This is one of them. They have others, but they assured me that this was the most elegant and it is true. The only thing that I will pay for is to tip the servants so that they will give us their best service."

"I don't see how it could be more beautiful than this." Nikki said. The bags were carried upstairs to the master suite which was magnificent. It alone was as large as an average size house with a long terrace. There were tables and chairs where she supposed they could be served their breakfast and they could sun bathe. The bathroom was made of marble and the tub was like a small swimming pool. She looked at it and turned to him and said, *"We can have lots of fun playing in this one!"*

He laughed and said, *"I was thinking the same thing! You know, we are acting like children!!"*

Nikki laughed and said, *"Isn't it fun being children again?"* He agreed.

One of the servants took them on a tour of the house. The living area was tremendous and beautifully furnished. There was a large, grand piano. *"This would be a great place to entertain if we had someone to invite." Nikki exclaimed.*

Marcel replied, *"You are the only one I want to entertain."* Again they laughed. It seemed that all they did was laugh. They were having the time of their lives and enjoying their freedom that they had so longed for.

The dining room had a long table that would probably seat at least thirty people. Nikki was wondering if they were going to eat there. As it turned out, they had most of their meals on the terrace, off of the living room area, except for breakfast, which was served to them on the terrace of the master suite.

When the tour was over the maid asked Nikki to show her which bags she wanted unpacked. Nikki felt like a queen. She had never had this kind of service before. She had packed her light weight clothes in one large bag and her shoes and bags in another. The maid began to unpack her bags and hang up her clothes. When she found a wrinkle in something, she would put it aside and say that she would press it. The valet was doing the same thing for Marcel. As the two of them walked out of the bedroom, Nikki told Marcel, *"I feel like I am of royalty. I have never had such service in my life!"* Marcel admitted that he too felt that way as it was the first time for him as well. Though he could have used the villas and had this kind of service, he had never accepted it, as he had no one he wanted to take there before Nikki.

When they finished unpacking, Marcel said, *"I am going to get out of this suit and get into something cooler."* When he left the living room Nikki found herself going to the piano. She had not had a piano to play since she and Roger had married and she could not resist it. She sat down and decided to see if she could remember anything that she had learned as a girl. She tried one of her favorites, which she had played so many times. It was Moonlight Sonata. Before she knew it, she was playing and had not forgotten it as she had played it so many times before. He fingers were a little stiff, but she kept on playing and by the time Marcel came out of the bedroom, she was so wrapped up in it that she did not even notice when he came into the room. She was in such a happy mood and it reflected in her music, the feeling was there. She had always had a beautiful touch to the piano and at one time in her life she had wanted to make a career of it, but she had never had the opportunity to continue with it, as she had married so young. When she finished, she heard Marcel applauding her. *"You are full of surprises, Nicole. I didn't know that you played the piano."*

She replied, *"I wanted to make it my career, but then I married so young and Roger never was able to buy me a piano. I have not played in a long time."* She finally played another piece that she had loved, *"Fur Elise"*.

Marcel was impressed now. He said, *"I expect you to play for me every day that we are here."* Her answer was that she could entertain him much better in the bedroom. He insisted that she would have to play for him every day.

As they relaxed and lay back on the terrace he asked her, *"What would you like to do tonight? Would you prefer to go out to the casino or would you like to spend a quiet even at home?"* Nikki thought a moment and replied, *"We have been running so much in Paris and I would love to relax tonight. We have plenty of time to see everything.*

"Good girl!" Marcel said happily. *"I was hoping that is what you would say."*

That evening they had their dinner served to them on the terrace. The chef informed them that he had selected the menu for them, as they had not been there to give him their preferences the night before. They sat on the terrace and could see the city as the lights went on as it was becoming dark. Nikki sighed and said, *"We could not have a more magnificent view. I am glad that we came here."*

"I told them to reserve the villa with the best view and the

best chef." They could not have asked for more. The dinner was excellent and was served with perfection. Marcel complimented the chef on the dinner and told him to make the selections on the menu every day. He told him that he would inform him when they would not be eating there. They could see that the chef could not have been more pleased. "*They are so proud of their profession.*" exclaimed Nikki after he left.

Marcel explained, "*In France they go to school to learn their profession. The chefs and waiters all go to school. That is why they are so proud and do everything so well.*"

Nikki was thinking about the restaurants at home. She said, "*At home most of the restaurants throw the food at you. You would hate it. Of course we have some fine restaurants that serve excellent food and wonderful service, but they are the ones that import them from Europe and they are very expensive. The average person cannot afford to eat there. Here no matter how insignificant a restaurant is, you always have delicious food and great service. It's a wonder the people here are not all fat.*"

Marcel explained that most of the people have their main meal at noon and eat out at night occasionally. "*We are tourists and therefore have been eating large dinners, but the average native does not do this. Also, they do a lot of walking here and they walk off their dinner.*" *She had noted that the* average Frenchman was not fat; in fact they were quite lean. She said, "*At home we do not have siesta as you do. People grab a quick bite at noon and their main meal is at night. That is why so many Americans are over-weight. The men would never come home at noon for their main meal. . Americans are very competitive, and many times they do not even stop to eat lunch. I know that when*

I worked, many times I did not go out to eat, as I had too much work to get out. Your way of life is much better than ours. You know that in New York you can come home at three o'clock in the morning and buy your groceries for the day. The competition is so great that many stores stay open all day and night."

"You do not know how to live and enjoy life in America," Marcel commented. I could never go at that pace. I would be no good for you in bed at night if I did."

Nikki thought of it and decided that was why the Frenchmen were so active sexually. She said *"At home the men come home tired and want their slippers and papers and fall asleep in their chairs. I realize that we are missing a lot in our country."*

Marcel remarked, *"You will find it difficult when you get home, as you have become accustomed to our way of life here. Are you not sorry to be going home?"*

"I have to go home to get my divorce." Nikki explained, *"And besides, I want to see my family. It has been two years since I have seen them and that was for only a week, as I had been living in New York for two years before that. After I get home I know that I will be sorry, but I don't know how I can live in this country. My French is not that adequate that I could work as a secretary. What could I do? I may be able to model in New York, but here the models are so tall and without curvses and I don't have that kind of figure. Your women are built like little boys."*

Marcel laughed and said, *"I never thought of that, but you are right. I prefer your figure any time. I like the curves!"*

They sat in silence for a while, just looking at the city lights and sipping their brandy. Finally Marcel said, *"Now I want a concert!"* Nikki refused saying that she had not played in a long time. She insisted she had played two pieces that she had known the best and she was very rusty. Marcel looked puzzled and asked her what she meant by rusty. She realized that she had used a term again that he was not familiar with. She explained to him what it meant and said, "*When you don't practice all the time, this is what happens.* She explained that her fingers were not as agile as they needed to be to play well and even if she had sheet music, she would not play as well as she had.

"It was beautiful. I want you to play it again."

She laughed and went inside and sat down at the piano. She said, *"I see that you are going to make me work for my supper!"* He followed her in with two glasses of brandy. He sat on the piano bench next to her as she began to play. As he closed his eyes she could see that he was relaxed and enjoying it. She was pleasing him and thought that is what it is all about! She wanted to please him more than anything in the world. He had been so good to her and she could never refuse him anything. As she played, she saw her diamond bracelet sparkling brilliantly under the soft lights. He had made her feel like a queen. She knew that if for the rest of her life she did not have anything wonderful happen to her, she was having enough now to last a lifetime.

Chapter Seventy-Four

After Nikki had left, Roger was feeling worse than he had ever felt in his life. He was wondering to himself how he could have let the one woman, whom he had loved more than any other in the world, walk out of his life. He knew that it would have been impossible to hold her, as he had lost her love. He was so angry with himself for having given her reason to leave him. He knew that it was his entire fault and could not understand what had driven him to do the things that he had done.

On the way back from the airport he had cried as he had never cried before. He could not forget how happy she looked when she boarded the plane to leave him. He knew that he had to let her go, but he could not accept the fact that she was lost to him forever. When they had all left the airport, Monique had put her hand on is arm and said, *"Roger, if you feel that you need someone to talk to, call me. I can see that you are hurt now and that you will need to talk."*

Roger thanked her and walked to his car.

It was now four days since Nikki had left and it seemed like a month to him. He supposed that she was on the ship, on her way back to the States, going further and further away from him. He felt that she might call his folks and decided to write them a letter. He sat down at his desk and started writing and before he knew it, he had written everything that had happened. He did not want them to hate Nikki, as he was sure that he never could. It had not been her fault and he knew he had been a rotten husband to her. He even told them that he had an affair while overseas. He wanted them to know how rotten he really was. He didn't know why he was doing this, but thought that by wiping his slate clean his sins would be forgiven. He imagined that it was like going to confession, except that he was not Catholic and there was no priest to confess to. He asked his parents to forgive him his weaknesses and as he wrote he cried. He had never felt so broken up in his entire life.

He was remembering how innocent Nikki was when he first met her and after they were married, how she had looked up to him and leaned on him for so many things. He knew that she had changed because of him and because of the fact that he was not any good.

That night he went out and got drunk. He got so drunk that he did not even know how he got home. At first he thought that Marcel must have brought him home, but then he remembered that Marcel was still in Paris and had put Nikki on the boat train. Suddenly he realized that Marcel had not returned and he knew that he had been gone for quite a while. He was curious about why he had been gone so long. It occurred to him that when he had so generously offered to help Nikki, he could have had something on his mind and his imagination began to run away with him. He remembered how he had looked at her from the time they had first come to Casablanca and he knew that Marcel would take advantage of a situation like this. After all, Nikki was going home for a divorce, why wouldn't he use this opportunity. He felt that he could be with her in Paris now, and he realized how stupid he had been when he had trusted him.

He looked at his watch and it was eleven o'clock. He had slept late, but he was hung over and not in the mood to do business today. He called the office and told them that he would not be in. Then he called Marcel's office and asked his secretary if she had heard from him. She knew which side her bread was buttered on and said only that he had extended his trip to Paris, as he had a lot of business to attend to. Roger asked her where he was staying and she replied *"I don't know. He said that if I needed to reach him that I should call the company in Paris."* Roger asked for the number of the company.

When Roger hung up, he called the steamship line that Nikki had sailed from. He asked if she had arrived safely. After holding the line for five minutes, the girl came back to the phone and said, *"She had her reservations cancelled."* Now Roger was sure that something was amiss. He called the company in Paris and asked where Marcel Beret was staying.

The secretary said, *"I don't know sir. I will have to put my employer on the phone."*

When the man answered, Roger tried to keep his voice calm. He said, *"This is a friend of Marcel Beret and it is very urgent that I reach him. Could you please tell me what hotel he is staying at?" The man's voice came back with an echo. He is not it Paris now, he went to the Riviera to rest before returning to Casablanca."*

Roger asked if there was a phone number where he could be reached and the man had no idea of where he was. He realized that someone was checking up on Marcel and he was sorry he had told the man where he was, as he had asked him not to tell anyone where he could be reached. When he hung up, he called the villa in Monte Carlo and when Marcel answered the phone he told him that a man had called and said that it was urgent that he talk to him. *"Where was he calling from?"* he asked. *"From Casablanca, I believe."* He then added, *"Before I realized what I was doing, I told him that you were in Monte Carlo, that you needed a rest. When he asked if you had a phone number where you could be reached, I told him that I didn't know where you were staying.*

"If he calls back, tell him that I have left the Riviera and you don't know where I am." Marcel commanded.

When Marcel hung up, he was concerned, but decided that he would figure out something to tell him when he got back. He was sure that it was Roger and that he was wondering why he had not returned yet. He decided not to say anything to Nicole, as he did not want her to worry. *"Who was that?"* Nikki asked.

Marcel said, *"You have to know everything, don't you? It was the company in Paris."*

"Who did you tell him to say that you were no longer at the Riviera? She was probing and he had to think fast. *"It was one of the men in Paris who has been trying to reach me. I don't want to talk to him now. I will see him when I get back."*

Nikki seemed satisfied with the answer. He wondered why Roger was trying to reach him and if he had figured out that they were together.

When Roger got the news that Nikki had not taken the ship he felt like there was something rotten in Denmark. Marcel had wired him that he had put her on the boat train and he had to have some reason for lying.

He called Monique and asked her what her plans were for that afternoon. It was raining and he knew that she would not be playing tennis. She answered, "*We can't play tennis, so I imagine we will wind up playing bridge as we usually do when it rains.*"

Roger said, "*Monique, I have not been with anyone since Renee and I cut that affair short. I am lonely and I need you. You know that I wanted you when I first met you and I want to spend the afternoon with you. Why don't you come over to my apartment? I am desperate for a friend.*"

Monique felt sorry for him and decided that she would go. She asked, "*When do you want me to come over?*"

Roger answered, "*As soon as you are free after siesta.*" They hung up and Roger went to clean up. He took a shower and shaved and dressed. He was ready and waiting for her to arrive. He decided what gave him the most satisfaction was the fact that Marcel had wanted her and she would have no part of him. She definitely went for Americans and had no use for Frenchmen. He had never been able to figure her out. He made up his mind that he was now single and he could do anything he wanted to do. He was certain that Nikki was living it up at the Riviera with Marcel and he may as well start living as well. He's been moping around like a sick cow, and he decided that he was going to make it without Nikki. He wondered if he was kidding himself. He still felt the hurt inside of him and he knew that it would be a long time before it would go away. He felt a void in his life that he had never felt before.

He decided not to question Marcel when he got back, as he did not want to give him the satisfaction. He was glad he had not given his name when he called Paris.

Chapter Seventy-Five

Nikki and Marcel were up early in the morning. They had their breakfast on the terrace and when they finished he asked her, *"What would you like to do today? Do you want to go to the beach or would you rather just look around and see what the shops are like?"*

She wanted to buy some gifts for her family and said she would rather look around and do some shopping. Marcel told her to dress up, as if they were not going to the beach; he wanted to take her to a special place for lunch. He told his valet to tell the driver to have the car ready in thirty minutes. They got dressed and were soon on their way.

Nikki was excited, as she had no idea of what they would do and she loved having Marcel take over. As they drove down to the shopping area, she realized how high up their villa was. Marcel told the driver to take them to the shopping area near the Hotel de Paris. He told him to inform the chef that they would not be eating at the villa and that he would call him when they were ready to return to the villa.

They got out of the car and started walking, looking in the different shops as they passed them. Finally he said, "*Wait, we have to go into this one.*" Nikki asked why and he told her she would see. The shop had lovely personal items such as accessories for men and women. He picked up a lovely hand made beaded bag and said, "*I think this is nice. Would you like to have it Nicole? It will go with the white formal dress I bought for you. Tonight we will dress formal, as we will go to the Casino de Monte Carlo.*"

Nikki was excited as she had never been to a casino before. She asked, "*What will we do there?*

He laughed and asked her, "*What do you think we'll do there?*"

Nikki asked, "*Do you like to gamble?*"

"*I don't gamble very often, but when I go to a casino, I gamble!*" he answered.

She told him that she loved the little bag and he purchased it for her. Then he went over to the perfume counter and started smelling the samples. He decided that he liked one of them and bought it for Nikki. She sighed and asked, "*When are you going to stop spoiling me?*"

Marcel was very serious when he said, "*I would like to do it forever. I now want to purchase some gifts for the children. Will you help me?* She told him that she would love to help him and they went into a store where there were many different kinds of clever toys. They selected beautiful dolls for the girls and for the baby they found a stuffed monkey that when wound up, performed for at least fifteen minutes. While he was performing on the trapeze, he smoked a real cigarette and actually puffed on it. They must have played with it for thirty minutes before they bought it. Then Nikki found a white cat that she had to have for her niece. It was dressed in a pink dress and held a fan and a pair of lorgnettes. When wound up, it would turn its head and fan itself and when it tuned its head back it would put the lorgnette up to its eyes. That also ran for about fifteen minutes when completely wound up. They found the animals to be so entertaining and were having such a good time playing with them; they didn't notice that it was time for lunch. Nikki put her own packages with the toys and they asked the shop keeper to hold them for them while they went to lunch. She was happy to do them the favor as they had already spent a lot of money in her shop. The animals themselves were very expensive. Nikki knew that Betty would never have anything like this, as she was sure they didn't have them at home. If they did, they would be imports from France and even more expensive. She had been away for a long time and she really didn't know what they would have at home by now. She was sure that she would have many surprises when she got there.

Marcel insisted on paying for Betty's gift. Nikki was upset, as she wanted to buy things for her sister and aunt and uncle and told him so. He said, "*You save the little money you have, as you will need it when you get home. I doubt that Roger will be sending very much, as he doesn't have any money of his own.*"

He took her arm and they headed for the special place where he wanted to take her for lunch. When they arrived, she was amazed when she looked around. They were going to the Hotel de Paris and across from that was the Casino de Monte Carlo. Also, in the same area was the Café de Paris.

The buildings were so magnificent; Nikki could not believe her eyes. She was sure that it must have taken years to build these buildings as they were so ornate. As they approached the Hotel de Paris, she noted that there were statues built in front of the building. When she looked across at the casino, it was the same type of architecture. She realized now why he had told her to dress up. When they entered the hotel and she saw the main lobby, she couldn't believe her eyes. It was magnificent, with a huge, ornate chandelier hanging from the dome in the center of the room. Surrounding the room were wide arches with columns ending with hand carved display cases with sculptured works of art behind the glass. The floral carpets were carefully laid so that one could see the designed marble floor in between. Nikki assumed that they were Persian carpets, but since she didn't know very much about these things, she didn't ask, as she didn't want to appear ignorant. There were fresh flower displays in the center and around the room. The whole effect was breathtaking. Marcel explained to her that the hotel had opened in Eighteen Sixty-Four along with the casino and the café.

She had even a more pleasant surprise as they entered the dining room. In the place of the carved ceilings and columns in the lobby, surrounding the room were beautiful murals, framed in arches which ended with baroque gold columns. The room was solidly carpeted with floral carpeting. The tables were elegantly set, and they had a buffet display fit for a king. Marcel explained to her that this hotel was probably the most luxurious, refined and prestigious hotel in Europe. He explained to her that all of the royalty had stayed there through the years and still did.

She was eager to go to the elaborate buffets, as they looked marvelous and were displayed beautifully, but Marcel insisted that they would order from the menu at the table. Though she was disappointed, she didn't say anything, as she was sure that Marcel knew what he was doing. When they sat down he said, *"From now on, we will have our main meal at noon and at night we will have a light meal. We are not walking as much as we did in Paris and are having a long holiday and if we eat large meals every night we will gain weight.*

Nikki agreed that it was a good idea as she certainly didn't want to gain weight and outgrow her beautiful wardrobe before she could show it off at home. Besides, the food was so superb that it was difficult to have to pass it up completely. She suddenly realized that Marcel was concerned with his own weight. He was thin and she had never realized that he would worry about these things.

After lunch, Marcel phoned the villa and asked that the driver come and pick them up at the hotel. They took their time having coffee and by the time they finished and he paid for the meal, the driver was there. He was instructed to drive back to the store where they made their purchases and Marcel had him wait while he and Nikki went into the first shop that they had visited to purchase a large bottle of Channel No. 5 for her sister, Shalimar for her aunt and a beautiful wallet for her uncle. Marcel insisted, *"You may as well get some perfume for yourself at the same time, as you might run out of it and I am sure that it is much more expensive at home."* She purchased another bottle of each of the fragrances that she had purchased for her sister and aunt and Marcel purchased some others that he wanted her to try.

They went back to the car and Marcel told the driver to take them home. He was ready for his siesta. Suddenly he turned to Nikki and asked, "*Would you like to see the Palace before we go back?*"

Nikki said she would love to and the driver took them up a winding road where the Palace stood. Though Nikki found it to be beautiful, it was not as ornate as the other buildings she had seen at the hotel and casino and she was not as impressed. Marcel explained that the palace was built in 1215, and though it had been modified through the years by different Emperors, it was still quite medieval. Through the years many new wings and pavilions had been added on to it. All of the rooms had been remodeled over and over again, and he had been informed that it was, indeed, very prestigious on the inside, although there was no such thing as a tour since the Prince lived there.

Finally the driver took them back to the villa. When they went to their bedroom, Marcel said, "*It is siesta time. We will play for a while and sleep a while so that we can enjoy our evening at the casino.*

Nikki agreed that it was a wonderful idea and she noticed that they had already turned down the bed for them.

Marcel went to the bathroom and ran the water in the large tub. In a few moments they were splashing and playing. Finally they washed each other, which had become a ritual by now, and then they dried off and headed for the bed. She loved the gigantic towels that they had in Europe.

"*What will I do when I don't have you anymore?*"

Marcel answered, "*It will not be permanent, I promise you that, Nicole. I will obtain a divorce, no matter how difficult it will be. I wish you would come back to Paris after your divorce is final and stay here and I could see you frequently before my divorce becomes final. I have no idea how long that will take."*

Nikki thought for a moment and said, "*What would I do alone in Paris? I would be very lonely in between visits.*"

Marcel could understand that it would be lonely for her and decided to wait and go to the States and get her when his divorce became final; however, he knew that even if he was able to get one, it would take a long time and he felt sad to think that he would have to wait so long before he would be with his beloved Nicole again.

He had already decided that he would start working on his plans for a new plant in Paris. He then told her, "*I promise you with my life, Nicole, I will never hurt you. I love you more than anything else in the world. I will want to have my children with me, however. Would you mind being an instant mother?*"

Nikki smiled and said, "*I adore your children, but what would poor Juanita do? I feel very badly for her. Here we are, happy, loving each other and making plans to be together while she is at home taking care of the children. Now you talk about taking them away from her as well. It makes me feel terrible. It is bad enough I have taken her husband away from her, but it breaks my heart to think of taking her children away from her as well.*"

Marcel said, "*In Casablanca, the women are used to these things, but I will let them go there for vacations and they will have some time with their mother. That is, if she is respectable and behaves herself. During those vacations, we can come back here to the villa*". He looked at her and said, "*Please say that you will marry me. I do not think that I could live without you Mon Cherie.*

She looked at him and said, "*I promise you I will decide soon. I just might get home and decided I miss you so much that I will write for you to come and get me as soon as we are both free. I feel this way now, but I want to give it a lot of thought.*" She then said, "*Enough of this serious talk for now, it is time to do your daily chores!*"

He smiled and said, "*That's what I love about you, you are so open and honest*".

They fell into bed and into each others arms. They belonged together; there was no doubt about it. Soon they were fast asleep.

Chapter Seventy-Six

Nikki and Marcel slept for the rest of the afternoon and when she awoke it was already dark. She woke Marcel and when he sat up he could not believe his eyes that they had slept into the night. "*We must have been more tired than we realized,*" he remarked. Start getting dressed. Wake me when you are almost ready, as it will not take me long.

Nikki took out the white formal that he had purchased for her in Paris. It was a gorgeous dress, very form fitting with the off the shoulder look. She put on her strapless bra and her panties and hose and went to the dressing table to put on her makeup and comb her hair. She was wearing it down on her shoulders now, and she thought she looked much younger than when she had been wearing it up in Casablanca. She sprayed herself with cologne, and then used the same scent of perfume behind her ears and on the inside of her wrists and elbows. Then she woke Marcel, as she was about to put on her dress and shoes. After she had zipped up her dress she looked in the mirror and said, "Now I wish we had gone to the beach today. This dress would look better if I had a good tan." Marcel looked at her and said, "*Nicole, you look fabulous. You have fair skin and dark hair and you don't need a tan. It is more striking as you are.*" She enjoyed the compliments that he continually fed her. One thing about him, he did not hold back about the way he felt, he was like her in that way. Roger had always been generous with compliments, but was not nearly as affectionate as Marcel was, even before they married. She was wishing that she had met Marcel first and could have come to him as a virgin, she loved him so much. She decided that when she did get back to the States she would behave herself and save herself for the day that they would be together again. Suddenly she realized that she was planning on spending her life with him and said, "*Marcel, I suddenly realized that I cannot bear the thought of being without you. I do not have to think about it. When we both have our freedom, I will marry you.*"

Marcel's face was radiant as he looked at her, almost with disbelief. She had never seen him like this before. He said, "*I knew that you did love me, and could not understand why you could not trust me, as the two things go hand in hand.*"

She answered, "*I know that I cannot live without you my darling. I have to know that when we do part that it will only be temporary. I will go home and get my divorce. When it is final I will go to New York and find a job and wait for you to be free.*"

"*In that case,*" he said, "*I will start working on my plans for the Paris plant as soon as you leave. Nicole, I will make you happy, I promise you that. Now the inscription on the bracelet is true. I feel that you are already my wife. We don't need a piece of paper for that. When I am free to marry you, we will have a civil ceremony when I come to get you. I will come to New York as soon as I am Free.*

They looked at each other, and knowing that their future was set, it took a great burden off of them. Now they would be able to thoroughly enjoy the remainder of their holiday together. The only thing that did sadden them was that there would have to be a temporary separation, for how long, they didn't know. Nikki knew that it would be seven months for her to obtain her freedom; six months to establish her residency again in Texas and thirty days for the final divorce, once it was filed. Marcel had no idea of how long he would have to fight to obtain his divorce, but if Nikki knew him, she was sure that he would do everything in his power to rush it up so that they could be back together again. Marcel said, *"Tomorrow we will go and buy you an engagement ring!"* He was so happy he was beside himself.

They got into the car and were driven to the casino. This time Marcel told the driver to wait for them. When they arrived Nikki thought that the building was even more exciting at night when it was all lit up. There was a magnificent clock centered between two towers on the top of the building. When they went inside, the casino was very plush and elegant with all of the carvings and arches that she had seen at the hotel and three exquisite chandeliers hanging along the center of the room, which had a dome that was all lit up. There were many people there, handling large oblong objects with different denominations of money printed on them and she realized that this was what they used as chips. Marcel took her over to the roulette table and purchased some chips for her. *"Play!" he said.*

Nikki asked, *"What do I do? I don't know how to play!"* The people around her started to laugh and said, *"She will have beginners luck."* Nikki finally selected numbers six, eight, twenty-five, twenty-nine and thirty-one and placed a chip on each one. The croupier started the wheel and the ball went round and round and finally landed on number twenty-nine. He pushed a large pile of chips to Nikki and her eyes had a surprised look on them. She was stunned. He smiled at her and asked, "Same numbers?" She nodded. Marcel told her to add a chip to each one, as when you win you should double your bet. He started the wheel again and the ball fell on number eight. Nikki let out a squeal of delight as he pushed even a larger amount of chips to her. When Marcel saw how delighted she was he said, *"Double your bets again!"* She did as he told her, placing two more chips on each number. She had no idea of how much the chips were worth. The ball fell on number twenty-nine again and Nikki was almost in hysterics, she was so excited. She had so many chips in front of her by now that she didn't know what to do with them and Marcel had begun cashing them in for francs. Occasionally the ball would miss her numbers and Marcel would say, *"Now go back to one chip again."* This went on for an hour. Nikki was so excited she didn't realize that a large crowd had gathered around watching her. Everyone was talking about the pretty woman in the white dress that was so lucky. After an hour, Marcel, trying to get her attention, asked, *"Have you had enough Nicole?"* She looked at him and knew that he wanted her to quit and said, *"I have had enough"*. When they walked away from the table, after cashing in all of the chips, everyone was looking at her and she felt very self-conscious. She asked Marcel, *"Why are they all staring at me?"*

He replied, "They are saying that the lovely lady is lucky." Nikki blushed. She wished that she could get away from that habit, but she always blushed.

Marcel had stuffed all of the money in his pockets and as they walked out of the casino he said, *"Nicole, you have won twenty-five thousand dollars in American money!"*

She couldn't believe her ears and said, *"I had no idea how much those chips were worth. Now you can make up for all f the money that you have spent on me, or at least part of it."*

He replied, *"No, it is your money, you won it."*

"But you are the one who bought the chips." she argued."

He insisted, *"Tomorrow we will go to the bank and get a cashiers' check made out to you. Then when you get home, you will not have to go to work. By the time it is gone we will be getting married."* "

Nikki said, *"That is a lot of money. I doubt that it will all be gone, unless you think that it will be more than a year before we will be getting married."*

Marcel said, *"Nicole, you have got to start living better and enjoying the better things in life. I want you to live this way when you get to New York. If you run out of money, I will send you more, but I do not want you to have to work. You must enjoy your life from now on."*.

Nikki reached up and kissed him. Then she said, *"How will I ever get along without you?"* She was serious and he knew it. He was glad that they had made a final decision. They went to the café and had a light supper. It was a popular café and was very busy. After they sat down, Marcel ordered a bottle of champagne to celebrate their engagement. They had a light supper and finally went to the car.

Chapter Seventy-Seven

Marcel had been concerned when they left the casino, but he didn't say anything to Nicole, as he was determined not to ruin this wonderful evening of their engagement. He knew that they would have to spend the rest of their time at the villa, or else go back to Paris for the rest of their time together, but was not sure how he would tell her without alarming her. While she was having her lucky streak at the roulette wheel, he had looked around and spotted an older couple from Casablanca. He knew that they were friends of Roger's parents. He felt sure they had seen her, as she had been attracting so much attention when she was winning. She always attracted attention, even when she was not doing anything, he thought, and he knew that they could not take the chance of running around Monte Carlo, as it was now too dangerous. He hoped that they had not realized that it was Nikki, as she did look different with her hair down. He wanted to be sure that she would be able to get her divorce when she got home, but if Roger were to find out that they were together in Monte Carlo, he might become stubborn about signing the papers. Marcel didn't sleep that night, he was trying to figure out an angle, but try as he may, he knew that he would have to tell her.

The next morning when they got up, he asked her if she had enjoyed the evening. Her answer was, "*I have enjoyed every morning, afternoon and night with you, darling. I don't have to win money to have a good time when we are together.* He smiled at her and said, "*We will go and pick out your ring today, but then we will not leave the villa again.*" Nikki looked at him and said, "*I would just as soon be alone with you, darling. We know that soon we will have to go our separate ways for a while. I want you every moment of the time. There is only one thing I want to know, because you seem so serious. Is there something wrong?*"

Marcel hesitated before he spoke and finally said, "*Nicole, I have to be honest with you. I could never lie to you and there is something that I am worried about. Last night at the casino I saw some friends of Roger's parents. I don't know if they saw us or not, but I am sure that with all of the attention that you were attracting, they might have recognized you. It is possible that they didn't, as they would not expect to see you in Monte Carlo. I am sure that by now everyone in Casablanca knows that you have left Roger. It is possible that they thought you resembled someone they knew if they did get a look at you. If they did recognize you and it gets back to Roger, I am afraid that he will give you trouble with the divorce. Up until now, he has felt that it was his entire fault, but now, if he hears that we are together, he might refuse you the divorce to make you suffer. I know how he thinks and I am worried. We must be very careful from now on as it is a small world.*"

Nikki was listening to Marcel, but at the same time he

could see the wheels turning in her head. Finally she said, "*Is that why you told me to quit playing? I thought it was funny that you told me that when I was having such a winning streak. I am not a gambler; that is the first time in my life I have gambled, but I have heard that you never quit when you are winning.*"

Marcel nodded, "*Do you think I would have let you quit? When I spotted them, I wanted to get out of there as fast as possible. I didn't want us to come face to face with them. I didn't want to alarm you, so I took you out of there as soon as possible without saying anything. I did not see them around as we left, but it was still early and I am sure they were still in the casino.*"

Nikki did not react as Marcel had expected. He was sure that she would be upset, but she just looked at him and said, "*If I am cheating on Roger, he gave me good reason. Even if he were to know that we were together he would have no right to say one word about it. After all, I am leaving him to get a divorce and I am sure that he is not sitting at home grieving by now. He is probably out screwing every available woman in Casablanca!*" She added, "*The only reason I do care, is that I know you have to go back there and face him. After all, you have been like brothers all of these years. It is you I feel sorry for.*"

Marcel said, *I am not afraid of facing Roger, he knows me well and he is acquainted with the way I react to an attractive woman. If he does find out, I will tell him that I did not infringe on his property until after he had lost it.*"

Nikki seemed satisfied with his decision, but she was wondering what kind of confrontation he and Roger would have. It did concern him, but he knew that Roger could not complain too much, since he and Nikki were through anyway.

In an hour they were dressed and Marcel called for the car. He told the driver to take them to the most prestigious jewelry store in Monte Carlo. He took Nikki's arm as they walked into the store. *"You had better take off your wedding ring if we are going to buy an engagement ring!"*

She laughed and apologized, *"I forgot all about it!"* She took her gold band off and put it in her purse.

When Marcel saw the owner, he told him that he wanted to see the most beautiful engagement ring in the store. The owner looked pleased as he led them to a counter and said, *"Sit here, I will bring out the rings."* He went back to the vault and removed a tray of rings. When he brought them over to the counter he picked up a magnificent heart shaped diamond. Then he said, *"I have larger stones, but this one is of the finest quality, as there are no flaws and the color is perfect. Also, it is the perfect ring for lovers as it is heart shaped."*

"How many carats is it? Marcel asked. The man looked at the tag to be certain and said, "Eight carats and thirty points. Not quite eight and a half carats." Marcel slipped it on Nikki's finger and said, *"Let us see how it looks."* Her fingers were long and tapered, perfect for the piano he was thinking. Also well manicured. He said, *"It is beautiful on you, Nicole, though it is too large.*

However we can have it made smaller for you if you like it.

She looked at him with so much love on her face and said, *"How could I not love it? I would love anything that you gave me. But we do not know yet how much it is."*

Marcel was annoyed and said, *"I have told you that you are not to worry about these things, Cherie. I would not have brought you here if I could not afford to. Do you want it?"*

"I love it!" Especially because of the fact that it is shaped like a heart, because you are my heart!"

He could see that she had already become very emotional and that there were signs of tears in her eyes. He turned to the owner and said, *"It is too large for her. How long would it take to have it made to fit her finger?"* The owner was elated by now, as he knew that he was going to make such a good sale. They were not browsers as he was afraid of when they had first entered the store. He was used to having browsers when it came to the tourists. He was also amazed that this young man had not even asked him the price, as he was sure that he must have known that not only was the size of the diamond expensive, but the shape made it even more costly. Marcel gave him the phone number at the villa and then told him that he would send his driver back to pick it up. He walked away from Nikki and quietly asked the man how much he owed him, then without blinking an eye, wrote out a check. He said, *"You can call my business associates in Paris for a credit reference."* After giving him orders that he wanted it by afternoon, he and Nikki went back to the villa.

"Well," Marcel said, *"We have over a week to entertain each other! Now I want you to play the piano."* Nikki teased him and asked,

"How do you plan to entertain me?" He replied "There is only one way I can entertain you. It seems that is where my talents lay."

Nikki sat down at the piano. She played for half an hour and stopped to stretch. Marcel stated, *"Your music is coming back to you. When we get married I am going to buy you the grandest piano that we can find!"*

"Well, I had better rent a piano when I get to New York." She replied, *"That way I can brush up on all of my old pieces and learn some new ones. In fact I may decide to study in New York now that I won't have to work. I think that I would enjoy that and it will make the time pass quickly if I keep busy. When I get serious about my music, the days pass swiftly, as I get very wrapped up in it when I am practicing. Since it pleases you so much, my darling, I want to play really well for you."*

Marcel looked at her and said, *"You play well now, but I think it is a good idea. It will keep you out of mischief!"*

She laughingly said, *"You don't think that I could look at anyone else, do you? After knowing you, I could never look at any other man."*

He smiled, *"I hope not."*

She asked, *"And what about you? What do you plan to do for that long year? I hope that you will not be playing around with every pretty girl that comes along!"*

He looked serious when he said, *"Nicole, I will be so busy getting my business set up in Paris, I will be too tired to play even if I wanted to. But I love you too much to be unfaithful to you. You have my promise."*

For some reason Nikki believed him. He had been so serious when he said this and she threw her arms around him and said, *"I love you so much, I suppose I will have to wear you out before we part so that you will have nothing left for anyone else!"*

They were informed that lunch was ready and went out on the terrace to eat. Afterwards they went up to their room and took their bath together, which by now had become a ritual, and made love. Their troubles seemed to dissolve when they were in each other's arms. The world did not exist. They fell asleep and slept for several hours when the phone rang. It was the jeweler saying that the ring was ready. He had evidently checked out Marcel's credit, as he told him that it could be picked up. Marcel sent the driver to get it. When he got back, he took the ring out of the box and put it on Nikki's finger saying, "*I do not want you to remove this ring from your finger, as I have placed it there for eternity.*"

As with the bracelet, Nikki could not stop looking at her ring and as she played the piano, she would watch it glisten as her fingers moved over the keys.

Chapter Seventy-Eight

After they had been in Monte Carlo for a week, Marcel asked Nikki if she had decided on how long she would stay. She answered, *"I would love to stay forever, but the sooner we both get home, the sooner we can be back together again in Paris, forever."*

He agreed with her that they would have a busy year ahead of them.

"I was thinking," she said. *"Instead of waiting six months in Texas for my residency and another month for my divorce to go through, I just may go to see my family for a few weeks and then go to Reno, Nevada where I can get my divorce in six weeks. Then I could go to New York and begin studying my music. I know that I will be bored to tears at home."* Before this, it had been out of the question, as she had not had the money, but now that she had twenty-five thousand dollars it would be the easiest way to go. Marcel agreed that it was a wonderful idea. Then he said, *"Why don't you come to Paris instead of New York? You can study music here, as they have very good schools of music here.*

I can get an apartment here and I will be here most of the time setting up my plant, so we can be together most of the time.

She excitedly exclaimed, "*You are right! We don't have to be away from each other more than eight or nine weeks! I will visit my family for two weeks, then go to Reno and get my divorce and be on my way back to Paris in about eight weeks.*" They were both so happy when they realized that they had solved their dilemma and realized that now, the parting would not be so difficult.

Marcel said, "*Instead of taking the ship you will fly home and fly back in about eight weeks. In the meantime I will find a nice apartment for us. That way everything will move along faster.*"

Nikki thought a moment and then said, "*This will be a terrible blow to my family when they find out that I will be living in Paris.*

He said, "*We can send your sister and her family tickets to fly over once a year and we could go there ourselves once a year so that you can see all of your family.*"

Nikki could not believe that this wonderful man could be so perfect. He was thoughtful and had every quality that a woman could possible hope for. She said, "*God has been good to me. I was beginning to doubt him for a while when I was so unhappy with Roger, but now I realize that there is an answer for everything. It's true that we have sinned. We've been having an affair for a long time, but have not been as bad as the others as we have truly loved each other. It makes a difference if it is true love. Roger has been with one woman after the other and even though I have loved Juanita, I realize that God is punishing her for the life she lived before the two of you married. I just pray he doesn't punish us for being together now, out of wedlock.*

Marcel assured her, "*What is happening now is right. We were meant for each other. It is true that I was not a good husband to Juanita, but I never truly loved her and it makes a difference. I did right by her, however, as I gave her children my name and she didn't have to go through life worrying. I have taken care of her as far as a home and food is concerned. She has suffered only because she made the mistake of loving a man who did not love her. She too will find someone, as will Roger. They are both young enough to start a new life with someone else. Maybe I did run around a lot in the old days, until I met you I didn't know the meaning of true love. You are the first woman that I have known that I want to share my life with, as well as my wealth.*"

After a couple more days at the villa, they decided to pack their bags and go back to Paris. Marcel was anxious to start things rolling with the Paris Plant and she was anxious to get home and finalize her divorce so that they could be back together permanently. They had decided that they would have a few more days in Paris and then they would both go home and start their divorce proceedings. He was anxious to tell Juanita that their marriage was to be terminated. He hoped that he would not have too much trouble persuading her to go through with it, but he knew that she was not happy either about their life together. She had never had a real husband. He was sure that he would be able to persuade her.

As they left the villa to be driven to the airport, Nikki looked longingly at the villa, went over and touched the piano and said, "*I hate to leave this place. These have been the happiest days of my life.*"

He assured her they would come back often once they

were settled in Paris. He called the company and asked them to get them another suite at the George V for a few days.

When they boarded the plane for Paris, Nikki looked at Marcel and said, "*Well, at least we won't have to be afraid of running into people and can go out of the hotel when we please. Not that I minded being with you. Even if we had been in one small room I would have loved it. I just hope that you don't miss your concerts when we get back to Paris.*" She was joking about the last statement, but he said, "*Who says that I will have to miss them. I will insist on a suite with a piano.*"

She asked if there was such a thing and he told her that if they didn't have one, they would have to find one.

"*You are always so sure of yourself, aren't you?*"

"*Now that I have you and know that you are mine forever, I am sure of everything! Now I have a purpose in life. It was never very important that I have money as I had no way of enjoying it. Now I want even more as I want to give you the best that life has to offer.*" For the rest of the trip they sat back and contentedly relaxed. They loved being together and holding hands. They didn't have to make conversation now that everything was settled. That was what was so comfortable about their relationship, no idle chatter when they didn't want it, no need to find clever words to entertain each other. All they needed was to be together, they belonged together and they both knew it.

When they arrived in Paris they took a taxi to the hotel. There was no need to have the company send a car, as they would not need it. Marcel went to check in and asked if they had a suite with a piano. The desk clerk seemed puzzled and Marcel explained, "*You see, my wife is a concert pianist and she has not been able to practice since we are in France. She has to give a performance in New York in a week and it is very important that she have a piano to practice on.*"

Nikki was trying to keep a straight face, as she knew that if they were to hear her play they would know that Marcel was lying to them. The clerk seemed quite impressed as he glanced towards Nikki and said, "*You will need a suite with a larger living room as I am sure she will need a concert grand piano. I will give you the Royal Suite as it is the largest one and we will rent a concert grand piano to place in there. You will have it by tomorrow.*" Marcel had not changed the serious expression on his face and thanked him.

They were finally taken to their new suite. As before, the room was filled with roses and there was champagne chilled with the cheese and fruit on the table. They had evidently changed it over from the other suite that had been reserved for them, as they had to wait a few minutes before they were finally taken to their suite. It was even more magnificent than the first one they had stayed in and Nikki assumed that the Royal families stayed here when in Paris. She remarked, "*It's almost the same as the first day I arrived in Paris, but it is even more wonderful, as then I thought that we would only have ten days together and it would be goodbye forever. I am so happy that we have solved all of our problems, as now we can be happy together and not have to worry about the things we worried about before.*

Marcel was evidently thinking as she was because he said, "*Nicole, when I think that we will be separated for eight weeks, I cannot stand the thought of it, but it is much better than what we had thought it would be. Now that our decisions are made, I know that I must keep very busy, as I have a lot to do before you get back and besides that, it will make the time pass quickly for me."*

Nikki answered, "*When we spoke of this before we would say that we would think about it tomorrow, but this time, tomorrow is just around the corner. Before we know it, we will be back together forever.*"

Marcel did not joke about her expressions this time, he knew that she was right and he was glad. He was anxious to get things on the road and moving and went to the phone and called the company. He said, "*I have decided to open a plant here in Paris. Please start searching for the right kind of property for my project.*"

He turned to Nikki and said, "*I have taken the first step towards our future together, Nicole. I will write you first and let you know where to send my letters. I do not want them coming to my office where my secretary will see them. It will be a pleasure the day I can fire her. After I break the news to Juanita I will move to a hotel room as I don't want to live at home with her. I'll contact you where to send my mail. Until that time, if you want to contact me for any reason, address it to the company here in Paris and they will forward it to me in their envelope, marked personal. We have made too much progress for us to take any foolish chances now.*"

Nikki answered, "I hope it will not take too long for you to get settled in Paris."

"Do not worry Cherie, when I get back to Casablanca I will start things rolling immediately. I am sure that I will move into a hotel within a week.

Chapter Seventy-Nine

Roger and Monique were seeing each other every day now. He tried to get her to admit that Nikki and Marcel were together, but Monique was faithful to Nikki and insisted that she knew nothing about their having an affair. He had told her about Nikki canceling out on the liner reservations that he had made for her and she said, *"Did it ever occur to you that she may have decided to fly home? She mentioned to me once that she was anxious to get home and did not like the idea of five days on the ship."* She was worried for Nicole, as she really valued her friendship and knew that if she ever managed to get a divorce and go to the States that she would want to continue their friendship. Nicole had told her that she would keep in touch with her. However, she assumed that she was still with Marcel in Paris, since she had not yet had a letter from her and she had promised that she would send her a letter as soon as she reached New York. She had said that she would write to her on the ship and tell her all about Paris. She was sure that Nicole would not go back on her word, as their friendship had been a special one and they had become very close. She also knew that Nicole would be happy to hear that she was consoling Roger. She was the only person besides Marcel who knew what the plans were. Nicole had confided in her because she knew that she could trust her and she was not about to ruin anything for her by telling Roger anything.

When Roger had told her that he suspected that Nikki was in Monte Carlo with Marcel she had laughed and said, *"I don't believe that! She was too anxious to get home."*

He decided to believe her as since they had started seeing each other he assumed she would not lie to him. However, it was still haunting him. He decided that when Marcel got back he would not do him the good of asking him. He said, *"Monique, I would not even suspect such a thing, except that Marcel wired me that he had already put Nikki on the boat train. He lied to me and there has to be a reason."*

Monique very calmly answered him, *"Maybe he didn't want you to worry. It could be that Nicole did not want you to know. There could be many reasons."*

Roger had thought about all of these things. He was sorry that he had called Paris, as he was sure that Marcel would know that it had been him who had called. He decided to deny it if Marcel should ask. He had talked to Juanita and asked her if she knew when Marcel would be back. She had said, *"I never know as he never tells me what he does and I do not ask as it would make him angry. When he gets here, he will be here. This is how it has always been."*

Roger wished that Nikki could have been more like Juanita. This poor, sweet creature just accepted things as they were. The only thing that she cared about was that he continue to support her and the children and that occasionally she could look forward to an evening with him. She was always grateful if she got a small part of his time. Usually he was home for lunch and siesta. He had not been one for staying home in the evenings and he had not wanted to have her with him. He chased his women and lived as he had before he had married. She seemed to accept the fact that the long nights alone came along with the marriage.

When he thought of Marcel and Nikki together, he laughed to himself and thought, He would be miserable if he were married to a woman like Nikki. He could never put up with the restrictions that an American wife would put on him. He realized that he should have married a girl like Juanita. He would have the comforts of home, but would be free to do as he pleased. He decided that when he got his divorce he would look for this type of woman . He liked the company of Monique, but she was too American in her ways, as far as her outlook on life went and he knew that he would never want to be married to her, even if she were single. She was attractive with her blonde hair and petite little figure, but really a complete opposite of Nikki. She lacked the softness that Nikki had and he knew that he was not in love with her, but he was using her as she was using him, because she was so unhappy with Michael. He was sure that he could get her to divorce him and marry him, but he knew that if he did remarry it would be to a woman like Juanita. Marcel had been right when he told him that he had make a mistake marrying a girl like Nikki if he did not plan to be faithful to her, as he truly did love her, but once he got away with it, he could not stop himself. He wondered why variety was so important to him and assumed it was because he had been raised in a country where it happened all the time.

When Roger got to the office one morning he found a wire from his father saying that they were on their way and would be arriving the following night. He decided not to tell them about his suspicions, as he knew that if Nikki was with Marcel, he had given her every reason to fall into another man's arms. No matter how he looked at it, he knew that it was his fault. She had given him her love and had been a very affectionate wife. He knew that had he not strayed, she would have remained faithful to him for the rest of her life. He could not tarnish her name when he knew he was to blame. He also wanted to remain friends with Marcel. He wanted to be close with him again and decided to forgive them if anything had happened, as he didn't blame either one of them.

Roger was on his way to the airport to pick up his parents. He was concerned about how they would act towards him. They had never answered his letter and he assumed it was because they wanted to tell him to his face what they thought of him. Now he was relieved, he was glad to get it over with. He parked his car at the airport parking lot and watched for the plane to come in. When he saw it making its approach, he got out of the car and went to meet them. His mother got off first and his father followed behind her. He waved to them and they waved back, but they were not smiling. They had a very sober look on their faces and he knew that he was in for it.

When he walked up to greet them, he found them to be

on the cold side. His mother looked at him and said, "*You look bad Roger. Have you been eating properly?*" It was just like her to ask a question like this now. She had always worried when she thought that he was too thin.

"*Yes mom, I have been eating. Why do you worry about such things all the time? I am not a child anymore.*"

Her answer was sharp and stinging. "*You don't act like a grown man.*" His father was more sympathetic. He had his own flings and knew that Roger was of his own blood. The difference was that he had been discrete. Finally he said, "*So, you have lost Nikki!*" He knew that it would hurt and it did. Finally Roger said, "*I wrote you all about it.*

What is the use of discussing it now? She has gone home to get a divorce and that is that." Then his father asked him, "*Do you think that if you were to go back to the States you could talk her out of it?*" Roger shook his head and said, "*She doesn't want any part of me, dad. I have admitted that it is my fault, but in a way it is yours.*" His father looked surprised when he asked what he meant by that remark. Finally Roger said, "*If I had not been raised in a country where these things happen all the time, in fact, they are taken for granted, or if we had remained in the States, I doubt that it would have happened. Over here, everyone does it and you know it. The men and women both have affairs.*"

His mother reproached him and said, "*Roger, you did not marry a girl from these parts. You should have realized that she would not put up with it. She comes from an area where these things seldom occur.*"

Roger disagreed with her and argued that it happens everywhere. It's just that the wife does not know about it.

Then he said, *"I love Nikki, but she is not the same girl I married and brought over here. When I married her she was naïve, but she left here a very self-sufficient woman, one who knew what she wanted and that she did not happen to want me anymore."*

"And who gave her that education?" his mother retorted angrily. *"If you had been a good husband to her, she would never have changed. I know that you are to blame and my only regret is that we have lost a wonderful daughter. You brought her to a country where she did not know the customs or the language and she tried her best to live up to what you wanted. She learned the language in three months; she made you very proud to be married to her. After all of her efforts to be a good wife to you, you turned around and treated her like a peasant. I do not feel sorry for you, Roger. I hope that you have learned a good lesson, but I am sure that it was the hard way. If you want to live like a barbarian, you should never marry again!"* She was having her say and did not even wait until they were out of customs before she let him have the tongue lashing.

Roger knew that he deserved it and he was almost glad she had said it. He was sure that it would take time before he could have a good relationship with his mother again. As for his father, he knew that he had been no angel and when they were alone he would tell him that he had set the example. Maybe this would make him help smooth things over with his mother. He could still remember the old days when his father had his mistresses, even to the point where he would have to get one of his friends to bring her to a party where he would be with his mother. Now he was older, he had stopped most of this, but he knew that his father still had his flings occasionally.

Finally his father said, "*Let's not dwell on this. It is true that we shall all miss Nikki, but there is nothing we can do about it now. I only hope she will find happiness, as she certainly does deserve it. She should not have any trouble finding another husband.*" As they drove home they were silent, each with their own thoughts. The main thing that they all had in common was that they all knew they would miss her.

His father questioned him about the business, and Roger was glad that he had taken care of it well. They were making money and he was glad that he had looked after things. Many nights after he had spent the afternoon with Monique, he had gone to the office and worked until one or two in the morning, as he knew he would have to keep up the paper work. That was one thing they had always done themselves, as they never trusted the help to do it. It would be too easy for them to steal from them in this kind of business. He had to keep records of all merchandise coming in and what had been sold for what price. The books had balanced perfectly, as he had worked most of the night before.

When his parents were settled at the apartment he told his father he was going to the office. "*When you are ready to come down, call me.*" His father answered that he would rest for awhile and probably come to the café at six. "*Ill take a cocher so don't worry about me. I'll see you there. Tomorrow we'll go over the books together.*"

When Roger got to the office he phoned Monique. "*I want to see you this afternoon, as we will not be able to meet anymore.*" Monique sounded unhappy when she asked why. He answered; "*I'll tell you later when I see you. The main thing is my parents have returned and I will have to go to the office or my dad will ship me home. He doesn't like it when he thinks I am not paying enough attention to the business."*

He could tell that she was angry when she said, *"I don't see any reason for meeting today. If it's over, why should I take the risk?"* Monique had not been all that important to him. She had only helped him fill the void for the time being.

Chapter Eighty

Nikki was playing the piano when the phone rang. She had been putting her whole heart into it, as she knew that she would be packing that night and that she and Marcel would have to say their farewells the next day, as she was leaving for the States and he was returning to Casablanca. She stopped playing the piano when the phone rang and Marcel answered it. It was the company calling. He asked, "Que' est-el que est ca?" He was annoyed, as he had told them that he did not want to be disturbed today. He did not want anything to ruin their last day together. He was told that Monsieur Roger Carpel had called and wanted to reach him. He told them at the office that he wanted to know when Marcel was coming back to Casablanca. Marcel answered *"Dire lui demain nuit!"* With that he hung up the phone.

Nikki asked, *"What is it?"* Marcel told her that Roger had tried to reach him and wanted to know when he was returning to Casablanca. He had told the office he would see him tomorrow night. Nikki looked frightened and asked,

"Do you think he knows that we are together?" Marcel answered, *"Nicole, you let me worry about that. I will deny it, that is all. He has no way of being sure.* He added, *"If those people did see us, they were probably not sure if it was us or not. You look completely different with you Paris look. You are even wearing your hair different. In Casablanca you had been wearing it up and you have let it down since you are here. I will even deny that it was us at the casino. I will say that I went to Monte Carlo to rest and sun as I was not feeling well. Let me do the worrying about all of this. You don't have to face anyone now. When we are married they can say what they wish, I don't care anymore. Let the whole world know!"*

Marcel went to draw the bath. Nikki smiled to herself and realized that he would not let this last day go to waste, nor would he let it be tarnished.

That evening they both packed. Then he asked her, *"Do you want to spend our last night out on the town, or would you prefer to be alone and order dinner in the room?"* Nikki decided that she would prefer for them to be alone the last night. *"Besides, I have already packed everything except what I am going to travel in."*

Marcel was pleased with her answer. She knew that he wanted their last evening together to be alone as she did.

Part Seven

Going Home

Chapter Eighty-One

When their wake-up call came the next morning, they both realized that this would be their final call for a while. The hotel was following their orders to wake them so that they could get to the airport in plenty of time. Nikki's heart was heavy. She looked at Marcel and said, *"I can't believe that our time has gone by so fast. It is true that we have done a lot, but the time has flown since we have been together. Even though we both knew that this would finally have to end, it is difficult to believe that the time has come. I feel like I am going to the death chamber!"*

Marcel answered her very quietly and she could see the tears in his eyes. *"Mon Cherie,"* he said, *"Let us just think of it as a short time before we will be back together forever. We will both be so busy that the time will go fast. You will see. Before we know it, we will be in each other's arms again."*

Nikki asked, *"You won't change your mind, will you?"*

He took her in his arms and said, "I could never live without you. *"As soon as I have everything underway and your divorce is final, we will be together. It will be as if we were never apart. You don't have to worry about me looking at other women. I will be so tired by the end of the day, I will be ready to fall into bed each night. I promise you that you have nothing to worry about. The most difficult part on my side is to obtain a divorce, but I will get it, you will see. If it takes time, it won't matter, as I will be in Paris by the time you return, watching the progress on my plant and we will still be able to live as man and wife until my divorce is final. Juanita will give me a divorce when she knows that I intend to move to Paris, as she would tire of living alone. She will want it as much as I do."*

Nikki had loved Juanita, but now she thought of her as an obstacle, she was standing in their way. Suddenly she wondered what had happened to her in the two years that she had been away from the States and decided that she had just grown up and learned that you have to grab your happiness where you find it. She too had been hurt in these years and she decided not to dwell on it. She gave no thought anymore to Roger, he was a thing of the past, as far as she was concerned and she knew that she would never see him again. He would have no way of contacting her, as she would tell her family not to give him any information about her whereabouts. Paris is a big city, and she was sure she would not have to worry about running into anyone she didn't want to see. She would have an unlisted phone number and even if someone were to learn of her whereabouts they would have no way of reaching her. She made up her mind that no one would find her unless she wanted to be found.

Marcel called for the bell boy to take their bags down. He was going to put her on the plane and then he would stay at the airport and wait for his flight to Casablanca two hours later. He did not want to go back into Paris without her today. It was too depressing.

He was thinking about his first encounter with Roger and was trying to decide what to tell him in case he asked a lot of questions. He was going to be prepared for any question that he might ask, as he didn't want him to do anything to stop Nicole from getting the divorce. His heart was heavy also, as he knew it would be at least two months before they would be together again. He couldn't bear the thought of the separation, but knew that they would have to go their separate ways so that they could finally be together permanently. When he expressed this to Nicole, she agreed. They may be separating now, but it was so that they could finally be together without any problems. This was actually the first link in getting back together soon. Nicole would not be going further away from him; she would actually be coming towards him. When he thought about it that way, he felt that two months was nothing when you compared it to a lifetime.

As Nikki got on the plane she no longer felt the heaviness in her heart that she had been feeling. She knew that she was on her way to freedom, as was Marcel. Freedom to be together without worrying every time they walked out of the hotel together that they might run into someone they knew. She could see Marcel standing there waving to her and she smiled and waved back to him.

As he watched the plane take off and go up and away from him, he could not help but feel sad. He had always hated goodbyes, but decided they had made a wise decision. There was no reason why they could not be back together in a couple of months. Now he knew that he had to go home and face the music with Roger and Juanita. He was not sure which would be the worst. He knew that Juanita would throw a tantrum when he told her he wanted a divorce. She was a devout Catholic and he knew that she would never feel free to marry again, as least as long as he was still alive. He was sorry that they had married in the church, as then it would be easier on both of them.

Finally he boarded his plane for Casablanca, on his way to face the whole rotten business. He was in such deep thought that he did not even realize that the plane was approaching Casablanca until the seat belt sign came on.

When he finally got through customs, he was surprised to find that Roger was waiting for him. He had wasted no time to have his confrontation. Marcel decided to let Roger lead the conversation on the way into town.

"Marcel!" Roger was trying to get his attention, as he had acted as it he had not seen him. He acted happy to see Roger and said, *"Roger, Mon Ami!" I am happy to see you, but I did not expect you to meet me."*

Roger answered, *"I have been waiting for you to come home. I need a friend. I have been miserable and lonesome. I hope that we can resume our friendship as it was before the war. I am not tied down with a wife anymore. I am free now and can live as a free man!"*

Marcel could see that Roger was putting on a good act and not as happy as he pretended to be; also that he had become very thin. He asked, *"What has happened to you? You are very thin."*

Roger finally poured out all of his heartache to Marcel. *"I still cannot believe that Nikki is gone for good. I tried to wire her flowers on the ship, but they told me that she had cancelled her reservation."* He was feeling Marcel out. He was determined to find out what had happened. He finally asked, "*You wired me that you had taken her to the boat train. How is it that she did not take the boat?"*

This was one question that Marcel had not been prepared to answer, as he has no idea that Roger had found out that she cancelled her reservation. "

"*She asked me not to tell you, but she decided to fly home, Roger, as she was not looking forward to five lonely days on the ship,"* *he lied*

Roger nodded and said, "*I suppose I don't blame her. That is what Monique figured happened. It's really no fun when you are alone and depressed. We always looked forward to taking a luxury liner together since we came over on a freighter and I can't say that I would want to do it alone. It is so sad when your dreams are not fulfilled."* He decided to accept Marcel's explanation and realized that he had probably imagined a lot of things that were not happening. Finally he said, "*I guess I let my imagination run away with me, Marcel. I was sure that she was with you in Monte Carlo."*.

Marcel acted surprised and said, "*So it was you who tried to reach me! Why didn't you leave your name when you called the company? "I had told them not to give my number out, as I went for a rest. I was not feeling well and I needed it."* He was glad that they had spent so much time on the terrace, as he had become tan from the sun and finally added, "*I went to the beach and relaxed. It was a good holiday and I have needed one for a long time. If I had known that it was you who called I would have called you back to join me. There were some beautiful women there!"*

Roger looked at him and said, "*Well, Now you are talking like my old friend. I have not been without a woman, Mon Ami. I have fully enjoyed my freedom once I realized that it was over between Nikki and me. Besides, I could not have left the office, as my father wasn't here and someone had to run the business."*

Marcel could see that he was lying about being happy. Then he asked, "*Who is the lucky woman?"*

Roger told him about his affair with Monique. Marcel smiled and said, "*She is a good looking woman, but she would never give me a chance. She likes Americans, everyone knows that."*

"*How was she?"*

Roger answered, "*She is a hot little number, but it is over. My parents have returned and I cannot do as I please in the afternoons now and since she is married we can't get together at night. My father would ship me home if I didn't show up at the office."*

Marcel looked at Roger and said, "*Roger, you will soon be thirty-one. Why is it that you let your father rule your life? You should be working on your own by now."*

Roger answered, "*He would not give me the money. There is no way I could do this."*

Marcel was feeling sorry for him and finally said, "*Roger, I have been gone for a while because I am opening a plant in Paris. I will be living there once it is opened and I was going to close my plant here in Casablanca. I will keep it a open if you want to run it. I can send you the materials from Paris and could train you before I leave. Also, I would send the imports as well from Paris. Maybe you would like to do this and have your independence from your father. You are smart and I know that I can teach you to run it in a short time. Though you would be tied down, at least you could breathe. You could get your own apartment and do as you please without your father breathing down your back. I have a man there who is very good and he has been running it for me when I am away. He will work with you also and show you the ropes. What do you think?*

Roger looked interested and Marcel was sure he was going to accept when he said, "*I don't know. My father is getting older and relies on me a lot. I think that I will tell him of this proposition and see if he will increase my salary to where I can become independent. You are right Marcel; they have been treating me like a kid. I realize that I will have to do something about it. Maybe if I had seen it before, I would not have lost Nikki. My father has not let me be my own man and I am going to talk to him first. I do appreciate the offer. Does this mean that you will not be living in Casablanca anymore?*

Marcel thought a moment and replied, "*It means that I will be spending more and more time in Paris until my new plant is finished and eventually I will live there.*" He could see the disappointment on Roger's face and finally said, "*Roger, you have many friends here besides me. You depend on one person too much. It is not good. Do you realize that if I should die tomorrow you would be in the same situation? It is time you make other friends. When Nicole was here, you did not seem to find the time for me. You were running around with other married couples. It is true that you are no longer married, but there are a lot of men that you knew before the war, and even though they are married, they live the same life as I do. You should get close to them again.*

Roger could not believe his ears. He knew that Marcel had been hurt when he had made new friends and that he had not accepted it very well. He wondered if he was trying to get even with him. "*Why are you opening a plant in Paris? You make plenty of money here. I can't understand your new move. It will cost you more money to live there than it does here.*"

Marcel answered, "*I have to get into the fashion end of it, Roger. In Paris I will be able to keep up with the latest trends. I did not realize how far behind I was until this trip to Paris. I saw the new styles and fashion is very big now. It is better for me to be in Paris.. That is the reason I was there so long. I have been looking at property to have my plant constructed on,*" he lied.

Roger asked him, "*Does Juanita know yet? Do you think that she will want to live there with the children? I am sure that your mother will be upset if she can't see her grandchildren.*"

Marcel was silent. He decided not to tell Roger that he had no intentions of taking Juanita with him, but only the children. He did not intend to tell him that he was asking for a divorce either. "Everything in its time." he thought.

Roger asked, "*Do you want to go to the club for a while before you go home?*"

Marcel could see that he was lonesome and suddenly he felt sorry for his old friend. "*Yes. Why do I have to go home? There is the whole night ahead of us!*" He tried to act eager, though it was the last thing he wanted to do, but he was still afraid that Roger was suspicious.

Roger laughed and said, "*Now you are talking like my old*

friend and not the serious one that I have seen since your return. Why is it that everyone changes so much?"

Marcel answered, *"You have also changed, Mon Ami, but you do not see yourself as you see others. Time moves on and we have to move on with it. We are no longer young boys as we were before the war. We have been through a lot since then and we have greater responsibilities. It was not pleasant here in Casablanca when the Vichy French were here. Even thou I didn't get involved in the war, life here was very difficult. There were many things we needed and could not get. Food was the main thing and we had problems getting milk for our children. The lines at the market were long and if you didn't get there at four in the morning, there would be no food left to buy. I may not have been in the war as you were, but if you think it was pleasant living here you are mistaken. We knew that in America you had rations, but it was distributed evenly. Here it was different and it was no picnic for any of us." Besides, we have grown older."*

This was the first time that Marcel had ever spoken about the hardships that they had gone through. Roger had heard it from others, but never Marcel. He assumed that Marcel had a way of getting things that the others couldn't get, but realized that it was only that Marcel didn't like to talk about it. That was the way he had always been. Roger had forgotten these things. Marcel had never been a complainer. Then he said, *"Let's go get drunk and forget about it!"*

Marcel answered, *"I will get drunk with you, but forget the girls. This is our night out together. Besides, I am worn out from the women in Paris and Monte Carlo!"*

"I never thought I would hear you say that, but I guess we are getting older. In fact, you have told me a lot of things tonight that

I never thought I would hear from you. You have always been a very private person as far as your thoughts were concerned. You are not the same person I knew before the war, but then, neither am I. I do miss Nikki, but I am sure that not seeing her will help me overcome it. I don't think that I will ever stop loving her."

"You will meet someone else one day and she will make you forget all about her." Marcel remarked. Roger answered, *"I hope you are right, but I doubt it."*

At the club, Roger started drinking seriously and Marcel had to take him home and pour him into bed. He left him a note that he had taken his car home and would have it back early in the morning.

When Juanita heard him at the door she was surprised. She had been asleep, but when the key turned she was immediately awake. She had not had a word from him, nor had they heard at his office that he was coming home, as she had checked there every day. She seemed happy to see him. When he looked at her, he could not help but feel sorry for her. She had been a good wife and mother. He was worried how she would react when he told her tomorrow that he wanted a divorce. Then he thought of Nicole's words that she had quoted from the movie, *"I'll worry about that tomorrow."*

He was very tired, physically and emotionally and all he wanted to do now was fall into bed and sleep.

Chapter Eighty-Two

Nikki arrived in New York safely, but was completely exhausted. She had wanted to try and make connections to go on to Texas, but she could not bear the long trip without having a few hours of sleep. She knew that it was too late to catch another plane. She had not been able to sleep on the plane and was sure that part of it was that she was thinking about Marcel and the other part of it was that she was very nervous. She had become nervous about flying again and supposed that it was because she wanted to live for Marcel, as she had felt that same way when she was first in love with Roger. She decided to make her reservation for the next day and check into a hotel near the airport. That way, she could also call her family and tell them what time she would be arriving. She had some problems with the American customs and was annoyed that it took her so long to get through. When they looked at her passport, they finally realized that she had lived in Casablanca for two years and finally allowed her the clothes she was bringing in, without paying duty on them. However, she had problems with the perfume and explained that some was hers and some were gifts, but they made her remove all of the seals. She wondered if they thought she was going to go into business with such a small amount of perfume. She could not smile her way through the customs here and it was obvious that she was back in America where a pretty face didn't get you what you wanted.

When she heard such terms as "Hey, lady!" It went right through her. She was used to the French accent when Marcel and the others had spoken English to her and she decided that it was much softer and more beautiful. Here she was, in her own country, and the language sounded so harsh to her. She wondered if she sounded the same way.

When she finally got through customs she managed to get her bags over to American Airlines and asked who went to San Antonio. They told her that she would have to go through Dallas and change planes. She wondered if it would not be easier to get on a train, but finally decided to make her reservation for the next day. She kept one bag and shipped the others ahead. She had packed a small one for use in New York just in case she could not make connections. She took a taxi and asked him to take her the nearest hotel and asked him to wait, as she didn't have a reservation. He said, "That won't be necessary, as this hotel is not that busy. Only people who are in transit use it and the traffic has been slow tonight. I am sure you won't have any trouble getting a room." She thanked him and paid her fare and gave him a generous tip. He looked pleased and said, "Have a good trip, lady!" She hated the way that word sounded, lady. With the New York accent it was sounded so harsh. She was accustomed to being addressed as "Madame" and she found it to be a much nicer sound.

When she got to her room she looked at her watch and tried to figure out the time difference since her watch was still on Paris time. She decided to wait until morning, as she knew it would be nighttime before she would arrive in San Antonio. Besides, she was too tired to start explaining things to anyone.

She looked around the room and thought it was a far cry from what she had become accustomed to in Paris with Marcel. She was spoiled now and would never want to go back to the poor days again, that she knew.

After leaving word at the desk for a wake-up call at ten o'clock, she climbed into bed, but couldn't sleep. She was thinking about how she would break the news to her family that she was going to live in Paris. She knew that they would not be able to accept her going all alone. She decided to tell them that her plans were already made. She was not a child anymore and they would have to accept her as she was. She had plenty of money and didn't have to ask for anything. Therefore, they had no right to tell her what to do.

She planned to tell her aunt and uncle that she was going to study music. However, Nora would know the truth. She knew that she could trust her not to say anything and decided that she wanted to stay with her. She decided to call Nora instead of Aunt Emma. Even though she would be living in Paris, she would still see Nora twice a year because of Marcel's generosity. She was anxious for her family to meet Marcel, and after they married there would definitely have to be a trip home with him.

When she finally called Nora, she was well received. They had all been waiting to hear from her and had become worried about the long delay in her return to the states. Nikki needed time to think and finally said, "I can talk to you for free when I see you. Don't worry though, everything is fine." She told Nora the flight number and the time of arrival and hung up.

As she dressed, she decided that she would tell the family that there was a mix-up about her reservation on the ship and that she had waited in Paris for a cancellation, and then finally decided to fly home. It was a believable story. She hated lying, but there was no way she could tell them what was really going on. They would never understand that she had already selected a new husband who was still married to his first wife and had three children. They would never understand such a thing as that and would think that she was nothing but a two bit whore. This sort of thing was not accepted here, but she knew that Nora would understand and found herself looking forward to telling her all of the wonderful experiences she had had in Paris and Monte Carlo. She wanted to show her the portrait and exquisite jewelry which she suddenly realized she would have to take off. This upset her, as she was hearing Marcel's words about never taking them off, but in this case, it was a necessity and she was sure he would understand. She zipped it in a side pocket in her hand bag and decided she would show it to Nora when everyone else was gone and the others asleep. She was glad that she was going to be staying with Nora.

As the plane landed and she was coming down the ramp, she could see all of the family there waiting. She was not looking forward to the barrage of questions that were waiting to be answered. She was eager to see them all, however, and when she stepped down from the plane, she ran to meet them. As they watched this lovely, self-reliant young woman walking towards them in her stylish suit, they realized that Nikki was now a woman of the world. She was lovelier in her maturity than she had been as a girl and they knew that there was no longer any reason to worry about her, as she was her own person.

After the hugs and kisses, Nora and Bob told her that they had brought their station wagon, as they were sure she would have a lot of luggage. She found it all waiting for her when she went to the baggage claim and they loaded it into their car. Nora remarked how beautiful the luggage was. Nikki nonchalantly said that they had bought it in Paris. No one seemed to think anything about it. She had packed her bags carefully. All of the dressy things, she decided, would not be unpacked, as she knew she would have no use for them. She was sure they would wonder where she got such a wardrobe. However, they all raved about her daytime clothes.

She explained that Roger and bought her some clothes in Paris and then she had gone to the couturieres in Casablanca to have her clothes made when the fashions had changed so much after the war. She explained that you did not go into a store in Casablanca and buy clothes, as they were not very stylish. She told them about her close call in Marrakech and they all sat with their mouths open listening to everything she had to say. They were so engrossed that up until now, no one had asked her any questions.

Finally, Uncle Frank asked, "Nikki, what happened between you and Roger? It was such a shock to us to hear that you were leaving him." Nikki went on to explain about Roger leaving her alone at nights and about all of the affairs he was having. She suddenly realized that Nora and her Aunt Emma were crying. Then she said, *"Don't cry, I am better off without him. I will find someone else one day."*

They were surprised to see that she was not at all upset. She added, *"By the time I left him, I couldn't stand to be in the same room with him. I fell out of love with him when he started running around on me and I was not unhappy to leave him. In fact, it was a big relief, because after all he had done to me, he insisted that he still loved me and didn't want me to go. When I got on that plane for Paris, I was so relieved, as I was afraid that he would change his mind at the last minute and not let me leave. I am happier now than I have been for the last two years. Please don't cry. You see, I am not crying." Nora spoke up and said, "We are not crying because you left him Nikki, we are crying because of what he put you through. How could you stand it for so long?" "When they were in Casablanca he behaved himself, as he is so afraid of his father, but when they would leave, he acted completely different. During those times when they were there he was so good to me and he could not have been a better husband. Of course I had already lost my love for him. How can you love a man when you know that he is running around with other women? I would have come home long ago, except for the fact that I had to have that operation. After that, he felt so much guilt that he could not be good enough to me. He took me to Paris and Marrakech and several times we went to Tangier. That is when I sent you those gifts, as we could not mail packages from Casablanca. I loved*

Tangier it was so picturesque. When you looked out on the water you could almost see the pirate ships that we studied about and saw movies about when we were kids. On a clear day, when you looked across the water, you would see the Rock of Gibraltar. When you walked on a street, suddenly you would have to go up steps to continue, as it is all hills. Most of the people who settled there were Spanish. We saw the flamenco dancers and they were marvelous. We always bought our shoes there, as the Spanish leather is so soft and in Casablanca it is impossible to buy shoes, as the leather is stiff and the shoes are ugly".

I was already forgetting what he had done to me when his parents went back to the States and he started up again. This time, though, he didn't leave me alone at night, but he cheated on me in the afternoons. When I found out what was happening, I told him that I wanted to go home. He pleaded with me to stay and I told him I was through. By that time, I knew that I could never love him again.

He fell apart at the seams when I left, but I am sure that by now he has found solace with some other woman, or I should say "women". He will never be satisfied with one woman. I do believe that."

Everyone saw that Nikki was talking and feeling no sorrow or emotion. She had not once cried and they assumed that she was definitely through with Roger. The subject was closed. They decided that it was best not to discuss it anymore.

Nikki then explained that she was exhausted, as she had not slept for so long and wanted to go to bed. Everyone got up to leave.

When they were gone she said, "*Nora, tomorrow I want*

to have a long talk with you alone. I am going to tell you some things in the strictest of confidence and you have to promise me you will tell no one."

Nora said, "*You are still my little sister, you know that what you tell me will go no further. You have always been able to trust me.*"

Nikki hugged her and said, "*I have missed you Nora. It was awful not having you to talk to. When I wake up tomorrow I will tell you everything.*"

When she went to bed, she fell sound asleep and never moved once during the whole night.

Chapter Eighty-Three

When she woke up she walked into the living room and saw Betty sitting on the floor, playing with the beautiful cat with the fan that she had bought for her. Betty seemed to be fascinated with it. Nikki said, *"I see you like what I bought for you."* Betty looked up and smiled. Then Nikki noticed that she was eating ice cream. *"What are you doing with that ice cream this time of morning?"* she asked. *"Does your mother know that you have it?"* Betty's eyes got big and she looked surprised.

About that time Nora came walking in from the kitchen. When she saw Nikki she looked surprised. *"Well, you have finally risen from the dead! I have been so worried about you; do you know what time it is?"*

Nikki shook her head.

Nora said, *"It is six o'clock in the evening!"* Nikki could not believe it. She had gone to sleep so early and she had slept for so many hours.

She explained, *"I suppose I was really tired. I had to catch up on all of the sleep I lost. It looks like I am going to have my days and nights mixed up for a while. Do you realize that there is eight hours difference between here and in Europe?"*

Nora didn't realize this and said, *"Any wonder!" I hope that you will not be sitting up every night and sleeping every day from now on!"*

Nikki laughed and said, *"It will take a few days to get back to normal, I guess. I went through the same thing when I first went to Casablanca, but it was not as bad since we went by ship and the time change was slower. Besides, I had not slept for two nights. I was up all night on the plane and could not sleep in New York."*

Nora smiled and said, *"You don't know how many times I came in to see if you were breathing! I was so worried about you."* She told her that Aunt Emma had called quite a few times and that she promised to let her know when she woke up.

Nikki said, *"After they leave tonight, we will have that talk when all is quiet and everyone is in bed".*

Nora agreed that it would be the best time. She was looking forward to being alone with Nikki after so long a time.

Nora had prepared dinner for the family and Aunt Emma and Uncle Frank were anxious to hear more about Nikki's life in Casablanca now that she had caught up on her sleep. When dinner was over, Nikki said, *"It's been a long time since I have had a good old American dinner and cooked by the best chef in the world! Nora has always been such a wonderful cook and that fried chicken was out of this world. It's almost like a dream."*

Then the questions began. What did you eat? How was

it cooked? They wanted to know about everything. Finally Nikki took over and described the feasts in Marrakech and the wonderful French dishes and how elegantly it was prepared and served.

Nora looked at Nikki and asked, "*How come you didn't get fat? It's just not fair!*" Poor Nora had always had weight problems and she could not imagine eating that rich food and not gaining weight. In fact, because of the example of Nora in front of her all through the years, that was the reason that Nikki had always worried about getting fat and had been careful about what she ate or at least how much she ate.

She finally explained, "*For one thing, I never finished what was put in front of me. If you eat small amounts, you don't gain weight. Many a chef in France was insulted when my plate was returned with food on it and would send out the waiter to see if there was something wrong with it. They take much pride in their cooking and service, as in France it is a profession. They go to school to learn their trade and they are very proud of what they do. Also, exercise is important. I played tennis just about every day. In Europe it is a very popular sport and a wonderful exercise.*" Then Nikki informed them about the siesta in Casablanca, how the men closed up their businesses and the children were let out of school from twelve to two and that the main meal was served at noon. She told them that they had many hours to work off the main meal and usually ate a light supper. She explained that there were very few fat people over there, as their customs were much different. "*They have the right idea over there. They really know how to relax and enjoy their lives. It is not the rushing around like we have in America. Everything goes at a slower pace. I have gotten used to it and I am sure it would be hard for me to go back to the old pace again."* She realized that she had almost let the cat out of the bag, but no one seemed to catch on to the fact that she did not intend to stay in America. They all agreed that it would be a good thing, but the men could not come home at noon, as it was not possible. Even the children only had thirty minutes for lunch. Nikki said, *"It's a shame, as that is the secret of eating well and staying slim. They know how to live and enjoy life over there and they don't seem to compete as much as they do here at home. Life is easy and we never had to do our own housework."*

They were all quite impressed with her. She was the only one in the family who had traveled to other countries and was very up on what the rest of the world was doing. Outside of going to the border towns of Mexico, no one else had been out of the country. They saw that Nikki had matured into a very sophisticated and interesting young woman and when she would accidentally say something with a French accent they would tease her. She explained to them that she had begun to think in French and without realizing it, she supposed she had picked up the French accent and sometimes even forgotten what a word was in English.

She was the center of attention as they all sat around and listened to her tell of her experiences. She even ate as the French did, to show them how it was done and told them that they had said that Americans let the food get cold before they got it to their mouths by just changing the fork from one hand to the other. Nora said, *"I never thought of that, but it's true."* She tried to eat as Nikki did, but had a bad time managing it and everyone laughed.

Nikki would have loved to tell them all about her experience in Monte Carlo, and about all the money she had won, but only Nora would know that story. She also wanted to show them her magnificent jewelry, but that too would only be shown to Nora. A couple of times she almost slipped and said Marcel when she was speaking of things that she and Roger had done.

When the others finally left, Bob said, *"I'm going to bed and let you two catch up on all of the gossip."* It was obvious that he could see that Nikki and Nora wanted to be alone and he made it easy for them. Nikki thought that he was nice. He was understanding when it came to women and she liked that in him and mentioned it to Nora.

When they were finally alone, Nikki said, *"Come on Nora, let's go to my room. I have a lot to tell you and show you."* She could see that Nora was curious, as she had talked about being alone with her since her arrival and knew that Nikki had something up her sleeve.

In a few moments she was pouring it all out. She was telling Nora all about Marcel and said, *"Now you can understand why I stayed in Casablanca when Roger was treating me so poorly. I was in love with Marcel and didn't care what Roger did anymore."* She told her all about their time together in Paris and Monte Carlo, describing the hotel suite and the villa. She stopped only to watch the expressions on Nora's face and to hear her comments. She had been right. Nora was excited and happy for her and she was not blaming Nikki for anything that she had done. In fact, she said, *"I would have done the same thing in your shoes. I don't look down on you because of it, but I am sure that the rest of the family would be shocked, so we will not tell them."* It was like they were kids again, confiding in one another and telling their secrets. Nikki was thinking how marvelous it was that they could be away from each other for such a long time and then pick up the same relationship when they got together. They were sisters at heart and they were close and always would be. She opened her handbag and unzipped the compartment and took out her ring and bracelet. Nora's eyes nearly popped out of their sockets. She looked at the inscription, *"A mon future femme"* and asked Nikki what it meant. Nikki told her that it meant *"To My Future Wife"* She then explained that Marcel had never loved his wife, but had married her to stay out of the service and to give their children a name. She told her that he was going to open a plant in Paris and of her own plans to go to Reno for a divorce after a two week visit here at home and then study music. She said, *"By that time he will be spending most of his time in Paris and we can be together. He is going to fix up an apartment for me. He loves for me to play the piano and made me play for him all the time at the villa and he insists that I should go to a good school of music in Paris and continue my education in music. I had planned to do it in New York, but the last few days, we got the idea that I could study in Paris and we would be able to be together. We were both so happy when we realized that we would not have the long separation that we thought we would have. It may take a year or longer before he can get his divorce, as he is Catholic and almost all of the Europeans in Casablanca are Catholic and it is under the French Protectorate and most of the people are either French or Spanish. In reality, it is a French country. All of the people, including the Arabs speak French, even though it is in Morocco."*

She continued, *"He says it will be difficult to obtain a divorce because of the church, but he is determined and I know that he will get one.*

"Nora, I love him too much to think of being away from him that long. You do understand, don't you? I will be living with him as his wife, long before we will be able to make it legal. Over there they think nothing of it. People feel that if they are truly in love they do not need a piece of paper to make it legal."

Nora nodded and said, *"I know how you feel, Nikki, and I do understand. It's just that I hate to think of you living so far away forever."*

Nikki interrupted, *"But Nora, Marcel is very rich and I will be able to come home and visit more often and he will send tickets for you, Bob and Betty to come and visit us in Paris. He has already promised me that. As soon as we are married, he has also promised that he will come home with me and meet my family. Actually, we will be able to see each other a lot more often than we have been in the past years.*

Nora looked dazed as she said, *"My God, Sis, I can't imagine going to Paris, it would be wonderful!" Now I have some incentive to lose weight and I am determined to do so before I do go. You know, the family will wonder why you are going to live in Paris alone and they will wonder where the money is coming from."*

Nikki answered, *'I have figured all of that out already. I had plenty of time to decide what I will tell them. That is one reason why I didn't sleep on the way home. My wheels were spinning so fast. It has been a long time since we have had to lie to Aunt Emma and Uncle Frank, and though I have always hated doing it, there is nothing else I can do. Once Marcel and I are married,*

I won't have to lie to anyone anymore and I will be glad. I will tell them that Roger has done well financially and that he is making a good settlement with me. I know that I will get some money from him anyway, but I am sure it will not be very much, as his father holds the purse strings. Aunt Emma and Uncle Frank will never see them again and will never know the difference. I am sure that Roger's father will see to it that I get something, though it will really be from him, as he loved me so much. My only regret was that I could not tell them goodbye. I am sure that Roger has caught hell from them by now."

Nora agreed, *"I guess you can pull it off, but I wouldn't tell them any of my plans if I were you, until shortly before you leave, as they will bug the hell out of you. They still don't realize that we have grown up!"*

Nikki confessed, *"I am glad that I got away from here when I did. I am not afraid to face them with it, but I will wait until the last few days and then tell them I am going to Reno to get my divorce so that I can go back to Paris to continue my study of music."* She added, *"Tomorrow I will call and make my reservations in Reno, as I don't know how hard it is to get them."*

Nikki began opening her cases and showed Nora the beautiful wardrobe that Marcel had bought for her. She told her the story about how they were hanging in her closet when she got to Paris and that he had even bought her the beautiful set of luggage. Nora was sure that he must be a wonderful, thoughtful man.

Then Nikki pulled out the portrait. When she looked at it, her heart began to swell with love and she realized how much she missed him already. Up until now she had been catching up on her sleep and visiting with the family, but now the realization was there that Marcel was in Casablanca and she in Texas. As she showed it to Nora she sighed, *"I miss him so much, Nora. God, I love that man. I didn't even know that he was so wealthy until I got to Paris, so you know that has nothing to do with it. He lived very simply in Casablanca, and even Roger never had any idea of how rich he is."*

Nora looked at the portrait and studied it for a while. Then she said, *"He has the most gorgeous eyes I have ever seen. I can see why you are in love with him. All that and money too! Boy, did my little sister luck out on this one."*

Nikki agreed. *"He never lived lavishly or put on a splash as the other wealthy people did in Casablanca. At least he knows that I was not after him for his money, as it certainly came as a surprise to me and I am sure that Roger would be shocked if he knew it."*

Nora thought a moment and said, *"Roger would absolutely die if he knew what was going on!"*

Nikki answered, *"I would never have had an affair with Marcel if Roger had not treated me as he did."*

Nora remarked, *"I'm glad to see you so happy and that you are going to be wealthy. I don't know what I would do if I had twenty-five thousand dollars in the bank!"*

Nikki said, *"Before I leave, I want to buy you something that you really want."*

Nora shook her head and said, *"You can't take the chance of running out of money before you and Marcel are back together."*

Nikki explained that Marcel had told her that he wanted

her to live well and not want for anything and that he would send her money if she did run out before she got back to Paris. "*Of course, that was before we knew that we would be back together so soon. I will be back in Paris in two months and there is no way I can spend all of this money.*"

Finally Nora agreed to accept a television set. They had just come out on the market and she was dying for one. They went out very little, as they were not fond of leaving Betty with sitters and they knew it would be wonderful to have this type of entertainment at home. "*You will not be able to tell anyone that I bought it for you. Of course you will have to tell Bob.*"

Nora agreed and said, "*We will say that we have been saving for one, or else that Bob got a bonus.*" He had always made a good living and they had never really wanted for anything. They depended on bonuses to buy this sort of thing. They had already started saving for one, but were far from the amount that they needed to get it.

Nikki was happy to be able to do things for Nora. She had always been good to her and now she would have a chance to repay her in some way. She said, "*As soon as I have rested up, we are going shopping. I want to buy you some stylish clothes as well. I also want to buy some things for Betty*"

Nora was excited. "*By the way,*" she said, "*Betty drank the Chanel Number five you sent me.*"

Nikki was shocked and asked if she had become very ill. Nora said that she had called the doctor and he had sent something out to make her throw up." *I'm the one who was sick!*"

Nikki took out the new, large bottle she had purchased

for her in Paris, as she had not had time to unpack the gifts. *"Once I get back to Paris I can keep you supplied with it."*

Nora was happy with her new bottle of perfume and said, *"This one will be put away where no one will drink it or use it except me!"*

Chapter Eighty-Four

The next morning Nikki, Nora and Betty went shopping. They had a wonderful day. First they went and picked out a television set. The screens were not very large, but the cost was high. Nora was very happy as she said, *"Do you realize that I will be the first of all of my friends to have one?"*

Nikki was happy to see her so excited and pleased. They insisted that they wanted the set delivered and installed the same day. The salesman promised that it would be there by four o'clock. They hurried out of the store and drove to a children's shop and Nikki bought some adorable dresses for Betty. She seemed very happy with them as she was already a little clothes horse.

Nora said that she took after her Aunt Nikki when it came to that and in many other ways. When Nikki said they were going to buy some clothes for Nora, she didn't want to go. She said, *"Let's face it. I am way too heavy to look good in anything!"*

Nikki insisted and finally they did find two pretty dresses

that were slimming and looked very well on her. She said, *"I never spend much on my clothes, as I know that they will look bad on me anyway, but I realize now that by paying more for them I can find things that are more flattering!"*

Nikki informed her that when she came to Paris they would have some beautiful things made for her. She loved Nora and was so happy to be able to do things for her. They happily went home with all of their purchases to wait for the television set. Nikki was the happiest one of all, as for the first time in her life, she found out the joy of being able to give.

By the time Bob came home, they were all glued to the TV, watching every commercial and hardly noticed that he had walked in.

He laughed and asked, *"Doesn't a fellow get dinner any more?"*

Nora's mouth fell open. In all of the excitement of the television set, she had completely forgotten to fix dinner.

Bob was very forgiving. *"Under the circumstances I can see that it would have been difficult to tear yourself away. I'll go get a bunch of hamburgers and we can all eat and watch television at the same time."*

It was obvious that he too was excited over the set. When he left, Nikki said, *"Bob has a wonderful sense of humor and is a very kind man. He understands women. You have been lucky Nora, as you do have a wonderful husband."* Nora agreed. He had always tried his best to give her nice things and she had more than most of her friends whose husbands made more money than Bob did, but he had always been generous with Nora and Betty. When he came back, none of them stopped watching the television set until it went off the air. There was only one channel at that time and it was all very new. Having been away so long, it was the first time Nikki had seen one and she wished that they had them in France. However, there was so much to do in Paris, she was sure she would never even use one if they had them there.

She tried to see most of her friends who were still living there, but most of her close friends had moved away since they had married men who had been stationed there in the service and were no longer living there. The few who were, were wrapped up in their little circles and doing club work and she found them to be not as friendly as before. It didn't bother her, as she knew that life had much more to offer her than what they were doing and she actually felt sorry for them, as she knew that the lives they were living would be boring to her after all of the things she had done. She felt certain that they were talking about her behind her back and saying that she had become affected, as she was still throwing in a few French words here and there when she wasn't thinking about it and they would look at each other as though to say, "*She thinks she is hot stuff!*" She didn't care what they thought or were saying about her, as in another ten days she would be on her way to Reno and then Paris where she knew she would have a much better life than they were having. All they cared about was outdoing each other and she wondered how much their husbands owed the banks.

It seemed funny, but the war had not seemed to touch these people. They had certainly not changed very much. The only ones who had been touched were the ones who had had a war casualty in their family, and even then, they already seemed to have forgotten about it. One of her friends had lost her husband in the war, but she was now remarried and didn't seem to give it a thought anymore. She wondered how they could forget something as horrible as that. Nikki decided that she would not like living here, as the life was not what she wanted. She had great ambitions to learn about other people and other countries and hoped that she and Marcel would be able to travel all over Europe. She was hungry for knowledge, the kind that you don't find over the bridge table or listening to gossip. She imagined that had she not been away for so long she would be satisfied with this kind of life and decided that was one good deed that Roger had done for her, as she wouldn't have known the difference otherwise.

Outside of a few close friends, the average woman that she knew considered her a threat. She looked better than any of them, as she had learned how to use make-up to her advantage and her clothes were of high fashion. The average American woman could not afford to buy the designer lines, as here in the States they were much more expensive than they had been in Paris and even in Paris they were far from cheap. Everyone assumed that she had been married to a very wealthy man and could not understand why she would want to divorce him. Nikki didn't tell her closest friends about Marcel. That was her secret with Nora. There was no one else that she would ever trust, as she knew how the gossip flew over the bridge games. She thought back to the bridge games in Casablanca and realized how much more down to earth the women there were. They didn't go in for petty gossip. All of them had their little secrets and for the most part kept them to themselves, except those that were close friends as she and Monique had been. Renee was not out-going about those things, but then she was having an affair with Nikki's husband, which would not have made for a very good conversation. However, they all understood each other and that was the important thing, and Nikki already knew that she would miss Monique, especially. After she got settled in Paris she would let her know where she was in case she decided she wanted to visit her. She was wondering if she had an affair with Roger yet and was sure that she had since Roger had always been attracted to her. She was curious to know how she felt about him. That was why she had decided not to reveal her plans until after her divorce. She knew that Monique would not tell Roger anything on purpose, but there is always that chance that she could slip and she didn't want anything to happen to prevent the divorce from going through. If Roger did accidentally find out, he might not sign the papers and in turn, he might tell Juanita what was going on.

One night when she and Nora were alone she asked, "*Do you think that anyone would be hurt if I left sooner than I had planned?*"

Nora looked surprised and said, "*I would hate to see you leave, but I know that you will be going soon anyway. Why do you want to rush your trip here?*" Nikki was hesitant as she said, "*I can't stand the women in this town anymore. I have outgrown them and the town. You are the only one I feel close to anymore, but I am anxious to go ahead and get my divorce over with. I am scared to death that Roger will change his mind about signing the papers. I am also very grateful that I can afford to go to Reno and get it in six weeks instead of sitting around here for six months waiting to file and another thirty days for the divorce to finalize."*

Nora could understand her impatience, as she knew that her sister had a restless nature anyway and now even more so than ever, since she was anxious to be back in Paris with Marcel. She said, *"I know, Nikki, and the sooner you get your divorce the sooner you can get back to Marcel!"*

Nikki nodded and said, *"Nora, I am so unhappy without him. When he first wanted me to go to Paris, I refused, but then when I realized that I could study in Paris and would have no trouble making friends on my own, I knew that it was the only thing to do, as Marcel will be there more and more as the plant progresses. I want to be there and see him whenever I can. We are so happy when we are together and nothing when apart."*

Nora understood and said, *"I will help ease things with Aunt Emma and Uncle Frank."* They made the decision to break the news to them that night, as they were going there for dinner. They would just say that Nikki was going to Reno to get her divorce and then to Paris to study music.

When dinner was over they all pitched in to do the dishes and finally sat down in the living room. By now the conversation had slowed down quite a bit, as they had heard all about Nikki's experiences and she had been caught up on all of the things going on at home. Evidently Nora had prepared Bob for what was coming, as when Nikki started talking, he sat there without showing any indication of surprise on his face.

She finally got up the courage *"Now, I want to tell you my plans for the future."* Both her Aunt and Uncle looked surprised, as they had assumed that she was home for good.

She looked at Nora for moral support and she could see that she was just as nervous as herself, but she knew that she would have to say it sooner or later and continued on. "*I do not intend to stay here, nor in the United States.*" They looked at her unbelievingly and no one could say anything, as it took them by such surprise. Before they had a chance to ask any questions, she continued on, "*I will tell you exactly what my plans are and they are already made, so there is no use in trying to talk me out of it. I am going to Reno to get my divorce. I am afraid that Roger will change his mind about signing the papers and I want to get it over with as soon as possible. I don't like being in limbo and that is where I am at the present time. I'm not married and I'm not single. I do not intend to sit around here for six months to wait for my residency and another month for the divorce to be finalized. Before you ask, I will tell you that I have plenty of money and nothing to worry about in that department. I have enough to go to Reno and get my divorce and then I intend to fly to Paris and study music. I have started playing again and this is what I want to do for my career. I don't want to go through life being a secretary, as I hate it. If I don't make it big, I can always teach, but these are my plans.*

Roger gave me enough money to get started on, but he thinks I am going to use it for furniture and things of that sort. I do not want him to ever find out that I am in Paris. If he should contact you, just tell him I am in New York. I will get more money in my settlement and I am sure that it will last me until I have finished my study, as you can live very cheaply in Paris as a student," she lied. "*If I see that I am running low on funds, I can always take a job in Paris playing at dinner clubs at night and going to school in the daytime. Even in the finer hotels in Paris, they have someone playing classical music in the lobbies. If not that, I can always play popular music and I know that I can earn a living there in this way. Even though the students there live cheaply, they live well. They have special restaurants where the food is marvelous and very reasonable. A student flat costs very little and I am hoping to meet a nice girl and share an apartment with her. That way it will even be easier on my pocketbook."* She was glad that she had been in the student area and knew so much about it, as she could talk about it and know what she was talking about. In fact, she even remembered writing them about it and also about running into a boy from her debate class, so they never guessed that she was lying.

Nora sat with a straight face and Nikki was sure that it was difficult for her to keep the secret to herself.

Aunt Emma was crying and said, *"I had no idea that you did not intend to stay here. I was so sure that you were home for good."*

Nikki was very honest in this way and said, *"Aunt Emma, I would suffocate in this town! I am used to living in a world where people are aware of what is happening. They have not grown up here, even though the city has grown. The people are still the same. When I am with my friends I can see that they have not changed. Even the war has not changed them. I can not go through life listening to the petty gossip they have to talk about, it bores me to tears. Even if I didn't go to Paris, I would go to New York. But I love Paris and I hope to make it my home. I fell in love with that city the first day I went there, and decided then, if given the opportunity, I would some day make it my home. Who knows? Maybe I will meet someone there who has a lot of money and then I can come home as often as I wish. Everyone is flying now and it doesn't take that long to come home. I am not saying that I would marry for money, but hopefully I will fall in love with someone who is wealthy. I know that I don't ever want to be poor again."* They could see that she knew what she wanted and it was obvious that she had made up her mind about her future.

Finally Uncle Frank asked, *"When do you plan to leave, Nikki?"*

She was relieved that the worst part was over with and said, *"I am not sure. It will depend on when I can get reservations in Reno. I will go to the travel bureau tomorrow and make arrangements. I will be in Reno for six weeks, as it takes that long to establish residence and then the divorce goes through immediately."* Then she decided to take the sting off and added, *"Before I leave for Paris, I will come home again and see everyone."* She was anxious to get to Paris and into the arms of Marcel, but she knew that she couldn't hurt the ones she loved and felt that it would at least make them feel as if she cared about them.

Finally her uncle said, *"If that is what will make you happy, Nikki, you should go. As long as there is enough money to last you until you finish your schooling. Who knows? Maybe some day you will be a famous musician! You do have the makings of one, as you have always had a beautiful touch to the piano."*

Nikki knew that she was doing it for Marcel and Marcel only, but she smiled and said, *"Who knows?"*

Nora spoke up and said, *"It takes luck as well as skill. There are many musicians who are extremely talented, but never have gotten anywhere."*

Aunt Emma said, *"Maybe you will meet someone nice and get married again."*

Nikki knew that was what Aunt Emma wanted for her

and she was happy that she would be accommodating her and sorry that she couldn't tell her the truth, but she realized that when all was final, she would know.

That night she wrote her first letter to Roger. She told him of her plans to go to Reno. She lied, saying that her aunt and uncle had given her the money to go. She suddenly thought that she was becoming a real pro at lying and didn't like herself for it at all. She told him that she wanted to get it over with and get on with her life. She signed it, *"Always, Nikki."* She knew that it was a cool letter, very matter of fact, and that she did not give him any false hopes that she might change her mind. If anything, she let him know that she wanted to get it over with as fast as possible. In her letter, she also informed him that she planned to go back to school and finish her education, but didn't say where she was going. There was no mention of regrets that their marriage had failed. It was just cold turkey about her plans.

Two days later she left for Reno. She would wait until her divorce was final before calling the company in Paris to inform Marcel when she would be returning to Paris. If Marcel did not have an apartment yet, she would stay in a hotel, but she wanted to go there as soon as possible. She was looking forward to the day that she could be herself once more and not have to lie any more to anyone. At the present she truly hated herself for having told so many lies to her family, but there was no other way she could have handled it. When she realized that she would have to wait for an answer, she decided to write to Marcel in care of the company, as he had told her to do. She gave him her return address in Reno and waited for the answer.

Chapter Eighty-Five

Roger received Nikki's letter about the same time that Marcel had told Juanita that he wanted a divorce. She had phoned him, crying, and said, "*Please try and talk to Marcel, he wants a divorce. I have put up with all of his running around and have been a good wife to him and a good mother to our children. I do not want a divorce.*"

Roger was so wrapped up in his own troubles that he found it difficult to comfort her just then. He knew that he would have to go to her house, as she had no phone, and he was not in the mood for dramatics. He read Nikki's letter over and over, trying to find some sign that she still cared about him, but it was not there. It was almost as if she was a complete stranger to him. He wondered why she was in such a hurry to finalize their divorce and wondered if she had already met someone else. She was just too eager to get it over with. He decided that he would agree, as there was no use letting it hang on and on and at least he too could be free to do as he pleased, but he was doing it anyway. He finally thought, why not? He called his secretary into his office and dictated a cold note to her saying to send the papers when they are ready and he will sign them. It was cold and to the point, just as Nikki's letter had been and he felt that she would assume that he too was already wrapped up in someone else. He wouldn't do her the good to let her think he gave a damn.

What surprised Roger the most was that Marcel had asked Juanita for a divorce. He had never dreamed that Marcel would do this, as in the first place they were Catholic and in the second place, he had had his comforts of home and freedom to do as he pleased at the same time. Also, there were the children who he knew Marcel adored with all his heart. He had always been so proud of them and had adored them and Roger could not imagine what would be the reason for him to make such a decision.

He picked up the phone and called Marcel. When he answered, he wasted no time asking, "*Why do you want a divorce?*"

Marcel seemed surprised that he already knew about it and finally said, "*I plan to live in Paris most of the time, Roger, and I will be better off if I don't have to worry about a wife in Casablanca. I will never take her to Paris with me; you know that I do not love her. Who knows? Maybe I will meet someone who I will truly love and eventually marry. I have not liked the life I am living, as it is a lie, and not right. I have always wished that I could love someone as you loved Nicole. I was envious of you. Paris is a big city and there is a lot of money there. I could fall in love with a rich woman who could help me financially and socially as well. Opening another plant is going to weigh heavy on my purse, you know.*"

Roger thought a moment; it was running through his mind that he and Nikki were both getting divorces at the same time. He thought, "*How convenient.*" Finally he said, "*I had a letter from Nikki. She has gone to Reno to get her divorce. In Reno it only takes six weeks, whereas in Texas it takes seven months. I have been trying to figure out why she is in such a hurry. Do your divorces have something to do with each other?*

Marcel became indignant, "*Roger, we have been friends for a long time.*" Marcel knew that he was feeling him out and said, "*She didn't mention anything about her plans to me. I knew that she was in a hurry to get home, which is why she decided to fly. Maybe she just wants to be free so that she can live her life as she pleases.*"

Finally Roger got up the courage and asked, "*Are you sure that your divorce and her divorce have nothing to do with each other. I know you when it comes to women. You have had your eye on Nikki since day one*".

Is that what you think of me? I cannot believe that you think so little of me after all we have been through together!" Marcel acted insulted.

Roger answered, "*I did at one time, Marcel, but when you met her, I watched you and saw the way you looked at her. I also saw the way you danced with her. You cannot keep secrets from me, remember, I am like a brother to you, or at least I was at one time. If this has happened, I know that it is my fault and I am not blaming you or Nikki. God only knows, I asked for it. The thing that worries me is that I know you, and I am afraid that you will break her heart as I did. I want her to find happiness, but with the right person. You are not the right person for her, Marcel, as you would run around on her and finally kill her, as she is not strong enough to go through this again. I am sure that you saw the change in her from when we first arrived and when she left, and it took a lot out of her. She is still beautiful and can still find happiness, but not with a man like you. With your upbringing and the atmosphere where you have lived all of your life, you will never be satisfied with one woman; you will never change, just as I can not. I do not want you to go through with this, Marcel."*

Marcel kept his calm and answered, "*I have nothing going on with Nicole, Roger. I don't know where you get such an idea from. It is simply a coincidence that we have both asked for divorces at the same time. Yes, I would have liked to have had her, but I would never do anything like this with your wife. I will be honest with you, now I wish I had, as I would have been good to her. You forget, she is not of the same breed as the women we have been going out with here. She is different and if I could respect a woman, I know that I could be faithful to her. Maybe you have given me an idea! You are no longer going to be married to her and now I would have every right to try and see her once I have my divorce.*" He knew that he was getting to Roger when he said this. Roger was sorry that he had brought up the subject. If it was not true, and he didn't have proof that it was, he certainly had put the idea in Marcel's head.

Then he said, "*Marcel, you don't have to tell me anything that you don't want to tell me. I have had my feelings about you and Nikki for a long time. If you do marry her, I hope you will treat her well, because if you don't, I personally, will beat your head in. I promise you that! You see, I still love her, in spite of everything that has happened and I would take her back in a minute and be good to her if I could get another chance. I could kick myself in the ass for the way I treated her. I know I will never find anyone like her again, this I am sure of. There is no slut in the world who could take her place and I lost her very foolishly."* Then he added, "*As I said, I love you like a brother, and if you go through with what I think you are planning to do, don't make the same mistake that I did. I began to feel that something was funny ever since I found out that she cancelled her reservations on the ship. Then, when you came home and told me of your plans to build a plant in Paris, I was almost certain. Now Nikki is rushing the divorce in Reno and you are divorcing Juanita. It all fits together."*

Marcel was sure that Roger knew what was happening, but he was not about to admit it. He was sure that he would find out some day after they were married, it was inevitable. The children would talk about her to when they went to Casablanca to visit Juanita and his mother. However, he did not want to chance it that Roger would refuse to sign the papers just to stop him from marrying her. He knew that it would not be a problem for him to get a divorce, just the time involved, which annoyed him, but he did know that he would eventually be free to marry Nicole. In the meantime they would live as husband and wife anyway.

He finally said, "*Roger, you have a vivid imagination. Nothing has happened between Nicole and I except a couple of dinners before she caught her plane back to the States.*"

Roger wanted to believe him, but he still had his doubts. He hoped that it was only a coincidence. Finally, he dropped the subject and told Marcel that Juanita had called him and pleaded with him to talk to him. Then he said, "*I assume that it would be a waste of time.*"

Marcel answered, "*Yes, it would be in vain. In Paris she*

would only be a burden to me, she would only be more miserable there, as she wouldn't know anyone. It is better for her to try and find a new life. I have always known that I would not want to be married to her for the rest of my life. You know why I married her, but it cannot last forever.

Roger replied, *"Yes, I know. Well, I guess I did my duty as far as Juanita is concerned and Nikki as well. Goodbye, Mon Ami."*

When Marcel hung up, he called the company in Paris and said, *"Start looking for an apartment for me in a good location of the city. When you find it, let me know, as I will come there. I want to find a decorator and have it fixed up as elegant as possible."* He smiled to himself when he hung up. Roger had just told him what he needed to know. Nicole was already in Reno. That would mean that she would be in Paris in six weeks and he wanted everything to be prefect for her.

Chapter Eighty-Six

When Nikki got to Reno, she was not as bored as she had thought she would be. She had opened a checking account in San Antonio to use until she left the States and had taken quite a bit of cash and travelers' checks with her. She met many other women who were in the same boat as she was.

She immediately found an attorney who was highly recommended to her by one of the other women who had been through this before and was back again for the second time. The divorce would be ready to go into process as soon as her residency was up. The attorney was getting the papers ready to send to Roger so that when the six weeks was over, they would already have them signed and returned. That was the biggest hurdle as far as Nikki was concerned. She decided not to ask for a settlement, as she knew that she would have no trouble with Roger that way. She wrote to him at the same time and told him that if he wanted to give her a settlement that she would appreciate it, but if he didn't wish to do so, she still wanted the divorce and would go to work as soon as possible, so that she could support herself while she was going to school. Knowing Roger, she was sure that he would send her something, but she knew that he didn't have anything of his own to send. She was sure that his father would insist on sending her something, and she decided to take it if he did, as otherwise they would become suspicious that she could be so independent. Besides, she had been married to his son. She told him in her letter that her aunt and uncle were sending her to a school of music as soon as the divorce was final. She was certain that they would assume that they would also support her.

When she had written to Marcel, she had been sorry that she had been unable to write directly to him, as he had not as yet sent her an address in Casablanca where she could write. She knew that he was busy with his plans for the Paris plant and was probably going through hell trying to talk Juanita into giving him a divorce. She wrote:

My Darling:

I have cut short my visit with my family and am now in Reno to help me get to Paris as soon as possible.

I hope this will fit into your plans. Have you asked Juanita for a divorce yet? I hope that you will not have problems of that nature, but I will be with you no matter what happens as my love for you is still in my heart and I will not let a small piece of paper stand in our way. I cannot wait until I am back in your arms again where I belong.

I am sending you my address here in Reno. I will be here for six weeks and I am anxiously awaiting a letter from you so that I will know that it was not just a beautiful dream.

With all of my love and devotion,

Your future wife,

Nicole

As she wrote the letter, she looked at her ring and bracelet and knew that it was not just a dream now she could also keep the portrait in full display in her room where she could look at it whenever she wished. She remembered that day so well and determined that it was then that she had made her decision to marry him, although she didn't know it at the time.

When she sealed the envelope she suddenly realized that she would be Nicole again once she returned to Paris. In fact, it would be Nicole for the rest of her life. She was happy that her name had transferred so well into French. All of her life, people had asked her if Nikki was a nickname and she had told them that it was her real name. Now she would no longer have to answer that question.

While she was waiting for her divorce, she and the other women went to the casinos and gambled. She had a small amount of luck, but nothing like Monte Carlo. She assumed that Marcel had brought her luck, or maybe it had been beginners' luck.

It was warm in Reno by June and she was wearing her

wardrobe that Marcel had bought her for Monte Carlo. However, it was very casual and she didn't wear the formals or dressy things that she had. The other women commented on the beautiful clothes she had and one of them said, "You must have had a rich husband to have bought you all of those designer clothes." Nikki knew that the woman was evidently familiar with designer clothes and was probably divorcing a wealthy man herself. As soon as she had gotten on the plane to go to Reno, she had immediately put on her ring and bracelet. The other women were eyeing them and were asking if her husband had bought them for her. She was honest with them and told them there was someone else waiting for her in Paris. They were enthralled with the fact that she was going to live in Paris. Some of the girls already had their next husbands picked out, but the others were busy looking around for men who were getting divorces. They were having a good time, as they were all there for the same purpose and had a lot in common. There was a feeling of comradery since they all had the same thing going on in their life. The women who were unattached were going out every night with different men. Several men had approached Nikki, but she told them she was going to Paris to marry someone and they finally stopped pestering her when it got around. Most of the men seemed to be quite wealthy, as they gambled heavily and wined and dined the women who were looking for male companionship. Nikki was glad that she didn't have to go through the process of shopping for a new husband. It didn't appeal to her and she assumed that it was because she was so in love with Marcel. She had him on her mind constantly and wondered if he would be as wonderful to her after they were married. She still had her doubts about marrying him, as much as she knew she loved him, but worried about how he would act when the novelty wore off. She couldn't get the idea out of her head. Roger had been wonderful to her in the beginning, but after they were married for six years he had changed towards her. Even before then, he had already had his affair with Carla. However, she still didn't want any part of the men who were seeking divorces. Most of them felt that once you had been married, you could not live without sex and when she heard some of the girls talking about their experiences, she was glad she didn't have that kind of a hassle. She knew in her heart that she would not be able to sleep with just any man. She had to know that she had a special feeling for a man to go to bed with him and she had not seen one man there that would appeal to her in that way. Most of the women were different and were sleeping with their dates just to get something from them. They were being gifted with jewelry, but there was nothing that came close to what Marcel had given her. She could see the envy on their faces when they looked at hers. They would tell her, "You will never have any problem; the men must really dig you." Nikki would reply,

"I really don't know, as I married when I was very young!"

Finally she got a letter from Marcel. He told her that Roger suspected that there was some sort of connection between their divorces. He said that he felt that something had gone on in between them in Paris. He also said that he had not admitted anything and had made excuses for her having flown home and for his staying in Paris for as long as he did. He told her that he had informed Roger that he was opening a plant in Paris and had been looking for a good piece of property in the right location and that she had been anxious to go home and get her divorce so that she could get on with her life. It fit perfectly with what she herself had written him and she was glad.

He then told her that his biggest problem was with Juanita. She was giving him a hard time about the divorce, but that he had started the procedure anyway. He said, "I threatened her that if she gave me trouble, I would take the children and she would never see them again. I told her that if she would consent to the divorce, I would let the children visit her every summer and when they were out of school for holidays. Now I really think she is giving it some serious thought and is about ready to give in, although she claims that she will never remarry, as she does not want to give up the church. It will take time, but I promise you I will have my freedom!" He went on to tell her he planned to put the girls in a very fine private school where they would live during the week. They would only have the boy at home with them until he was old enough to go away to school.

All Nikki really cared about was that they would be together and it didn't make any difference how long it would take for his divorce to go through. She wanted to marry him, but as far as she was concerned, they were already married.

In the next paragraph he told her that the company in Paris had already found them a stunning apartment in a very prestigious neighborhood and that he had already hired a very prominent decorator to create a beautiful atmosphere. Nikki would have enjoyed doing the decorating herself, as she felt that she had pretty good taste along those lines and had already thought about what she wanted to do, but she would never let him know it, as he thought he was doing her a favor and she would not hurt his feelings. He added, "*In the meantime, if the apartment is not ready by the time you arrive, there will be a suite reserved for us at the George V and I will meet your plane when it arrives in Paris. When you know the exact date and time, call the Paris office and let them know. They in turn will call me in Casablanca if I am not already in Paris.*" Nikki was ecstatic when she read this, as she had not hoped that he would already be in Paris when she first got there. She was now sure that he missed her as much as she was missing him. She read the letter over and over, realizing that he wrote in English far better than he spoke it, but then he had studied it in school and she felt that was the reason.

She felt as if the time would never pass. However, she kept busy, as between basking in the sun, talking to the other women and going to the casinos, it helped make the days go faster. The nights were long, however, and she would look at the portrait of Marcel and her and think about how happy they were when they had it made. She wondered where he was keeping his copy and assumed that it was locked in a drawer in his desk so that when he wanted to see it he could look at it. She wondered how he could stay in the same house with Juanita the way things were between them, but he had mentioned that he wanted to be with the children as much as possible as it would be a while before he could bring them to Paris. He also said that he would be spending more and more time in Paris as the plant progressed.

One night she called Nora and told her about the letter.

Then she said, *"Nikki, don't forget you have to come back here before you leave!"*

Nikki answered, *"I have to come back to get my money anyway, don't I? Besides, you know that I will not leave the country without a last farewell to my family. I will be with Marcel for the rest of my life and I know that many times I will miss all of you, no matter how happy I am. However, don't forget, Nora, you are coming to France to visit us every year. I want you to meet my wonderful man!"*

Nora could hear the happiness in her voice and she could not help but be happy for her. Nikki reminded her, *"Don't slip and let anything out, because they will kill me if they know!"*

Nora was hurt when she said, *"Have I ever revealed your secrets before?"*

Nikki admitted that she had always been faithful and said, *"I don't know what I would do without you Nora. You are the best sister a girl could have. I am very lucky."*

Nora insisted, *"You deserve a lot of the credit, Nikki, as you have always been a good sister to me as well."*

Finally Nikki said, *"I'll see you in a couple of weeks!"* and hung up.

Chapter Eighty-Seven

Marcel was having more problems than he thought he would have, trying to get Juanita to consent to a divorce. She was determined to hold onto him, no matter what he said or did. He was upset about it, as he had hoped it could be on a friendly basis. Finally he said, "*I plan to leave Casablanca and I am not taking you with me. Now you can do it any way you want. Either you will give me a divorce and I will continue to support you or I will leave you and send no money for your support. Take your pick.*"

Juanita looked at him and said, "*I have been a good wife to you and have always provided for your needs. I have given you three beautiful children. Now you want to cast me aside. I do not deserve this and you know it!*"

Marcel was trying to be patient and he did feel sorry for her, and said "*If you give me a divorce you can remarry and you might be lucky enough to find someone who will love you and be a good husband to you. What kind of existence do you have now? I am never at home and when I am, I cannot even be a good husband to you. We have not had any sexual relations for at least a year now. You cook for me and that is all there is to our marriage. I never take you out, and I will admit I have been a rotten husband to you. You know why I married you. I have never loved you and you know it. I cannot understand how you can even want to stay with me. Have you no pride at all? A real woman would have walked out a long time ago."*

With that, Juanita's Spanish blood began to boil and she began to throw things at him. Finally she said, "*You can have your divorce! I don't know why I have wanted to keep you anyway!* Then she added, "*But you will never see the children again!*

Marcel laughed and said, "*We will see about that Juanita! Remember what you were when I married you. You were a common little whore who slept with every man who came along. That kind of mother is not allowed to keep the children. The court will not permit you to have them. If you give me the divorce peacefully, I will let you have the children in the summers when they are out of school. Think about it carefully, because if you don't do it the right way, you will have plenty of trouble. It is the question now of giving me the divorce and my supporting you, plus the fact that you will have the children for three months out of the year. The alternative is that you will get no money and you will not see your children again! That is how it is, so make up your mind."*

Juanita looked very nervous. She knew that he meant business. She decided not to argue with him anymore. She finally said, "*I will give you your answer tomorrow.*" She knew that she would not be able to get an attorney to take her case, as Marcel was well known and liked in Casablanca. She could not bear the thought of never seeing her children again and having to go out and try to earn a living for herself. She was over the hill as far as dancing went and she didn't know how to do anything else. At least by giving him what he wanted she was sure that he would let her keep her villa and send her money and she would have the children with her three months out of each year. That would be better than the alternative.

Finally she called Roger and cried and asked him if he could help her in any way. Roger replied, "*Juanita, I wish I could help you. I have plenty of troubles of my own. I have no money to give you and really no advice. The only thing I can tell you is to give him what he wants. At least you know you will be able to live on what he sends you and you will see your children. As you know, Marcel has been like a brother to me. My true advice is to give him the divorce. I know him, and he will not change his mind. From what I have seen in this country, women have no rights when it comes to these things.*"

She thanked him, and when Marcel came home for lunch she said, "*You win. I will do what you want. However, you will have to support me for the rest of my life as I will never remarry. I do not want to be excommunicated from the church.*" She was certain that Marcel would be upset, as she had no idea of how much money he did have, but surprisingly he told her to do whatever she wanted. As far as he was concerned, if she never married he would go on supporting her.

Marcel had already made up his mind that he would put the children in a good boarding school in Paris so that he and Nicole would have their freedom. As for the baby, he would hire a good governess to take care of him. He had already decided to bring one in from England, as he wanted him to grow up speaking in fluent English. Between the governess and Nicole he would be speaking English most of the time at home. The apartment he had selected was large and there was a special wing for the children and the governess. He and Nicole would be in another wing of the apartment where they would have their privacy. Later on, he decided, he would build a home for them, but he wanted to wait for Nicole and let her have her say in this. He wanted it to be her home as well.

He could not wait to write to her and hurried back to his office where he would have his privacy. He was certain that there would still be time for her to receive his letter. It was a nuisance that he could not call her, as by now he was longing to hear her voice. He told his secretary that he did not want to be disturbed and sat down to write the letter.

Mon Cherie: It takes time for a divorce to go through here, but now that Juanita has consented, at least we know that we will be married by the end of the year. I have taken a beautiful apartment and we will have our privacy, as the girls will be in a private boarding school during the week and I am hiring a governess from England to attend to the boy.

Our bedroom is in a different wing from theirs, which will make it very private. I have told the decorator to hold off on some of the things since you will soon be here and I feel that you will want to add your touch to it and select the colors that appeal to you. In the meantime, we will stay in our suite at the George V.

After we are settled in the apartment, I plan to build a beautiful villa, but I want you to take part in that, as you have a right to select what you want for our permanent home. When I say permanent, I cannot believe that it means you and me together forever! You have no idea how happy it makes me when I think of that.

I will be in Paris in a few days and you may call me at the company office. If I am not there, leave the phone number where I can reach you. I long to hear your voice. I miss you so very much.

I will be waiting for your arrival with open arms and the day that we will finally be together again. Please hurry, as I am very lonesome for you and need you very much.

I still have to make two trips to Casablanca and that is all. One will be to close the plant when the Paris plant is completed and the other will be to collect my children when the divorce is final.

Remember that I love you with all my heart.

Eternally yours,

Marcel

When Nikki received the second letter it was only two days until she would be leaving Reno with her final divorce. She was so happy she didn't know whether to laugh or cry. It was all turning out so perfect and she wondered if it wasn't all too perfect and she could not help but worry about it. She had been so full of fear that something would go wrong and ruin everything. She had always been this way and decided that she would not let it bother her at this stage of the game. She would have a whole year with him before they would be married and by then, she was sure, she would know if he was the right man for her and if he was going to be a faithful husband.

It was true that she had had her share of problems in her life, first losing her parents at such a young age and then having to move to the south when her father died and leave all of her family and friends that she was familiar with and start all over again. Then Roger had mistreated her so much. Now it looked like the good Lord was trying to make things up to her. She could not have been happier.

She read parts of the letter to her friends and they too were happy for her, especially the ones who had someone waiting for them as well. The others seemed a little envious, but she was so happy, she wanted to tell the whole world and wished that she could. She could tell by Marcel's letter that he was happy and excited as she was. She knew that she would be a good wife and a good mother to his children. God willing, one day she would have a child of her own. She wanted to have Marcel's child as much as she wanted him and knew that she would tell him as soon as they were married. When she thought of being with him so soon, she couldn't think of anything else and as usual, lost her appetite. She was too excited to eat and found it difficult to sleep. She stayed awake most of the night and looked at his picture and dreamed of the day they would finally have their reunion.

Again, Marcel showed his thoughtfulness when he wrote that he told the decorator to hold up on certain things so that she could put her touch to it and select the colors. She was sure now that she was not making a mistake. She thought of Roger's cousins, Annette and Pierre and realized that a Frenchman could be a perfect husband and felt that Marcel would be more like Pierre, that he would be as thoughtful and generous and probably more romantic and loving. Yes, she thought, I have made the right decision.

Chapter Eighty-Eight

In a couple of days, she was on her way back home for the last time before leaving for Paris. As the plane was approaching San Antonio, she suddenly remembered the ring and bracelet and she slipped them off and back into the little zipper compartment in her bag. She decided that when she got to Paris she would have Marcel put them on her again, as she would have to explain why she had taken them off. She had gone too far now to give herself away. Once she left San Antonio she knew that she would be free to do as she pleased and felt very content knowing this. Of course she hated the day that she would have to say goodbye to Nora and dreaded the tears that would flow, but she knew what she wanted now and was happy that she was finally self-sufficient and mature enough to know what she wanted to do with her life. She had never been in such an independent position before in her life and she was enjoying it.

Roger received the letter and papers of the final divorce. He went to his father and showed it to him. *"I can't understand it," he said. Nikki has not asked for one dime. Do you think I should send her something anyway? After all, we were married for six years and she left here with very little money."*

His father was serious when he said, *"Roger, she gave you six beautiful years. I think that she is entitled to something after all that she has been put through. Had you not married her, I am sure that she would have done much better with someone else, who would have been good to her and would have provided her with more luxuries than you were able to give her."*

His father was rubbing it in and he knew it. He also knew that he was right. He did deserve it.

Finally he said, *"Look, I know that I did not do right by Nikki, and believe me, I am paying for it. Don't you think it hurts? I have paid for it since the day she walked out of my life. You don't have to rub it in, as I have learned my lesson the hard way. I was a fool and I know it, but it is too late to cry over spilled milk. I would like to make things up to her in some way and would like to send her some money, but as you know, I don't have any money of my own to send her. I live on my salary and it doesn't go very far. You have never let me be independent in that way. I don't know how I can handle this."*

His father thought a moment and finally said, *"I have not given you money, because we are actually starting over in business. Most of the money we are making now is going back into the business to order more merchandise. That is how one builds up a business. I have felt that you are not wanting for anything as far as your life goes, but I realize too that you have nothing to send her. I will send her a check. I know that it is not enough to make up for the years of happiness that she has given all of us, but at least it will be something to help her until she gets on her feet again."* He sat down and wrote out a check for ten thousand dollars and handed it to Roger. Then he said, "*Take this to the bank and get a cashiers' check so that she will not have any trouble cashing it in the States. Then write her a note from all of us and tell her that we wish we had more to send, but it would not be possible right now. Tell her that we all still love her and that we pray that she will find the happiness that she so well deserves. Never mind! I will write the letter. I want her to know that she can always count on me if she is in any kind of trouble. I love that girl and always will. I am afraid that if you should remarry, I would find myself comparing her to Nikki and I doubt seriously that anyone can fill her shoes."* He had tears in his eyes and Roger could see that he was becoming very sentimental.

Roger said, "*I'll go to the bank and get the cashiers' check while you write the letter. That way we can get it off to her today.*"

He thanked his father, realizing what a good man he really was. It was funny; his father had always attracted people. He had such sympathetic eyes and complete strangers would seek him out and then pour their troubles out to him. As a matter of fact, the refugees, who normally stayed to themselves, had taken him into their confidences. They told him of their horrible and terrifying experiences in the Nazi prison camps. One poor man had had is son with him, strapped to his back so that they would not be separated. They had pulled the child away from him and killed him before his very eyes. Others had watched. Others had watched their entire families go into the gas chambers and be killed. They would let some of them live so that they would suffer. He wondered how anyone could cope with such things. They had come to their apartment and told of their experiences, and he was remembering Nikki excusing herself and going to her bedroom crying. She had so much compassion for these people. He could still not believe that they would never see her again. Roger despised himself when he thought of what he had done to that wonderful, sensitive creature. What a fool he had been. Well, he thought, it is too late now, but he was happy that he could at least send her something, though he wished that it could have been a lot more.

When he left for the bank, his father sat and stared into space. He too was thinking about what a dear person she was and hated the thought that she was no longer a member of their family. He knew that he had been rough on Roger, but if Nikki had been any other person than she was, it would not have hurt so badly. He too was remembering her compassion for others and thinking what a special person she really was. Even with all of her beauty, she had never let it go to her head. He finally picked up a pen and began to write,

Dearest Nikki: Until now, I have not written to you because I could not believe that you were out of our lives for good. I know that Roger did wrong by you, but I only pray that you will remember mom and me with kindness. We have all loved you and we feel that there is a great void in our family by your absence.

As you know, we are just getting the business on it's feet

again and do not have a great sum of money However, we want you to have something for the six wonderful years you have given to us.. We have all suffered a great loss since your departure and we hope that you will find happiness with someone who deserves you, as you certainly do deserve happiness.

Mom joins me in wishing you the best that life has to offer.

Our fondest love, Dad

When Roger returned with the check, he inserted it into the letter and addressed it to Nikki. He told Roger to go to the post office and get it on its way, so that she would have it in case she needed the money to help her get an apartment set up for herself. He was feeling depressed now that he knew that it was all over with. Roger saw the tears in his father's eyes and said, "*I have hurt all of you. I hope that one day I can make it up to you.*"

His father just looked at him, but had no answer. When he left for the post office he knew that there was no way he could ever make this up to his parents. He had brought them a daughter and they had loved her, and he knew in his heart, that no one would ever take her place as far as he was concerned nor his father and mother. He had broken all of their hearts with his juvenile behavior and would pay for it the rest of his life.

Nikki had written that any mail should be sent to her sister's house and would be forwarded to her if she was not there. He wished that he could go there himself and persuade her to come back to him, but he knew that it was hopeless.

By the time the letter arrived, Nikki was on her way to Paris. Nora forwarded the letter to her in care of Marcel at the company in Paris, the address that she had given her to use until she could send her a new address. She said, "*As soon as we are settled I will let your know. In the meantime this is where you can write to me. At least I can call you from Paris.*"

Monique had just had a letter from Nicole from Paris. She seemed to be very happy and Monique was happy for her. She wished that her life could have turned out as Nicole's had, as she still loved her American major. He had written to her and told her that he hoped to get back over there one day and he wanted her to try and get a divorce. He told her that he would never marry, as he wanted her and no one else. She knew that if he ever did come back she would give up everything for him. She admired Nicole for her courage and realized that she had shown weakness when she had stayed with Michael. She had a right to happiness as well as anyone else.

Nicole had written that she had received a check from Roger's father, but had to mail the check and her reply to her sister so that it would have the Texas postal stamp on it. She had endorsed the check to her sister and told her to cash it and put it in her account, as she didn't need it. Monique was shocked when Nicole told her how wealthy Marcel was, as he had never given anyone that impression.

Nikki knew that it would take time for her letter to reach Roger's father and it worried her that he would think her ungrateful. She felt badly that she was depriving him of that money as she knew that he needed it for his business, but didn't dare return it, as they would become suspicious if she did. When the letter finally did arrive, Roger's father had given it to Roger to read and he was gratified to know that she appreciated the sacrifice his father had made. He knew that his father had been right. She had gone through a very traumatic time herself and it had taken a long time for her to finally get settled.

However, he had not been fooled by Marcel and all of his excuses. Now that he had closed down his Casablanca plant and Juanita was letting him go through with his divorce, he had already moved to Paris permanently. He was sure that Nikki had sent the letter to her sister to be mailed and that was why it had taken so long to reach his father. He was hoping that the two of them would find the happiness that they both longed for together. Suddenly it occurred to him that not only had he lost his wife whom he truly loved, but he had also lost his best friend, because he knew that under the circumstances, they could never be friends again. He also realized that because of his foolishness and stupidity that he was the one who had come out the big loser.

THE END